THE MAYA FOREST GARDEN

NEW FRONTIERS IN HISTORICAL ECOLOGY

Dynamic new research in the genuinely interdisciplinary field of historical ecology is flourishing in the fields of restoration and landscape ecology, geography, forestry and range management, park design, biology, cultural anthropology, and anthropological archaeology. Historical ecology corrects shifts the paradigms of ecosystem designs and disequilibrium by constructing transdisciplinary histories of landscapes and regions that recognize the significance of human activity and the power of all forms of knowledge. The preferred theoretical approach of younger scholars in many social and natural science disciplines, historical ecology is in active practice around the world by such organizations as UNESCO. This series fosters the next generation of scholars, offering a sophisticated grasp of human-environmental interrelationships. The series editors invite proposals for cutting edge books that break new ground in theory or in the practical application of the historical ecology paradigm to contemporary problems.

General Editors

William Balée, *Tulane University*
Carole L. Crumley, *University of North Carolina, Chapel Hill*

Editorial Advisory Board

Wendy Ashmore, *University of California, Riverside*
Peter Brosius, *University of Georgia*
Lyle Campbell, *University of Utah*
Philippe Descola, *Collège de France*
Dave Egan, *Northern Arizona University*
Rebecca Hardin, *University of Michigan*
Edvard Hviding, *University of Bergen*
William Marquardt, *University of Florida*
Kenneth R. Olwig, *Swedish University of Agricultural Sciences*
Gustavo Politis, *Universidad de la Plata*
Nathan Sayre, *University of California, Berkeley*
Stephan Schwartzman, *Environmental Defense Fund*

Series Titles

Vol. 1: *Social and Ecological History of the Pyrenees: State, Market, and Landscape,* Ismael Vaccaro and Oriol Beltran, eds.

Vol. 2: *The Ten-Thousand Year Fever: Rethinking Human and Wild Primate Malarias,* Loretta A. Cormier

Vol. 3: *Sacred Geographies of Ancient Amazonia: Historical Ecology of Social Complexity,* Denise P. Schaan

Vol. 4: *Islands in the Rainforest: Landscape Management in Pre-Columbian Amazonia,* Stéphen Rostain

Vol. 5: *Landesque Capital: The Historical Ecology of Enduring Landscape Modifications,* N. Thomas Håkansson and Mats Widgren, eds.

Vol. 6: *The Maya Forest Garden: Eight Millennia of Sustainable Cultivation of the Tropical Woodlands,* Anabel Ford and Ronald Nigh

THE MAYA FOREST GARDEN

Eight Millennia of Sustainable Cultivation of the Tropical Woodlands

Anabel Ford
and Ronald Nigh

Routledge
Taylor & Francis Group

LONDON AND NEW YORK

First published 2015 by Left Coast Press, Inc.

Published 2016 by Routledge
2 Park Square, Milton Park, Abingdon, Oxon OX14 4RN
711 Third Avenue, New York, NY 10017, USA

Routledge is an imprint of the Taylor & Francis Group, an informa business

Library of Congress Cataloging-in-Publication Data:
Ford, Anabel.
  Maya forest garden : eight millennia of sustainable cultivation of the tropical woodlands / Anabel Ford and Ronald Nigh.
      pages cm. -- (New frontiers in historical ecology ; Vol. 6)
  Includes bibliographical references and index.
  ISBN 978-1-61132-997-1 (hardback) -- ISBN 978-1-61132-998-8 (paperback) -- ISBN 978-1-61132-999-5 (institutional ebook) -- ISBN 978-1-61132-745-8 (consumer ebook)
  1. Mayas--Agriculture. 2. Indians of Mexico--Agriculture. 3. Indians of Central America--Agriculture. I. Nigh, Ronald. II. Title.
  F1435.3.A37F67 2015
  972'.6--dc23
                          2015002902

ISBN 978-1-61132-998-8 paperback
ISBN 978-1-61132-997-1 hardback

CONTENTS

CONTENTS

ILLUSTRATIONS

FIGURES

TABLES

ACKNOWLEDGMENTS

This book owes much of its inspiration to the Maya forest gardeners of Belize, Guatemala, and Mexico, who shared their traditional knowledge, dedicated passion, and insights. While there are many individuals who helped to clarify the big picture as well as the intimate details, we thank in particular and in alphabetical order: Alcario Cano, Manuel Castellanos, Alfonso Chankin, Heriberto Cocom, Alfonzo Tzul, Leonardo Obando, Zacarias Quixchan, Narciso Torres, and José Valenzuela. These remarkable individuals whose heritage stretch back into the prehistoric past remind us that they are not Indians but Maya, and have not disappeared. That we in fact have been talking to the Maya.

It goes without saying that we could not have brought together our collective intellectual depth—Ronald Nigh as an ethnographer with a focus on agroecology and ethnobotany and Anabel Ford as an archaeologist with a focus on settlement and environment—if we did not have the support and encouragement of many of our colleagues beyond our Maya champions. From the archaeological world we thank Scott Fedick, Joel Gunn, Christian Isendahl, Macduff Everton; from geography Keith Clarke, Bill Denevan, Bill Doolittle; from agroecology we thank David Campbell, Stewart A. W. Diemont, Steve Gleissman, Arturo Gomez-Pompa, Francisco Roman, Gene Wilken; from paleoecology there is Mark Brenner and David Hodell; from ethnology Betty Faust and Norman Schwartz; and from the conservation and development world Jim Nations.

The archaeological fieldwork was made possible with the long-term support and permits from the Belize Institute of Archaeology annually starting in 1983-84 with the essential settlement surveys upon which all the other work is based. Work at El Pilar owes a debt of gratitude to both the Belize Institute of Archaeology and Guatemala's Instituto de Antropología e Historia. We see the El Pilar model as a way to showcase the Maya forest as a garden.

There are many other people who have played a role in parts of the book. Addison Sani worked tirelessly on the graphics, taking great care to bring consistency to their execution. We were fortunate to find a good copy editor; Joan Tapper helped bring continuity to the original chapters with her keen eye for detail. Once in press the tireless work of Lisa Devenish on the layout and Erica Hill on the index have brought a new level of uniformity and improved the exposition immeasurably. We also thank Ryan Harris who spirited the production process to fruition.

Much of the core support for our late nights, long discussions, and meetings in the US, Mexico, Guatemala and Belize must go to our spouses. Mike Glassow and Kippy Nigh have stood by us and provided cherish times of critique as well as celebration, good company and good food, and certainly companionship. This book is the product of concentration and commitment. We have given it our most concerted effort.

Prosperity across Centuries

The Conundrum

The ancient Maya, one of the world's greatest civilizations, have long been recognized for their keen celestial observations, their mathematical genius, and their remarkable art and architecture. It is a mistake, however, to think of them as a vanished people. The language of their hieroglyphs lives on in the speech of today's inhabitants of the Maya Lowlands (Figure 0.1). We, the co-authors of this book, have spent our careers in the forest with these descendants of the ancient Maya, and we have been struck by their intimate relationship to their environment and their vision of the forest.

This book demonstrates not merely the possibility but also the probability that the Maya milpa system, a diverse agroforestry polyculture of today's Maya forest gardeners, is the reflection of the sustainable strategies of the Maya civilization that climaxed in the Classic period, A.D. 500-900, and endured to be recorded by the Spanish in 1524. Our interest in the relationship of settlements to the environment within the Maya region weaves our individual decades-long research together and reveals the secrets that supported their dense populations over millennia. The traditional Maya milpa, like any agricultural system, disturbs the natural environment, but this system works *with* the forest and is integral to its creation and sustainability.

Anabel Ford and Ronald Nigh, "Prosperity across Centuries" in *The Maya Forest Garden: Eight Millennia of Sustainable Cultivation of the Tropical Woodlands*, pp. 13-20. © 2015 Left Coast Press, Inc. All rights reserved.

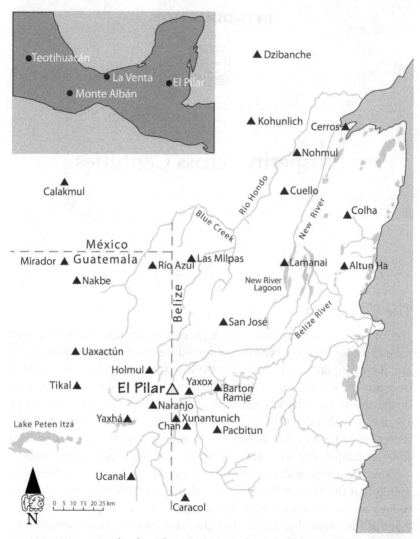

FIGURE 0.1. Maya Lowlands with major sites indicated. ©MesoAmerican Research Center, UCSB

We base our investigations on archaeological and ethnological observations, field data collection, and interdisciplinary scrutiny. We conclude that there is continuity in the sophisticated milpa practices of today's Maya forest gardeners that are preserved by generations of skillful farmers. The land use of the forest gardeners connects to the settlement patterns of their ancient ancestors. Our book shares the fruits of our rewarding collaboration.

Tropical Mesoamerica and the Maya Lowlands are favored with lush diversity, long recognized by early explorers and recently the focus of economic botanists, agroecologists, and foresters. The Maya forest, once thought to be a wild, pristine jungle, is, in reality, the result of prehistoric, colonial, and recent human activities (Denevan 1992a). Yet the human role in shaping the forest environment has been ignored in the historical ecology of the Maya region and the narrative of its people.

In our book, we collect diverse lines of evidence to examine traditional Maya livelihood and test ethnographic data within an archaeological context. Ethnobotanists have gathered a diversity of plant data with implications for the paleoecological record but have not linked with palynologists studying the fossil evidence of plants. Agroforestry and agroecology research details the complexity and flexibility of indigenous farming methods and strategies but has been published in journals not routinely read by historians and archaeologists. And accomplished traditional farmers are creatively thriving on the forested landscape that some archaeologists have called a "green hell." Each of these lines of evidence from the Maya Lowlands facilitates a fuller understanding and appreciation of ancient and contemporary Maya, with implications for the conservation of the area's valuable resources.

The contradiction between the glorified ancient Maya culture and the disparaged indigenous Maya agriculture bewilders us (see Diamond 2005; Dunning and Beach 2010; Turner and Sabloff 2012). Yes, the contemporary Maya forest is a threatened landscape, but not because of the integral indigenous milpa system that was developed within the forest. The culprit is the introduced European pasture and plow, which transformed lush, verdant moist forest into barren, brittle, dry grassland. In the past there was no extensive deforestation. The Maya and their ancestors have been living in this region for more than 10,000 years. Why would they cut down the forest that was their garden? Even after concerted efforts by governments and private interests to convert forest into pasture over the last half of the twentieth century, and after development schemes to introduce commercial annual monocrops into the perennial polycultivated croplands, and in spite of global trade agreements that have jeopardized the smallholder, the Maya forest has lived to tell the tale. We argue that conservation of the Maya forest must engage the traditional farmer, whose skills and knowledge created—and continue to maintain—the forest and its culture.

The Problem: Compatibility of Agriculture and Forest

A European plowed field or grazed pasture is a landscape designed to be treeless. Trees obstruct plowing, and only a few mature specimens can withstand the hooves and browsing of the likes of sheep and cows. This

FIGURE 0.2. Imagining the Maya landscape with Eurocentric eyes (top) and Maya eyes (bottom). ©MesoAmerican Research Center, UCSB

landscape management strategy, referred to as "ecological imperialism" by Crosby (1986), does more than change the agricultural picture. It imposes a panorama of neat rectangular plots of land like those of Normandy in 1066 (Adams 1986, Figure 0.2; see also Fedick 2010; Hervik 1999). This ecological imperialism has been so effective that in English colloquial use, the word "arable" is used synonymously for "cultivable" (see Wilson 2002:xxiii, 23, 27, 33–34, and especially 149; Trigger 2003:662). The root of "arable" in Latin means "to plow," and its precise English definition is "suitable for plowing" (New Webster's International Dictionary 1927; Webster's New World College Dictionary 2010; see Wikipedia 2013).

It is important to understand that the developed European culture views agriculture and forests as incompatible. That idea is embedded in our understanding of "arable" and in the Malthusian view that agricultural lands are finite, based on the medieval concept of "assart," the act of converting forest into arable land (see, for example, Bishop 1935; New Webster's International Dictionary 1927). Some scholars erroneously use the term "arable" to describe lands used for farming by the Maya or other prehispanic societies in the New World that developed innovative and successful strategies without any need for the plow or draft animals (which they did not have). Arable lands, lands that can be plowed, are flat or gently rolling, with deep soil amenable to furrows. We must be careful how we apply this vision to the Maya forest garden. There is no way to plow land covered with trees, nor is it possible to plow the stony ridges or steep slopes where most ancient Maya lived and farmed.

The lens of ecological imperialism makes implicit assumptions that persist in the scholarly literature on the tropics and on the Maya (Mann 2005; Snow 2006)—for example, that the tropics are unhealthy places and that the soils are infertile (Bates 1952). In fact, the Maya were able to feed cities that swelled to 20,000 or more inhabitants without draft animals, transportation to move food long distances, or deforestation.

For the Maya area, there would be no arable land. To evaluate ancient land use, we must conjure a world without the plow, without cattle or horses, where work in the fields was accomplished by hand, and where transport was on foot. Rojas Rabiela (1990) contrasts the agriculture of Europe, where mechanization could not reap benefits from micro-environmental variations, with that of Mesoamerica, where hand cultivators attended to individual plants. The world of tropical Mesoamerica and the Maya Lowlands, in which the ancient cultures lived and excelled, was facilitated by such individual care by its forest gardeners.

The Maya traditional agricultural system was aided by social sophistication and collective organization. Leaders supported local agricultural systems created in the familiar context of the forest; they invested in indigenous strategies and local land-use methods—proven successes that aggrandized the elite, underwrote their public infrastructure, and redistributed wealth. The structure and dynamics of the Maya milpa cycle integrates agricultural and other domestic activities with the complex historical and ecological patterns of the region.

Intensification is key to any subsistence system in times of population growth. With the Maya system, intensification of land use involved investments in knowledge, skill, and labor. The archaeological evidence found by mapping domestic structures shows how these factors materialized on the ancient landscape, as do the ethnographic records of the milpa system. Agriculture is based on the quality and suitability of the land for a wide variety of natural and agricultural products. In the case of the farmer, we are looking at a domestic enterprise that provides for the family and also produces enough for the taxes and tributes required by the elites. As these requirements change, so does the land use: More people means greater investment in land and labor; fewer people means less.

Lowland Maya subsistence is complex; it benefits the landscape by the cyclical management of plants, essentially creating a domesticated landscape that today is the feral forest. The cultural history of the Maya forest is embedded in its natural history. The plants are those that were encouraged in the fields, ensuring fertility and usefulness in diverse soil conditions and habitats. To understand the development of complex societies and civilizations in the Mesoamerican tropics, one must appreciate how agriculture and the forest work in tandem with labor, and how the Maya land-use intensification strategies leave little durable imprint on the landscape beyond the plants themselves. The Maya relied on intangible investments: knowledge and skill.

Maya strategies are essentially based on swidden. Conventionally, swidden has been described as shifting cultivation where there are the integral indigenous systems, like those of the Maya, and the partial systems that come from immigrants (Conklin 1957:3). This approach is often misrepresented as primitive and extensive and deprecated as "slash-and-burn," but that characterization is a far cry from what we have witnessed. In milpa swidden, "slashing" is equivalent to coppicing, pollarding, and pruning, worldwide practices vital to maintaining trees and shrubs.

Considering fire as destructive misses the mastery of its use where firebreaks are well established and burning is careful and strategic, taking into account conditions of wind, temperature, and time of day. Historically built around an ecological relationship with the environment, Maya croplands, as Geertz notes (1963:25), replicate in miniature the tropical forest. Cropping is a tightly woven fabric, where the planting of trees and shrubs and the leaving of choice trees make up the reforestation process. In fact, the pejorative word "primitive" belittles the elegant simplicity of the small-scale, basic technologies that are transportable, flexible, and tailored to the forest.

Our Exploration

In Chapter 1 we present the environmental and historical background for our investigation. We discuss the relationship of population, land, resources, and political factors as related to the ancient Maya chronology. In addition, we reflect on the way today's Maya traditions demonstrate adaptive management in varied landscapes and under difficult socio-ecological constraints.

To explore the historical ecology of the Maya, it is critical to understand the integration of the milpa and forest garden. We need to be aware of the qualities and characteristics of the Maya milpa cycle in order to dissect the paleoenvironmental data, consider ancient population, and discuss the forest cover. Chapter 2 establishes the productive capacity and complexity of the milpa and its related forest garden as one system. We contrast traditional systems that are integral to the forest with contemporary conventional milpas that are disassociated from it. We draw on examples of the milpa forest garden from the forests of the Petén, Yucatan, and Lacandon. The intricacy and finesse of the Maya milpa, particularly the detailed ethnographic data of the Lakantun[1] of the Lacandon forest, reveal the milpa's great value as an agroecosystem. Our pioneering compilation of these data is startling: It shows the remarkably diverse household resources made possible by land management that actually enhances the soil and biodiversity.

In Chapter 3 we turn to the paleoenvironmental data. In examining the ancient Maya region, the published evidence is a significant resource, but it has its limitations. A focus on specific taxa demonstrates that important pollen data has shortcomings as well. Accepting the data at face value is fraught with misinterpretation; some 98 percent of the plants of the forest are pollinated by birds, bees, or bats; whereas fossil pollen is predominately wind-borne. Yet despite the incompleteness of the fossil pollen record, that record is critical to understanding the milpa cycle and its impact on landscape dynamics.

In Chapter 4 we concentrate on the archaeological example of El Pilar, situated less than 50 km from Tikal at the edge of the interior uplands, and referred to as the mesoplano by Gunn and colleagues (2014). The geography and archaeology of the area surrounding the important Classic city center of El Pilar has been well studied. Using its environmental features and settlement patterns, we can estimate the population and model the Maya milpa system across approximately 1,300 square km to determine the potential of the milpa forest garden cycle to support the dense population of this area. Surprisingly, no one has done this before. Our illuminating analysis shows that the yields of maize more than cover the needs of the large population, providing a new appreciation for the great possibilities of land and labor intensification (the labor tasking of Scarborough 2003a).

Having sufficient maize for the population only begins to address the issue of land cover, and in Chapter 5 we consider forested areas. Deforestation has been widely proposed as an explanation for the demise of the Classic period Maya, approximately 1,000 years ago. That assumes, however, that the tropical landscape limits the development of civilization and that the milpa system, so primitive, cannot support large populations. Given the sophistication of the Maya milpa, the importance of land cover that moderates vagaries of rainfall, and the complexity of the subsistence system, we can see that managed forests are integral to the milpa. With our model of forest cover based on the maize field requirements for the El Pilar area, and relying on habitat classifications for Tikal, we show that significant forest cover remained under intensive cultivation. The milpa system manages the water cycle and prevents erosion, as the Maya accomplish today;[2] it also enhances soil quality and provides a rich array of natural resources for the family.

We conclude our study in Chapter 6 by considering the future of the Maya forest. From the earliest waves of human occupation at the close of the Pleistocene, people were living in Mesoamerica and the Maya Lowlands. The ecological dynamic of the Holocene that arose in the Archaic, between 8,000 and 4,000 years ago, resulted from the interrelationship among tropical plants and animals in which humans played a significant role. These precursors of the Maya contributed to the ecology of the forest environment. By the time the Maya became archaeologically visible, populations had grown and expanded throughout the region, as recorded in the early 1500s during the Spanish conquest.

What are the dimensions of Maya influence on the landscape? What do today's flora and fauna tell us about this relationship? Tracing the development of the Maya and their forest and considering how management—based on skill, knowledge, and the intensification of labor—shaped the historical ecology of their landscape brings us to the challenges we face today. Where is the smallholder in today's world, and what is happening to the skill and knowledge of the Maya? How has globalization increased and limited potentials? What have NAFTA, CAFTA, and similar trade agreements done to traditional land use? How can we recover the value that the Maya created with the forest? We see that the significance of the Maya forest today depends on the milpa forest gardener. The greatest threat to the conservation of the Maya forest is the loss of these knowledgeable forest farmers.

CHAPTER 1

The Context of the Maya Forest

The conventional story of the magnificent Maya civilization ends with the disappearance of the Maya people and destruction of their environment in Belize, Guatemala, and Mexico. This myth persists despite historical accounts that disprove it. Cortés, on his march to Lake Petén Itzá, describes the area as populated, feeding and housing his army of more than 3,000. Moreover, the continuous 30-century period of population development of the ancient Maya Lowlands—from the Preclassic to the Terminal Classic period, through the Colonial period and into present times—represents long-lasting continuity. The source of Maya wealth lay in their landscape and in their profound understanding of how to use it. In fact, the Maya's subtle patterns are embedded within the forest structure. The historical ecology of this forest is complex (cf. Balée 2006); to understand it means examining contemporary agroecology of traditional farming and the paleoenvironmental record of the Late Classic Maya. An overview of the Maya timeline and the chronology of the environmental record reveal the discrepancy between the growth and sophistication of the Classic period Maya and the imagined environmental destruction. While most studies of the Maya assume that the collapse of the civilization was related to deforestation, such as that caused by humans, today the Maya forest is known for its remarkable diversity and its abundance of useful plants.

Anabel Ford and Ronald Nigh, "The Context of the Maya Forest" in *The Maya Forest Garden: Eight Millennia of Sustainable Cultivation of the Tropical Woodlands*, pp. 21-39. © 2015 Left Coast Press, Inc. All rights reserved.

Introduction

The Lowland Maya region (Figure 0.1) was transformed by humans from the initial peopling of the New World. They influenced the landscape ecology from the outset, managing and domesticating plants in a setting that changed from an arid temperate zone to a wet tropical one around 10,000 to 8,000 years ago (Table 1.1). When early Maya settlements emerged, from 4,000 to 3,000 years ago, the community increasingly depended on horticulture and the expansion of agriculture while essentially living within the forest. The archaeological evidence from the Preclassic Maya focuses first on areas with secure water reserves, as noted by Dennis Puleston and Olga Puleston (1971). As populations grew, farming settlements went on to occupy virtually every locale with the potential for cultivation. At this time the Maya built major centers as impressive as anything from the Classic period, including Mirador and Nakbe, in the Guatemalan Petén, and Cerros and Cuello, in Northern Belize. Based on a survey around Tikal, Lake Yaxha, and the El Pilar area east of Tikal (Ford 1986, 1990; Puleston 1973; Rice 1976), by 2,800 years ago, in the Middle Preclassic, Maya farmers largely occupied the desirable, well-drained uplands of the region—the same zones that were most densely occupied centuries later during the Late Classic.

Between 2,000 and 1,000 years ago Maya centers and settlements grew and expanded over the landscape during the Classic. Much has been made of the so-called Terminal Classic collapse, a turbulent time when the culture of sacred monarchs underwent a major transformation and important centers in the southern area gradually ceased to be maintained (Webster 2002). The idea of collapse, however, exaggerates the reality and promotes a picture of population crash without evidence. Dramatic "collapses," or the gradual abandonment of impressive urban centers, appear to be a signature of Maya culture from the Preclassic and signals transformations of settlement patterns (Aimers and Iannone 2014; Iannone 2014; Chase and Scarborough 2014a). Nevertheless, the Maya persisted and significant numbers still lived around Postclassic centers when the first Spanish conquistadors arrived several centuries later (Alexander 2006).

Hernán Cortés's Fifth Letter to the emperor and king of Spain, Charles V, provides a unique glimpse of the Prehispanic Maya (Cortés 1985[1526]). In this letter of September 3, 1526 (1985:355-449), Cortés describes his epic *entrada* to the very heart of the southern lowlands at Lake Petén Itzá, some 70 km from the abandoned Classic city of Tikal. The "heavily settled region" (Jones 1998:31) that the Spaniards crossed was already feeling the first effects of the European invasion provoked by the dramatic demise of the Aztec civilization. Cortés's party traversed Tabasco, Acalan, and Central

TABLE 1.1. Occupation Chronology: Eight Thousand Years in the Maya Forest

Years Before Present	Human Ecology	Land Use	Cultural Period
8000-4000	Hunting & gathering	Mobile horticulture	Archaic
4000-3000	Early settlement	Settled horticultural forest gardens	Formative Preclassic
3000-2000	Emergent Preclassic centers	Settled forest gardens	Middle-Late Preclassic
2000-1400	Civic center expansion	Expanding milpa forest gardens	Late Preclassic -Early Classic
1400-1100	Center and settlement growth	Centralized milpa forest gardens	Late Classic
1100-800	Civic center demise	Community milpa forest gardens	Terminal Classic -Postclassic
800-500	Settlement refocus	Dispersed milpa forest gardens	Late Postclassic
500-Present	Conquest depopulation	Disrupted milpa forest gardens	Colonial, National, Global

Petén, where they encountered many large towns, often spaced less than a day's journey apart but separated by "dense forests," groves, and fields (Cortés 1985:363-386). Cortés's large army struggled to move overland in a region of Maya waterways and footpaths. Even with local maps, the Spanish spent many days lost among forests and bogged down in the swamps, often deliberately misled by terrified local guides, as Cortés admits in his letter (e.g., Cortés 1985:377). Cortés and his retinue were, nevertheless, nearly always well billeted and provisioned—willingly or not—by the Maya themselves (Jones 1998:32-33).

Though the Maya inhabitants fled before him, it is remarkable that Cortés found enough food left behind in well-ordered towns to maintain his huge entourage of 3,000 Mexican warriors and almost 100 Spanish horsemen. During a journey through a largely hostile territory with only walking trails, in what is generally considered a military disaster, Cortés mentions having to sleep in the open air just 17 or so nights over the more than 150 days it took to travel from Coatzacoalcos to Tayasal/Nohpeten, the Itzá capital (Cortés 1985:360-386). The rest of the time he and his vast army were comfortably housed and fed, if reluctantly, in Maya towns. Only between Tabasco and Acalan, what is now South-Central Campeche, in the Kejach territory near Calakmul of the greater Petén, did Cortés have to spend several nights in what he calls a "depopulated" area before finding a Maya settlement large enough to house his horde. A careful reading of Cortés's description and Jones's overview suggests that in the southern Yucatan Peninsula the Maya dwelt prosperously on the forest landscape in the early sixteenth century. This conjecture is underscored more than a century later, when Ursua, during his 1697 conquest, pleaded for support (Schwartz 1990:54-55) and detailed a list of the foods that he and his men were "forced" to eat, including chicozapote, macal, nance, and other foods found in the forest gardens. It was a veritable cornucopia, but the Spanish had culturally defined standards and found these foods inedible (Terán and Rasmussen 2008:134). Yet what allowed the Maya to succeed in their tropical ecosystem and produce the food they ate was what the Spanish called the *milpa*. The milpa is crucial to the resource-management system that shaped the Maya forest to meet subsistence and tribute needs, develop the political economy, and promote local and long-distance trade.

The Maya Lowland Environment: A Comprehensive Production Platform

The fundamental geographical feature of the Maya forest at the regional scale is the environmental gradient from the high cloud forests of the mountains of Chiapas and Guatemala in the south, around 15 degrees north latitude, through mountain ranges and ridges that gradually descend into the lowland limestone plain of the Yucatan Peninsula, around 21 degrees north. Average annual rainfall varies here (Figure 1.1) from less than 500 mm in the northwest Yucatan Peninsula to 4,000 mm in the far south (White and Hood 2004; West 1964). Commonly divided into the wet and dry season, local farmers see the rainy "winter" season as, first, the warm wet period associated with hurricanes, and then a cool wet period associated with the *nortes*, followed by the dry "summer." Along the environmental gradient, forests grow up over an essentially limestone base, though there are variations depending on local climate, water, and soil conditions (Chase et al. 2014; Dunning et al. 1998; Dunning et al. 2009; Liendo et al 2014).

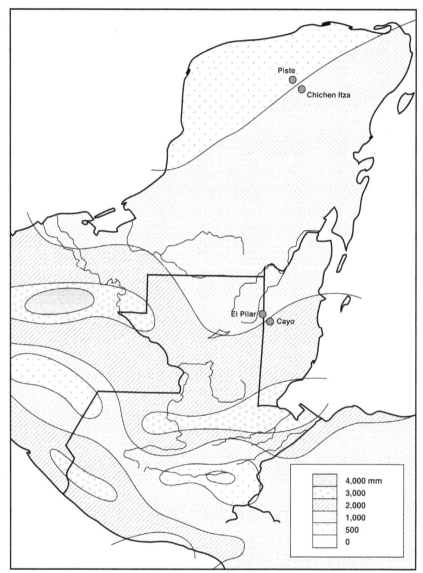

FIGURE 1.1. Annual rainfall distribution in the Maya area. ©MesoAmerican Research Center, UCSB

The capricious limestone bedrock creates unpredictable access to water: Water rarely flows on the surface (Chase and Scarborough 2014a, 2014b; Fedick 2014; Iannone 2014; Lucero et al. 2014). Instead it is absorbed through fissures into the bedrock or flows in underground streams within the limestone. Two major river systems and several smaller ones flank the east and west sides of the central lowlands: the Belize/New River on the east and the Usumacinta/Candelaria on the west. When openings in the limestone drop below the water level, lakes, lagoons, or, as in northern Yucatan, cenotes may form. In the wet season water collects within closed lowland depressions throughout the region. It is estimated that at least 40 percent of the region is wetlands (Dunning et al. 2002; see also Fedick and Ford 1990). This is consistent with data from El Pilar, 47 km to the east of Tikal, where poor drainage characterizes 38 percent of the area (Ford et al. 2009). These variations of karstic topography and water access generate the following four basic ecosystems (Figure 1.2) in the central Maya Lowlands (Fedick and Ford 1990), producing resources used by both the ancient and modern people of the region (Schwartz 1990, Turner 1978):

- well-drained ridges and uplands (high to low closed forest)
- poorly drained lowlands (low open forests and transitional wetlands)
- perennial riverine wetlands (riparian, aquatic, and semi-aquatic vegetation)
- seasonal closed wetlands (low open forest tolerant of hydric extremes)

The peopling of the New World, coinciding with the retreat of the northern ice sheets, changed the character of the landscape. In only a few millennia, humans occupied the Americas from the Arctic Circle to Tierra del Fuego. These early mobile groups, equipped with the essential knowledge of the use of fire and the ability to make stone tools, fanned out through myriad settings. Within approximately 2,000 years of their initial arrival more than 13,000 years ago, people had spread into all habitable areas (Steele et al. 1998), including the Maya Lowlands (Figure 1.3). These groups were the first to understand the topography of the area and to identify the sites of permanent water in a time when the climate was cold and arid and temperate vegetation prevailed (Leyden 1987).

As the climate warmed and precipitation increased, marked worldwide as the Holocene Thermal Maximum, around 8,000 years ago, vegetation changed. The register of plants of the Maya tropical forest is clear. The temperate pine-oak-grass complex diminishes, and tropical megathermal taxa (Morley 2000:14-17), such as *Brosimum*-type Moraceae, commonly known as ramon, are evident in the pollen lake cores (Leyden 2002; Vaughn et al. 1985; among others). A stable warm wet environment prevailed in the Maya Lowlands for approximately 4,000 years (Ford and Nigh 2009, 2014; Figure 1.4). By this time, with the basic knowledge of the regional geography—the ridges, the undulating slopes, the wetlands, the lakes, and rivers—Archaic mobile horticulturalists were expanding the domestic crops they used in the forest. In this long period of favorable stable climate conditions, their seasonal hunting and gathering activities were governed

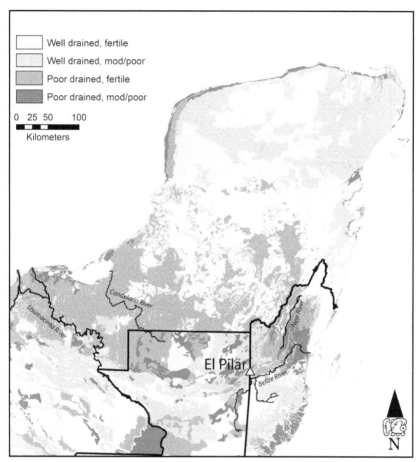

FIGURE 1.2. General resource zones of the Maya area. ©MesoAmerican Research Center, UCSB

by the rhythms of forest production. It was a time of incubation for the Mesoamerican culture that has endured to this day.

Because they were familiar with the lowland environment, the inhabitants could subsist here by building on their historical ecological experience. Their challenges helped establish the traditional ecological knowledge that continues to inform Mesoamerican agroecology. The paleoecological record of the region—from cores of the Petén Lakes (Mueller et al. 2010) to the Cariaco basin (Haug et al. 2003)—shows that beginning about 4,000 years ago precipitation became unstable and unpredictable (see Figure 1.4), marking a period of climate chaos. This caused environmental stress that dramatically changed the landscape. Alternating wet and dry cycles created radical changes that influenced flora and fauna and resulted in a new way of life for the Mesoamerican mobile horticulturalists.

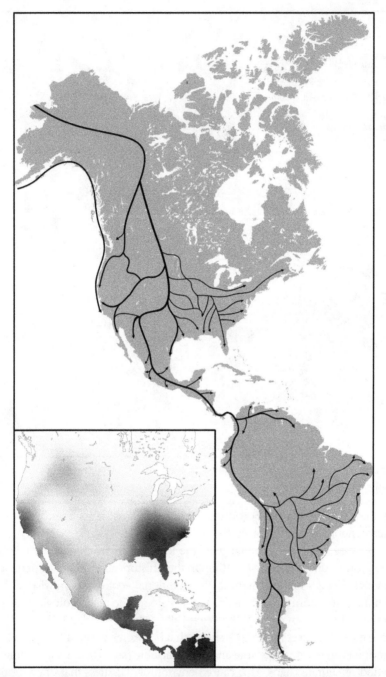

FIGURE 1.3. Peopling of the New World with an inset of population distribution after 2,000 years (after Steele et al. 1998). ©MesoAmerican Research Center, UCSB

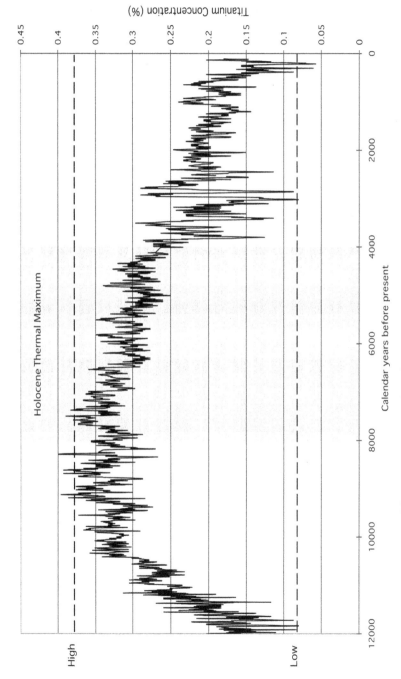

FIGURE 1.4. Precipitation record for Cariaco Basin with Holocene Thermal Maximum indicated (based on Haug et al. 2003). ©MesoAmerican Research Center, UCSB

The well-drained zones preferred by the ancient Maya for farming were the ridges and lower upland slopes above the annual flood line (Fedick 1988, 1989; Fedick and Ford 1990; Ford et al. 2009). Today, these are areas where moist closed canopy forests develop to their fullest (Schulze and Whitacre 1999). Such forested land is unevenly distributed across the region, resulting in dispersed human settlements that reflect this preference for well-drained zones (Bullard 1960, 1964; Culbert and Rice 1990; Freidel 1981; Puleston 1974; Rice 1976; Scarborough and Burnside 2010). Ancient centers—and later Spanish relocation—had to work against these centrifugal patterns (Fedick 1988, 1989; Ford 1991a; Ford et al. 2009). These well-drained slopes comprise less than one-sixth of the area of Northern Belize around the center of Nohmul but nearly half of the interior Petén around the large Classic center of Tikal, Guatemala (Fedick and Ford 1990), and they continue to be found, in varying proportions, to the west into Chiapas and north into the Yucatan Peninsula in Mexico (Figure 1.2). There is a direct relationship between the presence of well-drained ridges, high settlement density, and the location of elite cultural remains of the Classic Maya kingships (Fedick and Ford 1990; Ford 1986; Ford et al. 2009).

It is a mistake to view Maya urbanism through a European filter.[1] In this region the Preclassic settlement changes beginning 4,000 years ago involved a shift from scattered and temporary patterns to permanent occupation of desirable well-drained areas. As people began to settle in greater numbers in the preferred areas—where later centers eventually grew (Ford 2003a:115-116)—their use of milpa forest gardens became more intensive. Farming settlements were predicated upon agricultural resources, and the centers depended upon the farmers. Control of limited sources of water may also have become increasingly political, particularly in the Preclassic, drawing dispersed farmers into centers as the populations grew and the climate became drier (Ford 1996; Lucero 2002; Lucero et al. 2014; Scarborough 2003; see Haug et al. 2003). The historical ecology of the Maya Lowlands, however, was linked to their valuable upland resources. The source of Maya wealth lay in the landscape and in the Maya people's profound understanding of how to construct and use it.

Historical Setting of the Maya Lowlands

The currently accepted view of the Maya collapse identifies the Preclassic as the beginning of a period of *escalating* environmental disturbance, due to increasing human population density (Turner and Sabloff 2012). According to this interpretation, large areas of the central lowlands "were essentially deforested, with most available land given over to agriculture" (Dunning and Beach 2000:184). The perceived result was ecological vulnerability and degradation (cf. Hirshberg et al. 1957; Meggers 1954; see also Anselmetti et al. 2007; Dull et al. 2010). This vision of the ancient Maya landscape, however, conflicts with evidence of long-lasting cultural continuity—a continuous 30-century period of population growth and resilience of the ancient Maya Lowlands, from the Preclassic into present times.

There is no doubt that land use intensified with Maya societal expansion: The steady increase in the number of residential sites reflects population growth, as does the proliferation of exuberant monumental city centers. Traditionally, scholars have imagined this landscape overrun by people and fields. Our alternative landscape for the Classic Maya is one where living in the forest was integral to the human-environment relationship (Atran 1993; Folan et al. 1979; Graham 1992, 1999, 2006; Johnston 2003; Voorhies 1982; see also Conklin 1957). With population concentrated in rainforest cities, a "galactic" form of decentralized urbanism emerged in a largely forested landscape, resembling descriptions of the prehistoric Amazon and Southeast Asia (Fletcher 2009; Heckenberger et al. 2008; Scarborough; 2003 Scarborough and Burnside 2010; Scarborough and Lucero 2011; Scarborough and Valdez 2014; Tambiah 1976). This settlement pattern and landscape ecology were created by the "high-performance milpa" system (Wilken 1971, 1987) that we describe in Chapter 2.

Ancient Maya settlements and, by proxy, the farmers, were located near useful resources. The emergence of urban centers depended on these farmers, and farming requirements were integrated into land-use strategies. Archaeologists for some time have recognized that the population was dispersed in well-drained uplands, regardless of where the centers were (Bullard 1960, 1964; Ford 1986). Social phenomena, such as trade and markets (Freidel 1981; Gunn et al. 2002; Gunn et al. 2014; Scarborough and Burnside 2010), may help explain these patterns, but the ultimate roots have been left uninvestigated. Recently, with the power of the Geographic Information System (GIS), we have demonstrated statistically the strong connections between settlement patterns and the geographic environment (Ford et al. 2009). We will explore in detail the subtlety of the patterns and how they are embedded within the forest.

Prehistoric Chronology

The chronological development of the Maya follows a long, steady, and successful course. Maya occupation of Lowland Mesoamerica began with the expansion of hunters and gatherers into the Americas more than 10,000 years ago. These first people inhabited an arid and cool landscape founded on the karstic limestone platform that forms the Maya region. While the climate differed, the topography was essentially that of today, with undulating ridges and hills interspersed with flatlands. Initially cool, the climate was changing (Haug et al. 2001). Only 8,000 years ago the region became a warm and wet environment with its familiar tropical characteristics: evergreen and semi-deciduous, broadleaf forested uplands; seasonally and permanently inundated wetlands with lakes in the south and cenotes in the north. The region was—and remains—subject to periodic Atlantic hurricanes and volcanic eruptions; it also experiences annual and multiyear cycles of wet and dry periods (Iannone et al. 2014).

8,000-4,000 Years Ago

Archaeological data from the Archaic period is scant, yet the presence of domesticated plants shows that inhabitants were already manipulating flora. Maize, beans, squash, and chile supplemented hunting and gathering (Betz 1997; Clark and Cheetham 2002; Lohse 2010; McClung de Tapia 1992; Piperno and Pearsall 1998; B. Smith 1998). Little is known of the sparse Archaic settlements and their annual cycles. Records of sites, however, suggest widely ranging hunting and gathering in the emergent tropical forests of the lowlands (Kennett et al. 2010; Lohse et al. 2006; Rosenswig 2006a, 2006b; Rosenswig et al. 2014; Voorhies 1998).

4,000-3,000 Years Ago

Widespread small but permanent settlements point to major changes throughout Mesoamerica (Pohl et al. 1996; Vanderwarker 2006). By 3,000 B.P., settlements dominated the region (Blake et al. 1992; Clark and Cheetham 2002:283–286; Neff et al. 2006a; Voorhies 1998), including the Maya area (Fedick 1989; Ford 1986; Puleston and Puleston 1971; Rice 1976; Scarborough and Burnside 2010:337). This period marks the beginning of Maya civilization, the expansion of permanent structures concentrated in well-drained areas, and the use of pottery.

3,000-2000 Years Ago

All upland hills and ridges in the Maya area show evidence of settlements (Fedick 1989; Fedick and Ford 1990; Ford 1986,1991a; Fry 1969; Puleston 1974). These communities formed the foundation for Preclassic cities, such as Nakbe and Mirador (Clark and Cheetham 2002; Forsyth 1993a, 1993b;

Hansen et al. 2002) and later Tikal and El Pilar (Coe 1965; Fedick 1988, 1989; Ford 2004; Haviland 1969; Puleston 1973; Wernecke 1994, 2005). Small at the outset, these centers became major players in the ruling administrative hierarchies on both local and regional levels. Some expanded and grew, while others ebbed. The trajectory, however, was toward increasing population and land-use management, which required greater organization.

2,000-1,400 Years Ago

Classic Maya civilization is marked by the growth of settlements and centers in the Late Preclassic and the Early Classic, with increased social complexity. Settlements expanded to all well-drained areas, especially the prime upland agricultural areas that compose 25 to 49 percent of the region (Bullard 1960; Fedick and Ford 1990; Ford 1985, 1990, 1991a, 1992, 1996; 2003; Fry 1969; Graham 2003; Puleston 1974; Rice 1976), and reflect the intensification of land use (Ford and Nigh 2009; Johnston 2003; Robin 2012). Monumental hieroglyphic stones refer to warfare (Chase and Chase 2002; Kennett 2012:790), and settlements began to spread to less-optimal transitional wetland areas (Fedick 1988; Fedick and Ford 1990; Ford 1986; Ford et al. 2009; McAnany 1995).

1,400-1,100 Years Ago

The Late Classic, the apex of Maya civilization, includes the growth of civic centers and the proliferation of residential settlements (Culbert and Rice 1990; Webster 2002). Centers reached their most extensive size; Tikal, for example, covered approximately 150 hectares of monumental architecture (50 percent of the size of the medieval city of London c. A.D. 1300). Large, dense settlements occupied all the well-drained ridges, the same areas occupied in the Preclassic period (cf. Robin 2012). This was also a time of diversification in ceramics, with the sudden appearance of volcanic ash-tempered pottery in the fine wares (Coffey et al. 2014; Ford and Glicken 1987; Ford and Rose 1995; Ford and Spera 2007; Jones 1986; Sunahara 2003) and evidence of decaying volcanic ash in clay deposits (Tankersly 2011).

While settlement counts are straightforward and well reported (Chase and Chase 1987; Ford 1986, 1991a; Haviland 1972; Healy et al. 2007; Puleston 1973; Rice and Rice 1990; Robin 2012), and numbers of buildings have been used to indicate population size (Culbert and Rice 1990), actual population estimates are a source of major discord. For example, Chase and others (2011), based on research at Caracol, estimate regional population at 1,000 persons per square kilometer, while Ford and Clarke

(2015), based on modeling at El Pilar, put the figure at approximately 140 persons per square kilometer, a little more than one eighth the projection for Caracol. In the Maya context, reasoned estimates of 100-200 persons per square kilometer (Turner 1990) are viable, although these numbers have yet to be reconciled with land use.

1,100-800 Years Ago

The last stela erected at Tikal (Stela 11 dated to A.D. 869) marks the end of the Classic Maya civilization in the core area of the region. Known as the Terminal Classic, this is a period of decline lasting several centuries, identified by the abandonment of monumental buildings. The period has been linked to purported droughts (Gill et al. 2007; Haug et al. 2003, 2005; Hodell et al. 2001; Kennett et al. 2012), though the data are equivocal (Metcalfe et al. 2009; Rushton et al. 2012). The leading hypothesis considers the decline predominantly an environmental transformation (Chase and Scarborough 2014a; Demarest et al. 2004; Lentz et al. 2014), and attributes the cause to overpopulation, resulting in deforestation and soil degradation (e.g., Chase and Scarborough 2014b:3; Chase et al. 2014:24; Rice 1990; Turner 1990; Turner and Sabloff 2012; Webster 2002). The main evidence cited for environmental change comes from paleoecological records derived from lake sediments (e.g., Binford et al. 1987), although the interpretation of these data is ambiguous (Ford and Nigh 2009; see also Fedick 2010; Fedick and Islebe 2012; Gunn et al. 1995; McNeil et al. 2010; Everton 2012:18-21).

800-500 Years Ago

The demise of the major Classic centers, such as Tikal and El Pilar, has been interpreted as desertion of the area. We know that the public infrastructure—temples, palaces, plazas—were gradually left to the elements. The neglect of building maintenance speaks directly to the failure of the political economy, however, and not to the disappearance of the farmers. The Classic Maya regents' power to collect tribute and fund public projects clearly broke down. But, the collapse of the elite institutions does not imply the collapse of the population. That assumption is based on the notion that overpopulation and agricultural expansion drove deforestation (Chase et al. 2014; Diamond 2005; Turner and Sabloff 2012; Webster 2002), and supposes that agriculture and forest are incompatible, but the incompatibility of the forest and the fields has not been demonstrated.

The area between the sites of Tikal and Yaxhá shows continuous, undiminished occupation through the Terminal Classic (Ford 1986:64-65,

2003a:78-80). The El Pilar area, where excavations focused on residential units around centers and beyond (Ford 1990, 2004), shows that at least half of these units were occupied after the Late Classic. The areas without major public architecture, despite the demise of the centers, continued to flourish into the Postclassic (Alexander 2006; Robin 2012, 2013).

Furthermore, the abandonment of the temples, palaces, and plazas did not happen overnight but occurred gradually over decades and even centuries (Scarborough and Burnside 2010; Webster 2002:260-326), and probably not in any one individual's lifetime. First, portions of buildings were abandoned, then whole complexes, and finally, no resources remained for maintenance (e.g., Hammond et al 1998).[2]

Construction and maintenance of monumental architecture was a major issue in both the public and private sectors. Public construction was likely based on the corvée labor of those who were also responsible for maintaining their own private structures. As corvée resources for public buildings diminished, private constructions simplified. The Classic Maya signatures on the landscape dwindled; there was no more investment in stone quarries, and the bare maintenance of monuments was coupled with increasingly plain domestic structures. Farmers, freed from the burden of maintaining the monumental architecture, organized into smaller units and farmed in the traditional way that was encountered at the time of the conquest (Pugh et al. 2012; Terán and Rasmussen 1995).

The Paleoenvironmental and Pollen Records

The paleoenvironmental record for the Maya relies primarily on lake core sediments in the Petén of Guatemala (Binford et al. 1987; Deevey et al. 1979; Hodell et al. 2012). Vegetation changes for the Holocene are recorded in the pollen register of these cores (e.g., Vaughan et al. 1985; Leyden 2002), which are dominated by wind-borne pollen (Bradley 1999:362-362; Kellman and Tackaberry 1997:18) and associated with deposits that reveal the influx of sediment by turbid currents into the lakes (Anselmetti et al. 2007; Mueller et al. 2010; cf. Hartke and Hill 1974). These lake layers are believed to correspond to widespread erosion that formed sedimentary "Maya clay." The record of past precipitation is based on the concentration and ratios of the minor element titanium (Ti) and iron (Fe) in the marine and lake sediments. Titanium concentration is used as a proxy for rainfall, specifically summer monsoonal rain that is reflected in the annual sediment varves of cores from the Cariaco Basin (Haug et al. 2001) and corroborated in the Petén Lakes (Hodell et al. 2008; Metcalfe et al. 2010).

8,000-4,000 Years Ago

High precipitation characterizes the Holocene Thermal Maximum in the Maya area. Plant communities changed from temperate to tropical, and *Brosimum*-type Moraceae pollen, interpreted as representing mature forest cover, dominated (Brenner et al. 2002; Hillesheim et al. 2005). Temperate taxa, including pine and oak, maintain a presence but in low proportions (Leyden 2002).

4,000-3,000 Years Ago

The end of the Holocene Thermal Maximum was marked by more than 1,000 years of rapidly fluctuating precipitation (Ford and Nigh 2009). Although there were chaotic extremes of high and low annual precipitation, the trend was toward drier conditions that persist to the present (Haug et al. 2001; see also Aragón-Moreno et al. 2012; Curtis et al. 1996; Hodell et al. 1995; Islebe and Sánchez 2001; Islebe et al. 1996a; Islebe et al. 1996b; Wahl et al. 2007). Amid this variable rainfall, the diversity of fossil pollen increased with that of wind-pollinated forbs and grasses, relative to wind-pollinated trees (Vaughan et al. 1985; Mueller et al. 2009) and the initial presence of Maya clay (Anselmetti et al. 2007; Mueller et al. 2010), interpreted to be the result of local soil erosion into lakes and swamps, or *bajos* (Beach 1998; Beach et al. 2002; Beach et al. 2006; Brenner et al. 2003; Chase and Scarborough 2014b:3; Mueller et al. 2006).

3,000-2,000 Years Ago

Precipitation was still chaotic at first, but by 2,000 B.P. it had stabilized under somewhat drier conditions, suggested by a drop in titanium concentrations in the Cariaco core. The composition and relative abundance of pollen taxa in sediments hint at even greater species diversity, with a dominance of forbs and grasses. At the same time, the presence of the Maya clay rose to its highest levels (Anselmetti et al. 2007; Mueller 2010:1226), possibly because of erosion from agricultural deforestation or from other environmental change—for example, drier conditions or changes within the lakebed itself, as suggested by Mueller and others (2009:139; Anselmetti et al. 2006).

2,000-1,400 Years Ago

Precipitation stabilized at rates lower than those during the Holocene Thermal Maximum. The pollen record comprises stable vegetation that continues to be dominated by forbs and grasses, with less than 20 percent originating from the forest taxa (using the *Brosimum*-type Moraceae as the forest proxy, Leyden 1984, 1987). The Maya clay also stabilized at moderate levels (Mueller et al. 2010). In all, it is noteworthy that the paleoenvironmental data suggest steady continuity for this time period.

1,400-1,100 Years Ago

During this period there were few changes in pollen and sediment inputs (Leyden 1984, 1987; see also summary in Ford and Nigh 2014), yet new data on precipitation suggest more variability (Kennett et al. 2012). Interpretations during this stable period in Maya prehistory continue to emphasize deforestation yet suggest that this deforestation began at least two millennia earlier (Rosenmeier et al. 2002; Turner and Sabloff 2012; Wahl et al. 2006). Our reading of the data, however, indicates continued continuity in the paleoenvironmental indicators: Forbs make up the majority of the wind-pollinated pollen, with grasses and *Brosimum*-type Moraceae each making up less than one fifth.

1,100-800 Years Ago

No dramatic climactic changes have been resolved for this critical period of Maya prehistory (Medina-Elizalde and Rohling 2012), despite the search for evidence of drought and other environmental impacts (Aimers and Hodell 2011; Iannone et al. 2014). Precipitation was stable, with some rise in levels of titanium suggesting increased rainfall (Haug et al. 2001). Maya clay is present, and forbs and grasses dominate vegetation; all this is interpreted as a backdrop of deforestation (Brenner 1994; Rosenmeier et al. 2002).

800-500 Years Ago

The centuries leading up to the Spanish conquest show major shifts in pollen indicators (Binford et al. 1987), with the rise of *Brosimum*-type Moraceae and a drop in forbs and grasses. Rainfall, as interpreted in the Cariaco and Petén cores, increased at this time, presumably improving annual farming conditions, especially in the drying north. Yet, these data have been interpreted as the rebounding of the tree cover in the *absence* of farmers. This is hardly proven. While the *Brosimum*-type Moraceae pollen increases in the record, this marks a change in the *Brosimum* habitat. *Brosimum* is a pioneer, which is evident in the expansion of the tropics 8,000 years ago. The new habitat for *Brosimum* was the result of collapsing temples and palaces. Population abandonment is inconsistent with Cortés's observations at the time of the conquest. The so-called Classic Maya collapse lasted centuries (Webster 2002), and although the major centers ceased to be maintained, farmers stayed in their forest gardens.

The Fundamentals

The agricultural civilization of the Maya emerged naturally within the context of the Maya forest and the tropical lowland ecosystem of southern Mexico's Yucatan Peninsula, Petén of Guatemala, and Belize (cf. Conklin 1957). These forests were once considered pristine, but geographers and botanists now recognize that humans throughout millennia have influenced the composition of the vegetation (e.g., Denevan 1992a, 2011; Gómez-Pompa et al. 2003; Whitmore and Turner 1992). Today, the human impact is largely expressed in the European practices of cattle pasture and plowing that together threaten the integrity and biodiversity of the forest (Harvey et al. 2008; Nations 2006; Primack et al. 1998; TNC 2014; cf. Campbell 2005). In many respects, the population-deforestation relationship playing out in the Maya forest now is exactly what has been said to have happened a thousand years ago. But how can that be, if there were no sheep or cattle or plows during the period in question?

Despite scholars' broad recognition of human impacts on the Maya forest, they disagree on the timing and nature of these impacts. Turner and Sabloff (2012), summarizing current interpretations of received wisdom (Diamond 2005:176-177), posit that Lowland Maya interactions with the forest culminated in continued clearing for agriculture and were so destructive to the environment as to cause the collapse of Classic Maya society in the ninth century (Townsend 2009:60-69). This interpretation is in line with Webster's conclusion in his 2002 synthesis that the Maya are reenacting the same story today (2002:348). He implies that the milpa system is at the root of contemporary threats, when he refers to satellite imagery that clearly exposes the expansion of cattle pasturage, not milpa farming (Brook and Knudsen 2014). While most studies of the Maya assume that the collapse of the civilization was related to deforestation by people, the Maya forest today is known for its diversity and abundance of useful plants that remain as beneficial today as they were in the past (e.g., Atran et al. 2004; Balick et al. 2000; Campbell et al. 2006; Fedick and Islebe 2012; Levi 2003; Roys 1976).

Amid the expansion of "conventional" monoculture based on industrial production, the traditional Maya farmers continue to practice hand cultivation, making use of generations of ecological knowledge (Ferguson et al. 2003; Griffith 2000, 2004; Terán and Rasmussen 2009:23-30). What is behind the historical ecological transformation of the Maya forest? How can the prehistory of this people provide the background for understanding the transformation? Where are the lessons to be learned? The following chapters explore these questions in light of the conservation challenges we face today.

CHAPTER 2

Dwelling in the Maya Forest: The High-Performance Milpa

The exceptional qualities of the Maya milpa forest garden cycle disclose not only the success of an indigenous annual cropping strategy but also the well-developed management of successive perennials in a system linked to sacred beliefs. The astonishingly productive strategies are flexible and can be intensified. Tree nurturing, crop yields, and land-use methods balance land cover and harvests over countless generations. Far from being destructive, the Maya farmers we have come to know are spiritual caretakers and co-creators of the Maya forest.

Introduction

Any understanding of the historical ecology of the Maya forest is likely to be biased and inaccurate, unless we begin with a clear vision of how human activity has affected the landscape. For millennia the *milpa* (Yukatek *kol*), a form of perennial, multi-cropping swidden cultivation centered on maize (*Zea mays L.*), has been the crucial element in managing the neotropical woodlands of the Maya area and has shaped and conserved forest ecosystems. The "high-performance milpa"—sophisticated, intensive agroforestry—was widely practiced by Mesoamerican farmers (Palerm 1967, 1976; Wilken 1971, 1987). Understanding it helps us interpret the paleo-ecological and archaeological data on ancient Maya land use.

Anabel Ford and Ronald Nigh, "Dwelling in the Maya Forest: The High-Performance Milpa" in *The Maya Forest Garden: Eight Millennia of Sustainable Cultivation of the Tropical Woodlands*, pp. 41-76

FIGURE 2.1. (*Above and on facing page*) Diego Jiménez Chi with his grandson Roque Calderon, in his full-grown milpa, Quintana Roo, Mexico (Macduff Everton).

The Maya milpa entails a rotation of annual crops with a series of managed and enriched intermediate stages of short- and long-term perennial shrubs and trees (Figures 2.1, 2.2). It culminates in the reestablishment of long-lived, mature canopy trees on the once-cultivated parcel (Everton 2012; Ford and Nigh 2010; Gliessman 1993; Hernández Xolocotzi et al. 1995; Nations and Nigh 1980; Nigh 2008; Nigh and Diemont 2013; Terán and Rasmussen 1994; Terán et al. 1998). The integration of the milpa cycle into neotropical woodland ecology transformed the succession of plants (Table 2.1, Figure 2.3) and turned the Maya forest into a garden where more than 90 percent of the dominant tree species have benefits for humans (Campbell et al. 2006).

FIGURE 2.2. Lakantun Maya farmer Chan K'in in his milpa, showing the three stages of the cycle, Chiapas, Mexico (James D. Nations).

Milpa cultivation is much maligned and misunderstood and often accused of provoking widespread deforestation, soil degradation, and loss of biodiversity. This negative view of a venerable agroecological strategy is due in part to the peripheral role the milpa plays in today's commodity-oriented industrial agriculture (Everton, 2012:112-113; Schwartz and Corzo Márquez 2015). The contemporary milpa of marginalized smallholders—family farmers—is often little more than a rear-guard action to conserve seed and provide fresh corn and other products for domestic consumption (integral vs. incipient, cf. Conklin 1957:3-5), a far cry from the system described by Wilken (1971, 1987). Disparagingly referred to as "slash-and-burn" farmers, the ancient Maya are accused of having "burned, cut, and eventually in some regions removed large tracts of these wooded landscapes not long after they settled them" (Piperno 2011:206). Our research has shown that traditional Maya milpa swidden results in the enrichment of woodlands with species useful to humans and significantly improves the ecosystem (Atran et al. 1999; Diemont and Martin 2009; Snook and Capitanio 2012).

TABLE 2.1. Dominant Plants of the Milpa Forest Garden Cycle from the Greater Petén*

Milpa Cycle	Dominant Plants (Wind-pollinated spp. indicated in bold)
Open multi-crop maize field ~ favoring sun: Phase 1 initialization (1-4 yrs)	Cultigens: ~99 spp. such as Capsicum spp. **Chenopodium ambrosioides L.**, Cnidoscolus spp., Cucurbita spp., **Lycopersicon esculentum Mill.**, Phaseolus spp., Xanthosoma yucatanense Engl., **Zea mays L.** Several other genera found in: Leguminosae. Non-cultigens: **Ambrosia spp., Cecropia sp., Mimosa sp., Trema sp.,** and several genera found in: **Amaranthaceae, Asteraceae, Cyperaceae, Euphorbiaceae, Melastomataceae, Poaceae, Urticaceae.**
Long-lived perennial reforestation ~ producing shade: Phase 2 renewal cycle (4-12 yrs)	Acacia cornigera L. Wild, Ananas comosus L. Merr., Annona muricata L., Attalea cohune C., **Brosimum alicastrum Sw.**, Bucida buceras L., Cucurbita pepo L., **Bursera simarouba L.**, Byrsonima crassifolia L. Kunth, Calophyllum brasiliense Cambess, Carica papaya L., **Cecropia peltata L.**, Ceiba pentandra L., Cnidoscolus chayamansa McVaugh, Enterolobium cyclocarpum Jacq. Griseb., Guarea glabra Vahl, Guazuma ulmifolia Lam., Hamelia patens Jacq., Manihot esculenta Crantz, Manilkara zapota L. van Royen, Opuntia cochenillifera L. P. Mill, Pachyrhizus erosus L., Persea americana P. Mill, Pimenta dioica L. Merr., Pouteria sapota Jacq. Moore & Stearn, Psidium guajava L., **Quercus oleoides Schltdl. & Cham.**, Sabal morrisiana Bartlett, Simira salvadorensis Standl., Talisia oliviformis Radlk.
Closed canopy ~ favoring shade: Phase 3 culmination (>12 yrs)	Alseis yucatanensis Standley, Aspidosperma cruentum Woodson, Attalea cohune C. Mart., **Brosimum alicastrum Sw.**, Bursera simarouba L., Cryosophila stauracantha Heynh. R. Evans, Licania platypus Hemsley Fritsch, Lonchocarpus castilloi Standley, Manilkara zapota L. van Royen, Piscidia piscipula L. Sarg., Pouteria campechiana Kunth Baehni, Pouteria reticulata Engl., Sabal morrisiana Bartlett, Simira salvadorensis Standl., Spondias mombin L., Swietenia macrophylla King, Talisia oliviformis Radlk., Vitex gaumeri Greenman, Zuelania guidonia Britton & Millsp.

*Only native taxa included, bolded taxa are wind-pollinated

Note: Only Phase 1 dominated by wind-pollinated taxa

FIGURE 2.3. The milpa cycle from forest to field and back (Kippy Nigh).

The Maya Milpa: A Resource Management System

Milpa is the recognized agroecosystem of indigenous Mesoamerica and the Maya area (Gliessman 2004; Kelly and Palerm 1952:100-107). It has been practiced for thousands of years in all the region's settings. Even today, milpa is a central, sustainable activity in the traditional Maya management of the environment (Gliessman 2001; Terán and Rasmussen 1995). If we define milpa as an open-field polyculture centered on maize (Figures 2.4, 2.5), rotated with successive stages of woodland vegetation in a cycle of 16 to 30 years, then milpa is similar everywhere in Mesoamerica. Adaptable to the diverse ecosystems (cf. Scott 2009), milpa is found from sea level to highlands above 2,000 m; it can be integrated with house gardens or grown some km from the family dwelling and can be intensified to respond to environmental constraints, market demands, and domestic cycles. It also harbors enormous agrobiodiversity, the heritage of thousands of years of forest farming and experimentation (Cleveland 2013).

The Maya milpa has been well described in academic literature (Bernsten and Herdt 1977; Diemont and Martin 2009; Everton 2012; Gómez-Pompa 1987; Hernández Xolocotzi et al. 1995; Isakson 2009; Nations and Nigh 1980; Nigh 2008; Parsons et al. 2009; Steinberg 1998; Terán and Rasmussen 2009; Wilken 1987; and others). Yet it is still perceived through the European lens. In fact, Staller (2010) suggests that to consider maize a "staple grain"—and to compare the tortilla to the Spaniards' bread—is a Eurocentric idea that may not reflect the dietary reality of the Prehispanic Mesoamerican and Maya people. Maize was an important, even sacred, plant to the Maya, so it may not be analogous to wheat or rice in the Old World.[1] The Spanish demand that maize be used for tribute in the Colonial period, along with introduced steel tools, helped reshape the emphasis of milpa practices and even influenced the varieties of maize commonly planted after the conquest (Staller 2010).

In the Eurocentric view, the milpa is simply a cornfield, an investment in cropland only, and so it was seen by the first conquistadors, who coined the word *"milpa"* to define the Mesoamerican maize field. The milpa is not a maize monoculture like a Spanish wheat field, however. While maize is visually dominant, it is interplanted with beans, squash, and other plants from a basket of more than 90 Mesoamerican possibilities (Appendix A). Moreover the multi-cropped maize field is just one stage of a recurring cycle (Table 2.1). Traced back to its Nahuatl origin, the word "milpa" is based on the word *"millipan,"* where *"milli"* means "to cultivate" and *"pan"* means "place" (Bierhorst 1985:213, 259). Thus it is a cultivated place.

FIGURE 2.4. Lakantun Maya polyculture milpa featuring macal, banana, tobacco, sugarcane, and maize in the background, Chiapas, Mexico (James D. Nations).

FIGURE 2.5. Milpa polyculture in Petén, Guatemala (Macduff Everton).

FIGURE 2.6. Lakantun farmer José Valensuela in his recently burned milpa, Chiapas, Mexico; note the considerable charred and partially burned organic surface remains (James D. Nations).

Perhaps the most misunderstood aspect of milpa is its relationship to the forest. For centuries this silvi-horticultural system has formed and conserved neotropical woodlands (Goméz-Pompa 1987), and our research has been directed at exploring the impact it has had on the woodland environment. To understand the power of the milpa to affect the landscape, we need to scrutinize milpa practices and reflect on their consequences. We characterize milpa as an agroforestry system because annual cropping is one stage in a managed, regenerating woodland environment. In a traditional milpa, the space for annual crops is opened and burned to prepare for planting (Figures 2.6, 2.7), but from the first year farmers take measures that ensure the regeneration of forest vegetation.

FIGURE 2.7. *(Above and on facing page)* One burn establishes the open field gap and initiates the milpa cycle, Yucatan, Mexico (Macduff Everton).

The Yukatek Maya word *"k'ax"* is usually translated as "forest" (*bosque* in Spanish) in colonial documents (e.g., Roys 1976; erroneously translated by Dunning et al. 2012[2]). Our notion of forest as woodland, however, as implied in Roys's use of the term, is an oversimplification of the Maya concept of *k'ax*. The dictionary of Yukatek Maya published by Cordemex (Barrera Vásquez 1980) indicates *k'ax* or *k'aax* may be translated into Spanish as *bosque* or *selva* (forest or jungle) or *montaña* or *monte* (tall forest or bush) but also as *arboleda* (grove), and, especially, *campo donde hay monte*, that is, an agricultural field with bushes and trees. *Kanan k'ax* is a well-tended forest or, alternately, a deity considered a guardian of the forest (Terán and Rasmussen 2008:195, 196-107). McAnany (1995:67; see Kintz 1990) also points out that these managed forests were privately owned and considered part of a Maya family's heritage from Prehispanic times into the Colonial period.

The products that are derived from the milpa and the activities related to its management are highly dependent on the skill of the Maya farmers. The literature repeatedly refers to the protection of trees when the maize field is established (Arias Reyes 1995b; Cowgill 1961; Emerson 1953; Everton 2012:72; Hernández Xolocotzi et al. 1995:274; Lundell 1937; Nations and Nigh 1980; Roman Dañobeytia et al. 2011; Terán and Rasmussen 2009). Hunting, beekeeping, and wildlife management also are all related to the milpa management cycle (Diemont and Martin 2009; Terán and Rasmussen 1995).

Ethnographic literature specifically mentions trees associated with milpa. Lundell (1933:66-67) and Emerson (1953:55) specify that chicozapote (*Manilkara zapota*) and ramon (*Brosimum alicastrum*) are systematically maintained in cultivated areas, along with the native species of *Annona* spp., caimito (*Chrysophyllum cainito*), cedro (*Cedrela odorata*), ceiba (*Ceiba petandra*), cocoyol (*Acrocomia aculeata*), corozo (*Attalea cohune*), guayaba *(Psidium guajava)*, guano (*Sabal morrisiana*), nance (*Byrsonima crassifolia*), papaya (*Carica papaya*), pimienta gorda (*Pimenta dioica*), siricote (*Cordia dodecandra*), and zapote negro (*Diospyros digyna*) (cf. Cowgill 1961:17). Lundell (1933:66, 71) adds avocado (*Persea americana*), cacao (*Theobroma cacao*), chayote (*Sechium edule*), cotton (*Gossypium hirsutum*), mamey (*Pouteria sapota*), and tobacco *(Nicotiana tabacum)*, along with ornamental shrubs and trees, as well as medicinal plants (Table 2.2). The tomb of the seventh century Maya king of Palenque, Pakal, illustrates ancestral fruit trees—avocado, nance, mamey, guayaba, and cacao (Schele and Mathews 1998:119-122), all found in infield home gardens and protected outfield orchards (Cowgill 1961:17; Emerson 1953:55; FLAAR 2008; Lundell 1933:66-68, 71, 75; Palerm 1976:39-43). Native forest trees, palms, and shrubs have characterized the Maya ethnobotanical literature of the milpa in the twentieth century (Roys 1976) and maintain importance as we move into the twenty-first century (Balick 2000).

The Milpa Forest Garden Cycle

The neotropical woodlands in which Maya civilization developed was a landscape profoundly influenced by the human societies it nurtured. Archaeologists and paleoecologists in the Maya area have assumed that the presence of agriculture implied woodland reduction and ultimately deforestation, but agroecologists understand that this is not what usually happens in the milpa. Economic botanists, agroecologists, and ecological restorationists recognize the importance of cutting and burning to increase soil fertility and promote local biodiversity (Altieri 1995, 1999, 2008; Altieri and Merrick 1987; Altieri and Toledo 2005, 2011; Gliessman 1982; Gliessman et al. 1981; Ferguson

TABLE 2.2. Sample Protected Trees of the Milpa

Common Name	Scientific Name	Pollination	Uses
Annona	*Annona* sp.	insects^	food
Avocado*	*Persea americana* Mill.	honey bees	food
Cacao*	*Theobroma cacao* L.	insects	food
Caimito	*Chrysophyllum cainito* L.	insects, bats	food
Cedro	*Cedrela mexicana* M. Roem.	insects	construction
Ceiba	*Ceiba pentandra* (L.) Gaertn	bat^	construction
Chayote	*Sechium edule* [Jacq.] Sw.	insects, bees	food
Chicozapote	*Manilkara zapota* (L.) P. Royen	bats	food
Cocoyol	*Acrocomia mexicana* Karw.	insects	food
Corozo	*Attalea cohune* Mart.	insects, wind	food, medicine
Cotton	*Gossypium* sp.	bees	production
Guayaba*	*Psidium guajava* L.	insects	food
Guayo	*Talisia oliviformis* Radlk.	bees	food
Guano	*Sabal morrisiana* Bartlett	insects^	construction
Huano de Sombrero	*Sabal mexicana* Mart.	insects	products
Nance*	*Byrsonima crassifolia* (L.) DC.	insects, bees	food
Papaya	*Carica papaya* L.	insects, wind	food
Pimienta	*Pimenta dioica* Lindl.	insects, birds^	food, medicine
Ramon	*Brosimum alicastrum* Sw.	wind	food
Siricote	*Cordia dodecandra* Dc.	insects	fruit
Tobacco	*Nicotiana tabacum* L.	bees	stimulant

^Pollinator was found for genus only

Trees compiled from: Cowgill 1961, Emerson 1953, Lundell 1933, *Schele & Mathews 1998, Schwartz 1999

FIGURE 2.8. *(Above and on facing page)* Establishing perennial shrubs and trees in the milpa directs forest succession, Petén, Guatemala (Macduff Everton).

et al. 2003; Griffith 2000; Hernández Xolocotzi 1985; Hernández Xoloco tzi et al. 1995:565-566; Toledo 2010; Toledo et al. 2003; Toledo et al. 2008; Woodworth 2013:325-350). The Maya forest, like other wooded areas of Mesoamerica, has been structured by the ancient and contemporary milpa cycle (Finegan 2004; Ford and Nigh 2009, 2014).

As a cultural landscape (Atran 1993; Everton 2012; Gómez-Pompa and Kaus 1990), this forest developed over generations because of the opportunities and challenges of the tropical lowland environment. The adaptive response that we call the milpa forest garden cycle arose during a millennium of climatic chaos 4,000 years ago (Ford and Nigh 2014; see Haug et al. 2001; Hodell et al. 2008; see Chapter 3). The product of a historical ecology arising as early as 8,000 years ago, the milpa is widely misrepresented in historical (Cook 1921; Lundell 1937), scientific (Piperno 2006; Reina 1967; Steggerda

1941; Turner 1978; Villa Rojas 1945; Webster 2002:348), and development literature (Camacho Villa 2011:107; Haney 1968; Pilcher 1998).

A major objective of the milpa forest garden cycle is to increase the beneficial makeup of the managed landscapes and the forest as a whole (Everton 2012; Ford and Nigh 2009; Levy Tacher et al. 2005). The stages of the cycle are strategically directed with utility in mind, employing practices based on the skilled selection of species (Atran 1993; Atran and Medin 1997; Atran et al. 1999; Atran et al. 2000; Rätsch 1992). Planting and plant selection in the early reforestation phases favor fast-growing, short-lived woody species to achieve rapid closure of the canopy (Figure 2.8). These create the conditions that long-lived perennials need to sprout and grow (Gómez-Pompa 1987; Gómez-Pompa et al. 1972; Levy Tacher et al. 2005:71).

Recognizing the nature of the high-performance milpa and the sequence of land-cover changes that the cycle implies (see Table 2.1; Figure 2.3), it is not surprising to find that scholars affirm the significance of humans in shaping the Maya forest as we know it (Atran 1999; Campbell et al. 2006; Dunning et al. 2012:3652; Dunning and Beach 2010; Ferguson et al. 2003; Ford and Nigh 2009; Gómez-Pompa 1987; Ross 2008). Sample plots in varied settings show astonishing homogeneity across woodland ecosystems, not to be expected in unmanaged forests (Campbell et al. 2006). In the Petén, the 20 dominant trees forming the Maya forest oligarchy (Table 2.3)—where core species account for a majority of the trees—are all found among traditional forest gardens in the region (Ford 2008) and fulfill household needs. A detailed examination of the forest species in areas with ancient residential architecture confirms the emphasis on plant utility (Campbell et al. 2006; Ross 2008, 2011). Well-managed, these milpas will also provide products for trade (Figure 2.9). This traditional agricultural knowledge of the Maya is an 8,000-year experiment in successful productive tropical landscapes.

The "young" ecological successional stages of crops and sequential rotations are the building phase of the forest cycle, producing a rapid increase in carbon sequestration, biomass, and diversity. All agricultural systems are based on the high primary productivity of these early phases of agroecosystems. Among other things, these systems can result in significant storage of carbon in soils.

> Atmospheric concentrations of carbon dioxide can be lowered either by reducing emissions or by taking carbon dioxide out of the atmosphere and storing in terrestrial, oceanic, or freshwater aquatic ecosystems. A sink is defined as a process or an activity that removes greenhouse gas from the atmosphere. The long-term conversion of grassland and forestland to cropland (and grazing lands) has resulted in historic losses of soil carbon worldwide but there is a major potential for increasing soil carbon through restoration of degraded soils and widespread adoption of soil conservation practices. (FAO 2014b)

The Yukatek Maya employ specialists known as "wind-tenders" (*yum ik'ob*), who control milpa fires by burning against the prevailing winds and spreading the brush out to achieve an even, low-temperature burn throughout the process (Figure 2.10). Our research with the Lakantun Maya (also known in the literature as Lacandon) has shown that such practices result in a significant cumulative input of black carbon to the soil and the enhancement of other physical and chemical characteristics of anthropogenic dark earths (Figure 2.11, Glaser et al. 2001; Nigh and Diemont 2013). There

TABLE 2.3. Dominant Plants of the Maya Forest^

Scientific Name	Common Name	Pollination	Uses
Alseis yucatanensis	wild mamey	moths	food
Aspidosperma cruentum	malerio	insects	construction
Attalea cohune *	corozo	insects	food
Brosimum alicastrum*	ramon	wind	food
Bursera simarouba*	chaca	bees	medicine
Cryosophila stauracantha	escoba	beetles	production
Licania platypus	succotz	moths	food
Lonchocarpus castilloi	manchiche	insects	construction
Manilkara zapota*	chicozapote	bats	food
Piscidia piscipula	jabin	bees	poison
Pouteria campechiana	zapotillo rojo	insects	food
Pouteria reticulata	zapotillo	insects	food
Sabal morrisiana*	guano	insects	production
Simira salvadorensis*	palo colorado	moths	construction
Spondias radlkoferi	jocote	insects	food
Swietenia macrophylla	mahogany	insects	construction
Tabebuia rosea	macuelizo	bees	construction
Talisia oliviformis*	kinep	bees	food
Vitex gaumeri	yaxnik	bats	construction
Zuelania guidonia	tamay	bees	medicine

^After Campbell et al. 2006 and Ford 2008
* Dominant in home gardens

has been a focus, especially in tropical ecology, on the "above-ground biomass" as a major carbon source. However, now we know that soil is the largest and most durable pool of terrestrial organic carbon and interacts strongly with vegetation cover and climate reservoir. The soil store is four to five times larger than the above-ground reservoirs, with a much longer turnover time—around 1,200 years (Lal 2004). Restoration agriculture, as defined by Shepard (2013), describes what we see in the high-performance Maya milpa. The cycles of production provide abundant products for family subsistence, while increasing soil fertility, water conservation, long-term carbon sequestration in the soil, and the carbon sequestration in the short-term regeneration of woodland biodiversity.

FIGURE 2.9. Tobacco was produced for trade by the Lakantun, Chiapas, Mexico (James D. Nations).

FIGURE 2.10. Dario Tuz Caamal, a Yukatek Maya "wind-tender," spreads fire to obtain a controlled burn, Yucatan, Mexico (Macduff Everton).

FIGURE 2.11. In Chan K'in's Lakantun milpa, frequent small-scale fires create ash and charcoal without damaging soil life, Chiapas, Mexico (James D. Nations).

Following the Spanish conquest, the Maya area underwent a sequence of severe droughts (Farriss 1984) that are now associated with the global Little Ice Age (Dull et al. 2010; Hodell et al. 2002). As depopulation, relocation, and forced labor recruitment left the dispersed forest gardens unattended in the Colonial period, they changed into what can be called the feral forest (Campbell et al. 2006), likely the dominant form of old-growth forest in the neotropics. A similar process probably occurred after the Terminal Classic, as temples and plazas went unattended (see Lambert and Arnason 1982).

Since virtually all of the Maya forest reflects millennia of human dwelling and use, it is difficult to gauge the extent of Maya modification versus a natural adaptation to existing conditions and resources (Schulze and Whitacre 1999). In western Belize, three inventoried Maya forest sites with evidence of Late Classic occupation and little evidence of subsequent human activity provide a vivid picture of the domesticated landscape (Campbell et al. 2006). Testing the hypothesis that the human signature is visible in the forest today, the authors report both *alpha* and *beta* diversity indices were low, compared to similar tropical latitudes in areas relatively free of human influence. Campbell and colleagues (2006) also showed that the three forest patches with ancient Maya settlements were highly oligarchic (defined by relative dominance of the top 10 or top 20 trees in the sample) and featured species of economic value to humans, with the top 10 species accounting for 57 to 61 percent of the forests' footprint measured in area based on tree diameter.

This degree of homogeneity suggests that these forest sites have been submitted to pervasive human disturbances such as fire, selection, and enrichment with species of economic value to people. While a forest's soil conditions clearly play a key role in the abundance and distribution of woody species (Sanchez 2012), the predominance of useful species strongly supports the priorities of ancient agroforestry management (Ross 2008, 2011; Ross and Rangel 2011).

This locally adapted agricultural cycle supplies households with food, trade items, and other useful products at every stage. It is noteworthy that the stages Maya farmers recognize are equivalent to the ecological stages defined by forest ecologists (Capers et al. 2005; Chazdon 2008, 2014; Kellman and Tackaberry 1997:146-151; cf. Nigh 2008; Finegan 2004). The economic plants that make up the Maya forest today, including plants kept to attract and feed animals such as deer (Greenberg 1992; Hernández Xolocotzi et al. 1995:62-63; Terán and Rasmussen 2009:309-320), owe their resilience to persistent selection during the past eight millennia (Atran 1993; Campbell et al. 2006; Ford and Nigh 2009, 2014). Many of the prominent plants of contemporary Maya ethnobotany are those commonly disturbed by human activity (Chazdon and Coe 1999; Voeks 2004), particularly the *Attalea* sp. (cf. Anderson et al. 1991) noted in the pollen cores of Lamanai (Rushton et al. 2012). Of the 456 plant species collected in the forested area of Lacanjá Chan Sayab, the Lakantun Maya recognize more than 73 percent as useful in at least one specific way (Levy Tacher et al. 2002).

Every stage of growth is skillfully managed to select and establish a useful and beneficial inventory of plants that serve the short- and long-term needs of the family (Figure 2.12), at the same time managing the water regime, soil fertility, and organic content of the soil. The successive woody stages serve not only as a reservoir for useful plants, but also support the animals that are needed for pollination, seed dispersal, hunting, and beekeeping (Everton 2012; Greenberg 1992; Hernández Xolocotzi et al. 1995:63-64; Terán and Rasmussen 2009:321). The maize cycles are staggered so that, at any one time, different plots create diverse habitats (see Figure 2.3). The result is a complex mosaic landscape of woodlands and fields at varied levels of development that we will examine in detail in Chapters 4 and 5.

The field-to-forest cycle has shaped the changing landscape around permanent Maya residential units. Native forbs and grasses cohabited the landscape as part of the sun-loving species that typically flourish over the average

FIGURE 2.12. Labor, skill, and scheduling are critical to the succession process in which Zacarias Quixchan trims lower siricote branches, Petén, Guatemala (Macduff Everton).

four-year period of the multi-crop maize field (Ford and Nigh 2010; Kellman and Adams 1970; Steggerda 1941:99-107), comparable to the initial stages of natural succession in forest tree-fall gaps (Chazdon 2014). With the development of perennial plants, representing the next stage of the milpa cycle, woody species are encouraged, selected, and planted. At the same time, the Maya favor species shown to be beneficial in reforestation and soil restoration (Diemont et al. 2006; Diemont et al. 2011; Nigh 2008; Roman Dañobeytia et al. 2009; Douterlungne et al. 2010). Among these are trumpet tree (*Cecropia* sp.), balsa (*Ochroma pyramidale*), bobtob (*Sapium lateriflorum*), and guapuruvú (*Schizolobium parahyba*) (Table 2.4; Appendix B).

In the perennial stages of the milpa cycle, economic needs would be met by the canopy trees (Figure 2.13). Among these are trees and palms found in traditional forest gardens today: avocado, allspice, achotillo, achiote, annona, balsa, bayal, cacao, calabash, cedar, ceiba, chaya, cherimoya, copal, corozo, fiddlewood, guano, gumbolimbo, hogplum, jabin, kinep, mahogany, malerio, mamey, manchiche, poisonwood, ramon, siricote, succotz, and zapote (see Appendix B for Latin names and a larger list; Everton 2012; Hernández Xolocotzi et al. 1995:232; de Miguel 2000; Terán and Rasmussen 2009:332-338). These plants are part of traditional Maya forest gardens and are largely pollinated by insects, birds, or bats (Ford 2008).

FIGURE 2.13. *(Above and on facing page)* This outfield orchard includes traditional Maya forest and introduced trees; note the profusion of annuals during this stage of succession. Petén, Guatemala (Macduff Everton).

TABLE 2.4. Plants Used by Lakantun Maya for Soil Restoration

Species Name	Lakantun Maya
Astrocaryum mexicanum Liebmann ex Martius	ak te
Belotia mexicana K. Schum	tao
Brosimum sp.	ba'am bax
Bucida buceras L.	sä puk te
Calophyllum brasiliense Camb.	baba
Cedrela sp.	kulche
Cordia alliodora Oken	bajum
Dialium guianeense Willd.	we' ech
Guatteria anomala R. E. Fries	ek bache
Hampea stipitata S. Watson	ts'uk tok

Species Name	Lakantun Maya
Hibiscus sp.	jor
Mucuna pruriens L.	Ka abe
Ochroma pyramidale Urban	chujum
Piper auritum H. B. K.	jo'ber
Piper aduncum L.	makarum
Sapium lateriflorum Hemsl.	u'cunte
Simira salvadorensis Standl.	chak'ax
Sterculia apetala Jacq.	anis
Swietenia macrophylla King	puna
Unidentified	pok te

Source: Diemont 2006

As a multi-crop cultivation system, the milpa forest garden cycles over decades. With the opening of the field as the initial phase, every plot cycle starts with selective harvesting, coppicing, pollarding, and cutting of the forest, followed by a careful hot burn (Everton 2012:75; Terán and Rasmussen 2009:201-231. This process clears the field of dried brush for the planting of maize and other annual crops (Hernández Xolocotzi et al. 1995:71; Terán and Rasmussen 2009:235-258). Domesticated crops and useful weedy herbs are cultivated annually over approximately four years, while woody shrubs, fruit trees, and hardwoods sprout and grow in the shade of the tall maize, progressing toward the next stage in the cycle. Some perennial crops are established at this time as well. When the woody shrubs and trees have grown enough to shade the annuals, the field advances through successive stages of guided reforestation, transforming from an open field into a managed forest (Everton 2012:16-18; Hernández Xolocotzi et al. 1995:131-139; Levy Tacher and Golicher 2004).

An Example from Chiapas: the Lakantun Maya Milpa

We can gain some insight to the interdependence of Maya milpa agriculture and the tropical forest by examining a recent ethnographic example of the Lakantun from Chiapas. The ancient Maya undoubtedly employed a wide variety of farming systems, and while the example of the Lakantun milpa cannot be taken as a general model of ancient Maya subsistence, it illustrates the sophisticated cultural engagement with the neotropical woodland environment characteristic of indigenous Mesoamerican systems (Alcorn 1990; Nigh 2008; Toledo et al. 2003; Wilken 1971, 1987; see also Conklin 1957). An understanding of Lakantun land-use management reveals the flexibility of the Maya milpa forest garden system.

The Lacandon rainforest is currently home to some 500,000 indigenous people largely of Maya cultural and linguistic affiliation. The Lakantun are the smallest of the Maya groups, but they have a long history of continuous occupation of the lowland forest (Palka 2005). Traditionally, they subsist by managing and exploiting land in several ecological zones concurrently. These zones include home gardens, fields, mature woodlands, and aquatic and semi-aquatic ecosystems. Regenerating forest parcels have been perceived as "abandoned" after maize cultivation. In fact, they demonstrate the enormous diversity of plants and animals intentionally and directly managed by the Lakantun (Durán Fernández 1999; Levy Tacher et al. 2002; Nations and Nigh 1980; Nigh 2008).

The historical background of the Lakantun as an ethnic group is shrouded in mystery, but what is not debated is their successful move away from the changing world of Mesoamerica after the conquest. Isolating themselves in the rugged terrain of the Lacandon Forest of modern-day Mexico and Guatemala, perhaps since the late seventeenth century (Palka 2005), these groups were able to maintain a traditional production system well into the twentieth century. The Lakantun agricultural system described by Nations and Nigh (1980) is therefore a glimpse into the past—a quintessential example of the high-performance milpa. The Lakantun approach to cultivation flourished in the absence of the political and social constraints of the globalizing world of the colonial sixteenth to nineteenth centuries (cf. Scott 2009). Families lived where they worked; food and other needs were derived directly and almost entirely from the milpa and woodlands.

Lakantun men traditionally dedicated the greater part of their days to milpa work, in addition to hunting and gathering forest resources. Women and children helped during harvest, when more labor was required, as is common in Mesoamerica. Such dedication to milpa work allowed plant diversification and productivity rarely noted in recent times (cf. Campbell 2010).

The impact of Lakantun management practices on regenerating forests is where the true subtlety of the system is revealed. The farmers chose cultivation sites surrounded by mature forest to maintain a source of tree seeds, many of which were transported across the maize fields by animals (Medellin 1994b; Medellin and Equihua 1998; Medellin and Gaona 1999; Vargas Contreras et al. 2009). This practice, combined with intensive daily selection and weeding of the cropping area accelerated and directed ecological succession and thus achieved rapid forest regeneration (Nigh 2008). Careful weed management extended the useful life of the field for annual crops, allowing high yields during extended periods from four to eight years. In contrast, less-intensive conventional milpas in this region are only planted for a maximum of three consecutive years before being overwhelmed by herb and shrub competition (Kellman and Adams 1970; see also Conklin 1957:3).

Weeding included a judicious use of fire, avoiding negative effects on soil ecology (Nigh and Diemont 2013; Nigh 2008; see also Gliessman et al. 1981). Lakantun weed management is radically different in philosophy and practice from the conventional milpa "cleaning," widely practiced by contemporary Mesoamerican farmers. In conventional milpa, the entire field is weeded once over several days, followed by two or three additional weedings during maize cultivation. Weeds are allowed to proliferate after the last cleaning as the maize crop grows to harvest size. This means that the entire field must be cleared and burned in preparation for the next planting season, damaging soil ecology.

In the high-performance Maya milpa, a complete burn over the entire field occurs only once in a cultivation cycle (see Table 2.1), when the primary vegetation is cleared to initiate field cropping. Even that initial burn is carefully controlled to maintain lower temperatures and keep the vegetation from converting entirely to ash, thus assuring the presence of charcoal (see Terán and Rasmussen 2009:225-231). Throughout the year, weeds and crop residues are accumulated in small piles and burned periodically (see Figure 2.11); the resulting ash and charcoal are spread over the field. Most weeds that are pulled or cut are not burned but left in the field to decompose as green manure (Everton 2012:17). These practices provide a continuous supply of organic matter and biochar, and result in the highly enriched anthropogenic soil observed on Lakantun fields (cf. Wilken 1987), similar in some ways to the *terra preta* of the Amazon (Balée 2010; Glaser et al. 2001; Guimaraes Vieira and Proctor 2007; Hecht 2007, 2009; McCann et al. 2001; Nigh and Diemont 2013; Peterson et al. 2001; Woods and McCann 1999).

Control of the seed bank has a profound effect on what follows the suspension of annual cropping. The idea of abandonment after cultivation is universally referred to as "fallow" in the literature, implying that the farmer simply lets the fields rest and allows the natural processes of regeneration to take its course. This notion is not an accurate characterization of traditional milpa management (see Table 2.1). For the Lakantun Maya, the phases that come after cultivation receive attention comparable to that of the maize field itself and gainsay the notion of abandoned fields.

Ecologists no longer subscribe to the equilibrium models of succession, in which woodlands were believed to return to a climax state after a disturbance (fire, blow-down, or clearing for cultivation). They recognize forest succession as a series of stages usually leading to some form of closed-canopy forest where the relations among dominant woody species characterize the stages (Chazdon 2008, 2014). The Lakantun identify such successional stages and their associated species of trees (Nigh 2008), so their traditional fields encompass a great diversity of species, especially compared to conventional milpa practices. Thus, forest recovery is hastened under this traditional management system.

For example, in one management practice, Lakantun farmers spread balsa seed (*Ochroma pyramidale*) in order to create thick stands of this fast-growing tree (Diemont et al. 2006; Douterlungne et al. 2010). Balsa has been used by generations of Lakantun farmers to accelerate forest regeneration, replenish soil organic matter, and enhance weed control. It is used in particular for the control of bracken (*Pteridium aquilinum*), which can be a serious invasive problem (Cooper-Driver 1990; Gliessman 1978; Schneider 2004; Suazo 1998; Turner et al. 2001, 2003, 2004; Turner and Sabloff 2012).

Bracken becomes invasive under specific conditions where the tree canopy is opened and bracken is able to establish its deep rhizomes and form dense swards (Berget 2012; Booth et al. 2003; Den Ouden 2000; Earp 2011; Schneider 2004). Schneider (2004:230) discovered that bracken invasion in Campeche was linked to land-use strategies: Parcel size and land-use intensity are fundamental. Where land was scarce and parcels were less than 40 hectares per household, bracken density was low. Where parcel size was large, 80 hectares or more per household, bracken was prevalent (Schneider 2004:237). Control of bracken is a matter of labor and skill (Berget 2012), as the Lakantun demonstrate (Levy Tacher 2012).

Perhaps a dozen other trees were also managed for their beneficial effects on soil fertility, retaining species of interest and value during the process of reforestation (Roman Dañobeytia et al. 2011; Diemont and Martin 2009; Levy Tacher 2000; see Table 2.4). In sum, as the Lakantun example illustrates, the milpa cycle is a complex multi-cropping system built around the rotation of maize fields with secondary stages of forest (Chazdon 2014). Forest succession and regeneration are carefully managed; tree species are selected—eliminated, planted, or encouraged to grow—so that woodland composition and regeneration are aimed at economic and cultural usefulness (Diemont and Martin 2009; cf. Campbell et al. 2006; Ross 2011; Ross and Rangel 2011; cf. Snook 2005; Snook et al. 2005).

An understanding of the Lakantun milpa system and the importance of the milpa cycle in the management of the Maya forest provides insight into the possible nature of Archaic mobile horticulturalists and the deep historical ecology of the area more than 4,000 years ago. These proto-forest farmers would have exploited and expanded small clearings in the forest, observing and eventually intervening in forest succession, along the lines of the Lakantun system. Other skills would have been available to the early inhabitants of the Maya Lowlands, anticipating the sophisticated forms of agroforestry that characterize indigenous peoples throughout the neotropics (Alcorn 1990; Linares 1976; Peters 2000; Stahl and Pearsall 2012). These practices left their imprint on the woodland environment long after these territories had been depopulated.

Another example of Maya agroforestry is the *pet kot*, a form of woodland modification practiced up until recently by the Yukatek Maya, first described by Gómez-Pompa and colleagues (1987). In this stony region of the Maya forest, the *pet kot* creates niches that support tall, managed stands of trees that often contrast greatly with surrounding lower vegetation. *Pet kot* were developed in fields by accumulating stones covering 19,000 to 24,000 square meters, where especially useful species were cultivated as a protected forest ecosystem (Gómez-Pompa et al. 1987:11, 13). Many of these are common to local home gardens, such as the genera *Brosimum, Spondias, Pithecellobium, Malmea, Bursera,* and *Sabal,* and others (Gómez-Pompa et al. 1987:11-12). In similarly enriched areas around cenotes, Gómez-Pompa's team observed cacao trees of a variety commonly found far to the south in Chiapas (Gómez-Pompa and Kaus 1990). By providing shade and windbreaks, these microenvironments in the arid Yucatan create their own water regime, producing more mist and humidity than the general area (Peters 2000).

The Yukatek *pet kot* and Lakantun milpa likely arose during the "long transition," as the Mesoamerican mobile horticulturalists extended their reach during the early Holocene. Eventually a true agrarian society emerged, with increasing dependence on settled agriculture. This resulted in a domesticated landscape that transformed the forest into a cultural feature (Fedick 2010; Everton 2012:1-37). The creation of the Maya forest garden is therefore the result of an accumulated investment in and intensification of the milpa cycle as part of a dynamic silvicultural system (Everton 2012:57-96; Ford and Nigh 2009; see Scarborough and Burnside 2010:327).

High-Performance Milpa
—Non-Industrial Agricultural Growth

An enduring question in ancient Maya studies is how could a sophisticated and populous civilization be maintained in a humid tropical environment and with an apparently "primitive" agricultural technology, the milpa swidden (see Beckerman 1983; Conklin 1954, 1957, 1971; Cook 1921). As we have shown, the Maya high-performance milpa is hardly primitive. It employs farmer knowledge- and labor-intensive strategies that greatly increases the production and restoration potential of the field (Cleveland 2013). A few archaeologists have pointed to this strategy to explain the apparent mystery of Maya cultural advancement and population growth over 20 centuries beginning by 1000 B.C.

> From an archaeological perspective, the fact that intensive bush fallow cultivation is ecologically feasible under certain conditions is significant because use of the practice in antiquity could account for processes that have long resisted explanation. Among these is the relationship in south-

ern lowland Classic Maya (ca. AD 550–800) society between population growth, agricultural intensification, and profound cultural change. On the basis of population estimates derived from settlement data and estimates of the productive capacity of the agricultural technologies known to have been employed by the Maya, several archaeologists have concluded that during the seventh and eighth centuries AD, some high-density southern lowland Maya populations must have exceeded the productive capacity of their agricultural systems. If current estimates of Maya maximum population densities are reasonable—an assumption that some Mayanists (Ford, 1991b; Webster, 2002:174, 264) reject—then archaeologists must ask, How did high-density Maya populations support themselves agriculturally? One intensification strategy not previously considered by Mesoamericanists is intensive bush fallow cultivation. (Johnston 2003:127)

The high-performance milpa, a form of "intensive bush fallow cultivation" in Johnston's terms (2003), permits agricultural growth through intensification of skilled labor and ecological knowledge (Ploeg 2013). Fallow reduction is usually seen by ecologists as negative, an unsought result of population growth and land pressure that leads to a loss of biodiversity and soil fertility (Karthnik et al. 2009; Schmook et al. 2004; Van Vliet et al. 2013; among others). Speeding up the process of reforestation in the milpa cycle, however, can be seen as agricultural intensification achieved by the management of secondary succession (cf. Snook 2005; Snook and Negreros-Castillo 2004; Snook et al. 2005; Valdez Hernández et al. 2014). This is what we saw with the Lakantun.

The milpa cycle is the foundation of the constructed landscape, composed of species selected by milpa farmers, especially in the annual cropping and early stages of succession where intense plant selection occurs. As a human-enriched ecosystem, it reflects the values of the culture, where investments emanate from a household base. For the infield-outfield strategy (see Netting 1977, 1993; Netting et al. 1989; Pyburn 1998), time, labor, and scheduling are balanced with the distance to fields. Home-garden infields (Caballero 1992; Corzo Márquez and Schwartz 2008; De Clerck and Negreros-Castillo 2000; Kintz 1990; Mariaca Méndez 2012; Negreros-Castillo and Hall 2000) and diverse, cultivated outfields take advantage of microenvironmental gradients of moisture, slope, and soil conditions to provide for the myriad demands of daily life.

The primary residence of a family is most often located in an established community with other families and will usually have an infield milpa and orchards surrounding the house compound (Figure 2.14). These household infield features are well known in Colonial times, and the Spanish, who saw

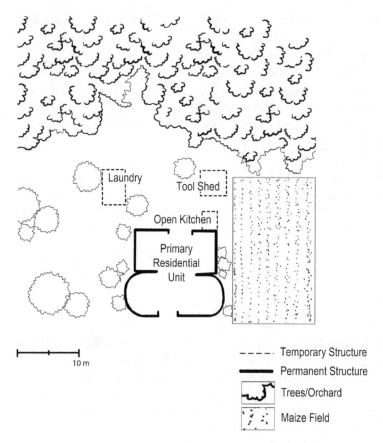

FIGURE 2.14. Infield Maya house and forest garden, the primary residential unit. ©MesoAmerican Research Ce nter, UCSB

these urban agricultural plots as intrusions on the order of proper city life, forbade them. An early Yucatan ordinance issued by Viceroy Governor To-mas Lopez Medel in 1552 reveals the conquistador's view of humans in the forest landscape:

> Therefore I order that all the natives...construct houses close to one an-other. And they should not sow any milpas within the town, but it shall be very clean. There shall not be groves, but they shall cut them all...so that they shall be clean, without sown land or groves; and if there were any, they should be burned. (quoted in Roys 1952:137)

Such policies clearly had a tremendous impact on traditional land use and residence patterns and wreaked havoc on the welfare of the Maya (Terán and Rasmussen 1995; 2008:133-134). Prior to the Spanish conquest, their farming systems were supported by the elite administration. Both infields and outfields would have been integrated into Prehispanic society.

Outfields are located at varying distances from the home base. As many as five fields might have been planted at a time (Terán and Rasmussen 1995:367), and many would have a shelter or rancho for periodic use (Everton, 2012:119-120; Faust 2001; Hanks 1990:380-387; Kintz 1990; Schwartz and Corzo Márquez 2015; Zetina G. and Faust 2011; see Chapter 4). These fields are situated among different habitats to provide a range of resources to hedge against uncertainties of rainfall (cf. Beaglehole 1937; Hack 1942; Soleri and Cleveland 1993). Because of distance, outfields are not as intensively managed as home gardens. Nearby fields may well be visited from the home, but those farther away would require a secondary base to accommodate periodic work. This infield-outfield model of land use is known worldwide as a means of managing household-based agriculture (Fedick 1992; Netting 1977; Pyburn 1998; Sanders 1981).

The productivity of maize and other crops grown by Maya households has been documented. Yield data on the maize from traditional, high-performance milpas vary widely, yet on the average, production ranges from 1,100 to 1,300 kg per hectare (see Chapter 4). Schwartz and Corzo Márquez (2015) argue that these data do not include *mulca*, or *molcate*, smaller ears that are separated from the main harvest for the immediate use for the household and animals. Looking at the 1950s data from the Petén, Cowgill (1961) gives an average yield of 855 kg per hectare. Yields for maize in the northern Yucatan gathered by researchers of the Carnegie Institution from comparable traditional milpa are greater, averaging 1,155 kg per hectare (Redfield and Villa Rojas 1962; Steggerda 1941; Villa Rojas 1945). These yields are contrasted with the skillful and labor-intensive system of the Lakantun discussed earlier, where yields reach 2,800 kg per hectare (Nations and Nigh 1980). These figures are only a fraction of the potential. Emigrating milpa farmers report that, upon initial colonization of the Lacandon Forest, yields from fields newly established in mature forest range from 6 to 10 tons per hectare, levels that quickly drop off with subsequent cultivation.

Reporting for yields of many other milpa crops is not as systematic as for maize. Cowgill (1961:22-26) itemizes 26 crops in the milpa, including five types of beans (several *Phaseolus* spp. and *Vigna elegans*) and three types of squash (*Cucurbita* spp.). She maintains, however, that estimating yields is problematic, as each farmer uses a different formula for plant combinations, making averages difficult to calculate (Cowgill 1961:22). Yields of beans vary in accordance with the kinds and amounts planted in a field. Cowgill reports yields of beans ranging from 125-2,500 kg per hectare to an average of 747 kg per hectare. Cowgill's reports are relatively high compared with the records of Terán and Rasmussen (2009:290-291), who record three types of beans in the traditional milpas of Xocen that together total 51 kg per hectare. Arias Reyes (1995b) records only one type of bean yield at 11 kg per hectare. Considering Cowgill's records of low maize yields (Schwartz and Corzo Márquez 2015), we can take these numbers as evidence of the wide variation within the milpa system.

Squash records are also variable, with as many as four types recorded in different fields. Cowgill (1961:22) offers some estimates in numbers of plants and one in yields that convert to 1,000 kg per hectare. The difficulty is that some records are based on the pulp or meat of the squash and others on the seeds, where the greatest nutrition lies. Terán and Rasmussen (1994:292-93) record from 15 kg per hectare and Arias Reyes (1995b) documents 28-49 kg per hectare for the seeds alone.

Both Cowgill and Steggerda record the number of "weeds" in the milpa, indicating a great deal of plant diversity that may be acting as cover to conserve humidity, inhibit erosion, and provide useful food and medicines for the household (Ankli et al. 1999; Ford 2008; Vieyra-Odilon and Vibrans 2001). Some weedy plants can inhibit growth of nearby vegetation or attract insects or provide allelopathic compounds that improve yields (Gliessman 1983). Cowgill (1961:22) estimates 5,727 plants/mecate, which comes to 14,318 per hectare. Steggerda (1941:24) estimates 1,135/4 square meters for a total of 28,375 per hectare and itemizes them by species.[3] Clearly there is a lot going on in these traditional milpas (Ford et al. 2012). These data on productivity will concern us in Chapter 4, where we address the question of the milpa system's capacity to support the regional population.

Maya Sacred Agriculture

Agriculture is a fundamental expression of the relationship between people and nature. In the case of the Maya, as with many traditional cultures, agriculture is not just a matter of soil fertility and crop genetics. Farming involves a relationship with a world of spirits, believed to rule the material world and to claim fundamental ritual and moral obligations for humans (Trigger 2003:649-650; 670-672). Scientists who focus on the material dimensions of farming practice and knowledge often ignore the spiritual aspect (Terán and Rasmussen 2008, 2009:27-28, 49-50). Yet, we can hardly understand the behavior of traditional Maya farmers if we do not take into account their cosmology—the relationship they perceive between natural processes and the elemental beings believed to animate those processes.

The Maya world is a moral one. Not only do actions have consequences but those consequences also depend on human intentions (Terán and Rasmussen 2008:137). Bad intentions, egotistical attitudes, or lack of respect for nature leads to negative consequences for all. It is not only in the actions directly related to agriculture where one must be careful. All aspects of behavior require respect for other humans and the nature spirits. "According to the elders, everything has its *secret,*" said one of our informants in Chiapas. These "secrets" are ritual actions that complete one's obligations to the spirit world. So success in agriculture is dependent not only on material and ecological factors, but also on the harmony that farmers and their communities establish with the spiritual beings that animate nature (Terán and Rasmussen 2008:136-137). This idea is fundamental to traditional Maya agriculture even today.

To farm a parcel of land, the Maya must ask permission of the owner, who is the lord of the earth, recognizing reciprocal obligations. In preparing the parcel, the farmer marks out the four cardinal directions and the center where he stands and faces each direction as he prays and makes offerings to bring the milpa into harmony with cosmic forces (Freidel et al. 1993:29-33; Everton 2012:67-74). The philosophy expressed here is one of partnership and reciprocity with the land and the spirits in every natural process. The idea is co-responsibility, not control over nature, similar to the reciprocity that governs social relations in the Maya community (Atran 1999).

The living, spiritual being that animates the species maize *Zea mays* is known in Maya as the soul or heart of maize. The actions and virtues of the farm family and community motivate the soul of maize to stay with them. If they waste maize or otherwise offend the soul, it will complain to the earth lord and perhaps abandon the family or the entire community. If the soul of maize leaves, one's maize supply and even the seed may be lost.

This view pertains to what is called the common tradition: the idea that humans are sinners and misfortune results from the normal will of God to punish. Most Mesoamericans have believed this since Prehispanic times. Other ceremonies involve acts to purify one's sins to lessen punishment. The Maya of the Yucatan Peninsula seem to have conserved more of these rituals directly associated with milpa, though all Maya peoples participate in this milpa tradition (Everton 2012:116). In reflecting on the religious aspects of Maya milpa, Terán and Rasmussen write:

> The high variability of the pluvial regime and the uncertainty it generates seem to be the basis of agricultural religious beliefs, as they affirm the

idea that rainfall expresses the will of God to pardon sinners. Drought, damaging rains, hurricanes, and pests are punishments He sends when He does not pardon. Just as the technical aspects produce practices and plants adapted to ecological limitation, spiritual aspects have generated beliefs and ceremonies such as the request for rain (*ch'a chaak*), mentioned in 16th-century sources, that have permitted humans to adapt to this difficult and uncertain environment. (2009:355, translation ours)

There is another uncommon tradition characteristic of the Maya appropriated by shamans—the curers and ritual specialists (Terán and Rasmussen 2008). Such specialists (*hmen* in Yukatek) participate as advisors to common folk, conduct the proper ceremonies such as *ch'a chaak*, and can communicate directly with spiritual entities (Everton 2012:67; Freidel et al. 1993; Schele and Freidel 1990:44; Terán and Rasmussen 2008:30-32). This special talent permits them to intervene directly with spirits to prevent misfortune—drought, hail, wind—or to cure disease. The shaman does not simply supplicate as a common sinner but requires a special ritual preparation and purification, as well as an internal spiritual state that allows him or her to communicate with supernatural beings (Terán and Rasmussen 2008:29).

Initiating the milpa cycle comes with petition and thanksgiving (Everton 2012:76). Farmers may make offerings of prayer and food before cutting the vegetation, once it is burned, before planting, and also when the corn is mature (Everton 2012:67-74; Hernández Xolocotzi et al. 1995:181; Terán and Rasmussen 2008:36-42). The ceremonial prayers of the *ch'a chaak* (Figure 2.15) will last three days (Terán and Rasmussen 2008:61-110) and name the specific features to protect in the particular milpa—for example, rocky spots, low areas, discrete trees, night birds, and the spirits of trails (Terán and Rasmussen 2008). But these customs have changed in recent years. Traditional Milpa farmers, or *milperos*, are being ridiculed by evangelists, and farmers no longer get together to do the *ch'a chaak*, though some will perform it individually (Everton 2012:112, 260, 284-285; Terán and Rasmussen 2008:61-110, 2009:259).

These recent developments are illustrated by a group of Ch'ol Maya schoolchildren from northern Chiapas who were participating in what became *laboratorios para la vida*, a school garden program. They carried out a research project to find out why the people of their village no longer planted their own maize (ECOSUR 2003; Nigh 1999). Questioning their parents and grandparents, they were told that around 10 years earlier the community had suffered a religious division. New converts to a Protestant sect had criticized their neighbors, who remained traditional Catholics, for

FIGURE 2.15. The ceremonial *ch'a chaak*, performed by *hmen* Agapito May, forges the connection of the farmer to his land in San Ramón, Yucatan, Mexico (Macduff Everton).

their rituals, including those accompanying the planting of milpa. This ridicule made the farmers ashamed, and even though they did not become Protestants, they ultimately abandoned those ritual practices. As a result, the children learned from the elders that the soul of maize abandoned the village, and the farmers lost their seed. The religious conflict affected all aspects of the community, and even the town assembly stopped meeting to decide collective issues.

According to Maya cosmology, these problems can be corrected by readjusting one's relation to the spirit world and modifying the offending behavior. In the case of the Ch'ol schoolchildren, the students decided they would recover the seed of the community and plant a school milpa. They visited a nearby community to obtain the varieties of maize seed previously planted by their forbears. On the appointed day the students planted traditional milpa and carried out the planting rituals, marking the four corners and the center and making an offering to the earth lord to request permission to puncture his skin to plant the seed. The entire community was invited, and the turnout was impressive. Even the Protestants came and observed from a distance. The earth lord was apparently pleased, because that year the milpa gave a particularly abundant harvest. Thanks to the children, the heart of maize had returned.

There is no real separation of nature and culture for the Maya. No word exists that equates with our term "nature" (Everton 2012:87). The knowledge of the landscape, the spirits of the natural world, and the respect for the common good pervade daily life and its rhythms. The milpa cycle embodies the relationship of the Maya to their fields, forests, and gardens.

Summary

The Maya forest is the result of smallholder farmers engaged in plant selection (Terán and Rasmussen 2009:44), using skills honed in a variable environment at the local landscape level (Ferguson et al. 2003; Griffith 2000). Traditional Maya farming, still practiced today, represents an investment in the conservation of the landscape, from the intricacies of soil management to the usefulness of trees and the spirits of that landscape. The farming strategy promotes biodiversity and animal habitats essential to the sustainability of an integrated subsistence system. The ancient and contemporary Maya rely on the intensity and productivity of their resource-management systems. As we have shown, the milpa cycle itself accommodates varied intensification, depending on the amount of labor devoted to the different phases of cultivation and managed succession. The result is a dynamic and resilient historical ecology that builds a diversified landscape and creates the required mosaic of successional stages.

The long-term historical response to the developing tropical forest included foraging, horticulture, arboriculture, and agroforestry. The strategies that favored the domestication of the ancient Maya forest landscape have influenced the composition and dynamics of the contemporary forest ecosystem. The Maya imprint is so extensive that the wealth of species that awakened the interest of conservation biologists (Mittermeier et al. 2000) should be seen largely as the result of millennia of human selection and management. If the Maya have transformed this diversity over the last 8,000 years to favor human needs, then flora and fauna now recognized by conservationists to be endangered and in need of protection must have evolved under intensive human management (Fedick 2003, 2010). In the following chapters, we will examine the landscape created by the milpa forest garden cycle, using specific data to interpret ancient Maya historical ecology and build an alternative explanation to the current view that the Maya destroyed their woodland ecosystem.

CHAPTER 3

Environmental Change and the Historical Ecology of the Maya Forest

People are always a part of the landscape, but to assume that cropping is inconsistent with forests is simply to follow the European experience and mock the nuanced sophistication we know to be a part of Maya cultivation. For the milpa of Mesoamerica and the Maya, the forest is integral to the cycle. Recognizing the cyclic quality of Maya farming emphasizes the impact of this forest enrichment and its reflection in the human ecology of the forest. The combined records for precipitation and pollen provide a baseline for interpreting environmental change.

Introduction

Human entrance into the New World and the occupation of Mesoamerica and the Maya area roughly coincide with the great transition of the Pleistocene to the Holocene epoch around 10,000 years ago, but at what point are humans actually present in the paleoecological record? Recent studies show that the questions encountered in interpreting data and determining the proper dating of phases revolve around distinguishing climate change from human impact. The human imprint was light in the Archaic period, from 8,000 to 4,000 years ago, becoming evident archaeologically around 3,000 years ago with agricultural settlements in the Preclassic. Any changes before that time are more likely attributable to climate change associated with the Holocene warming and the climatic chaos of 4,000 years ago (Ford and Nigh 2014). Once the Maya settled on the landscape, the forest was increasingly shaped by human management of the milpa cycle (Toledo et al. 2003). In this chapter, we analyze paleoecological data for consistency with this interpretation.

The Maya Forest Paleoenvironmental Context

The first peoples of the Americas, who arrived more than 13,000 years ago, possessed basic hunting and gathering skills, including stone tool production and the use of fire. These pioneers expanded rapidly across the hemisphere from north to south (Figure 1.3) and established a detectable presence throughout the Americas within 2,000 years (Goebel et al. 2008; Steele et al. 1998). The occupation of greater Mesoamerica and the Maya Lowlands dates from the earliest time period, when the climate was colder and drier than it is today (Leyden 2002:88-90; Steele et al. 1998).

The climatic transition that ended the final Pleistocene Ice Age created a dry landscape characterized in the Maya Lowlands by scrub, grasses, and cacti (Burroughs 2005; Piperno 2006, 2011). With the warming Holocene, there was a shift to a temperate oak and pine savanna. Paleoclimatic studies in the Petén of Guatemala suggest that as the world warmed, that change brought increased precipitation and humid conditions that, around 8,000 years ago, promoted the tropical evergreen forests of today (Carillo-Bastos et al. 2010; Leyden 2002; Leyden et al. 1993). This interpretation correlates with regional Circum-Caribbean Cariaco climate data (Haug et al. 2001; Hillesheim et al. 2005, Hodell et al. 2008; Peterson et al. 2001).

While archaeological evidence is scant for the early Holocene (Neff et al. 2006b; Rosenswig et al. 2006a, 2006b), there is every reason to consider that the Maya area was occupied early on, as was most of the continent (Kelly and Thomas 2013; Steele et al. 1998:297). Archaeological data for the hunting and gathering periods of the Paleoindian and Archaic occupation in the Maya area, prior to 4,000 years ago (Table 3.1), are gaining more attention (Kennett et al. 2002; Lohse 2005; Lohse et al. 2006; Voorhies 2004). The inhabitants of the Lowlands initially encountered an arid, cold, and temperate environment, which changed as tropical vegetation expanded.

The pollen data indicate a thinning of frost-tolerant plants like *Quercus* and *Pinus* and the rise of *Brosimum*-type Moraceae, tropical plants intolerant

TABLE 3.1. Paleoenvironmental and Cultural Chronology of the Maya Lowlands

Years Before Present	8000-4000	4000-3000	3000-2000	2000-1400	1400-1100	1100-800	800-500	500-Present
Human Ecology	Hunting & gathering	Early settlement	Emergent centers	Civic center expansion	Center and settlement growth	Civic center demise	Settlement refocus	Conquest depopulation
Precipitation	Long stable wet	Initial climate chaos	Continued climate chaos	Return stability dry	Stable dry	Medieval warm wet	Little Ice Age extremes	Instability
Wind-Borne Plants	Moraceae dominate	Moraceae varies, forbs rise	Moraceae drop, forbs climb	Forbs dominate, pines peak	Forbs dominate, grass variable	Moraceae rise, forbs decline	Moraceae expansion forbs decline	Moraceae continuity, forbs drop
Land Use	Mobile horticulture	Settled horticultural forest gardens	Settled forest gardens	Expansion of milpa forest gardens	Centralized milpa forest gardens	Community milpa forest gardens	Dispersed milpa forest gardens	Disrupted milpa forest gardens
Cultural Period	Archaic	Formative Preclassic	Middle–Late Preclassic	Late Preclassic-Early Classic	Late Classic	Terminal Classic Postclassic	Late Postclassic	Colonial, National, Global

of frost (Deevey et al. 1979; Leyden 2002:91; Morley 2000:13). The Middle Holocene, known as the Thermal Maximum or Climactic Optimum, from about 8,000 to 4,000 years ago (Burroughs 2005; Rosen 2007:80-88; see also Burn et al. 2010), was among the wettest periods in the history of the Maya Lowlands. We can imagine the Pleistocene landscape as a mosaic of open woodlands ranging from grasses to closed, semi-deciduous wood-lands. With warmer and moister conditions, the result was a more complex landscape in which tall evergreen forest expanded to become the dominant vegetation (Kellman and Tackaberry 1997:22-25; Morley 2000:126-129).

The change from an arid temperate environment to a humid neotropical one would have represented a fresh opportunity for the Archaic inhabitants, and indeed their numbers evidently grew over the millennia of the stable Holocene Thermal Maximum. Though these populations were relatively small and dispersed, we should not underestimate the potential long-term effect on the environment of their skillful use of fire and stone tools (Dene-van 1992b, 2012; Neff et al. 2006b; see also Piperno 2011). Through inter-action with their environment, the early occupants of the Maya Lowlands affected the composition and distribution of the rainforest.

The karstic landscape that characterizes much of the Maya area absorbs surface water and moves it quickly into subterranean deposits or to surface wetlands known as *bajos* (Dunning et al. 2002). Relying on rainfall for drink-ing water would have been a challenge in the more arid periods of the Early Holocene. The notably wet climate period of the Middle Holocene, begin-ning 8,000 years ago (Haug et al. 2001; Mueller et al. 2009), dramatically improved water availability in the Maya Lowlands. People could therefore spread out, initially as hunters and gatherers, then gradually adding horticul-ture to their seasonal rounds (Betz 1997; McClung de Tapia 1992; Piperno and Pearsall 1998; Pohl et al. 1996; Rosenswig 2006a; B. Smith 1998).

The four millennia of the Holocene Thermal Maximum in the Maya forest was a relatively consistent wet period. Predictable high precipitation (Mueller et al. 2009:138) provided a stable environment and coincides with the expansion of pioneering megathermal tropical plants, such as *Bro-simum alicastrum*, identified in the Petén lake-core pollen sequence (Leyden 2002). Around 4,000 years ago a period of climatic chaos began, associat-ed with the appearance of settled farmers in Mesoamerica and marking the Formative or Preclassic phase of Maya prehistory. Archaeologists have not fully recognized the importance of climate stability in the Archaic and the impact of the unpredictable climate chaos in the Formative.

The paleoecological record of sediment cores from the Cariaco Basin, off the Venezuelan coast of South America, provides valuable geochemical proxies for climate change (Figure 1.4). Titanium (Ti) and iron (Fe) are

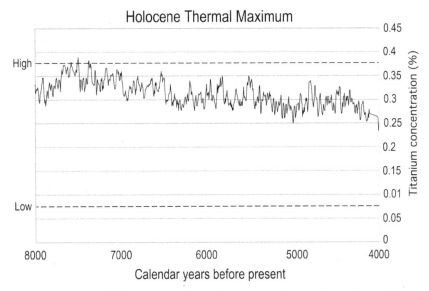

FIGURE 3.1. Stable high precipitation of the Holocene Thermal Maximum from 8,000 to 4,000 years ago (based on Haug et al. 2003). ©MesoAmerican Research Center, UCSB

trace elements that rise and fall with water runoff identified in sea cores for the past 14,000 years (Haug et al. 2001). The oxygen-free conditions of the Cariaco Basin create undisturbed sediment deposits, called varves, forming alternating light and dark strata that correspond with annual dry and wet seasons (Haug et al. 2001; Peterson et al. 2001). The precipitation changes in the Cariaco deep-sea core (Haug et al. 2001:1304-1305) have been corroborated with climatic trends reflected in local data throughout the region, in particular in the Maya area (Hodell et al. 2008; Mueller et al. 2009:137-140; Neff et al. 2006a; Neff et al. 2006b). Pollen shifts identified by the palynologists (Leyden 2002), as well the isotopic data reviewed by Brenner and others (2002:144; Hodell et al. 2008), coincide with the dramatic chaotic changes noted in the Cariaco data. The major precipitation fluctuations recognized in the Holocene have been attributed to the movements of the Intertropical Convergence Zone (ITCZ) and the increasing intensity of El Niño events (Haug et al. 2001; Hillesheim et al. 2005; Mayewski et al. 2004; Peterson et al. 2000).

This stable four-millennia-long Holocene wet period ended about 4,000 years ago (Figure 3.1) and was followed by approximately 2,000 years of significant instability and chaos (Figure 3.2). Variations in the precipitation

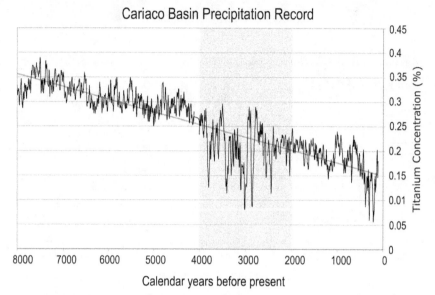

FIGURE 3.2. 8,000 years of precipitation featuring the period of climate chaos and the overall-best-fit drying trend (based on Haug et al. 2003). ©MesoAmerican Research Center, UCSB

chart for the Cariaco are so extreme that the amplitudes equal the difference between the driest periods recorded in the Pleistocene and the wettest periods recorded in the Holocene Thermal Maximum (Haug et al. 2001:1306). This chaotic period of radical differences in precipitation (Figures 3.2, 3.3), along with a general drying trend (Gunn et al. 2002; Haug et al. 2001; Neff et al. 2006b), would have provoked major changes over the landscape, as is evident in the pollen (Leyden 2002) and sediments of the Petén lakes (Anselmetti et al. 2007; Mueller et al. 2009; Mueller et al. 2010).

A number of environmental changes are associated with the period of climate chaos (Table 3.1, Figures 3.4, 3.5). One change is the reduction of the presence of *Brosimum* pollen and the increase of forbs and the fluctuation of grass pollen, classed as "disturbance" (Curtis et al. 1998; Islebe et al. 1996a; Islebe et al. 1996b; Mueller et al. 2009; Vaughan et al. 1985). These sun-loving, early successional annuals appeared where tall vegetation opened (Booth et al. 2003), either through natural disturbances such as drought or hurricanes or by intentional clearance for fields and construction (Ford et al. 2012; Kellman and Adams 1970; Steggerda 1941; Voeks 2004).

Another change noted in lake sediments is the identification of clay deposits, long assumed to be caused by Maya land-use practices (Anselmetti et al. 2007; Chase and Scarborough 2014b:3; Dunning et al. 2014). Now, with absolute dates for some of these records, it is clear that initial influx of

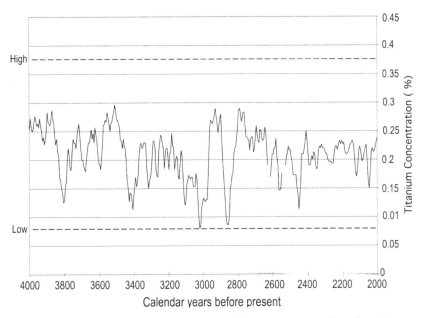

FIGURE 3.3. Climate chaos between 4,000 and 2,000 years ago (based on Haug et al. 2003). ©MesoAmerican Research Center, UCSB

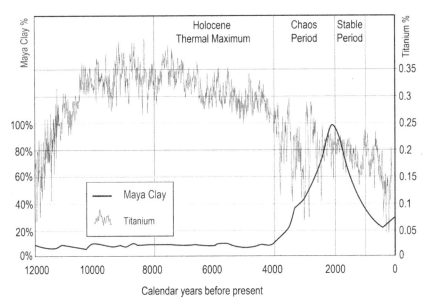

FIGURE 3.4. Precipitation change indicated by titanium percent over time showing Maya clay and climate chaos (based on Haug et al. 2003; Anselmetti et al. 2007; Brenner et al. 2002). ©MesoAmerican Research Center, UCSB

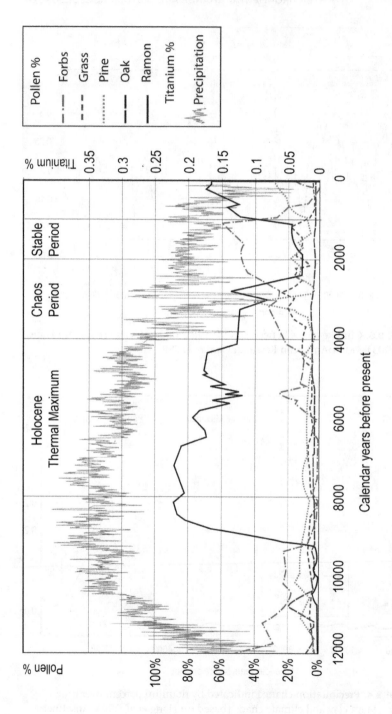

FIGURE 3.5. Precipitation and select pollen over time in the Maya forest (after Brenner et al. 2002; Curtis et al. 1998; Leyden 2002). ©MesoAmerican Research Center, UCSB

so-called Maya Clay *predates* the establishment of Maya settlements (Mueller et al. 2009). The sediments are likely the result of internal lake changes known as turbidites (Anselmetti et al. 2006; Mueller et al. 2010: 1226) and coincide with the precipitation chaos (Figure 3.4) that must have had significant impact on the landscape and may have contributed to the deposits (Ford and Nigh 2014). Rather than being caused by humans, radical precipitation variations beginning around 4,000 years ago are probably responsible for the clay (Mueller et al. 2009; see Ford and Nigh 2009). Increasingly permanent settlements that built on stability were the Maya response to the dramatic climatic changes.

Historical Foundations of Paleoenvironmental Research in the Maya Forest

The paleoenvironmental study of the Maya area began more than 50 years ago (Brenner et al. 2002:142-144). Much has changed since Deevey initiated his pioneering interdisciplinary work on lake-core sediments in the 1960s. Initially, although the stratigraphy of lake cores was clear, dating methods were crude. Since that time, methods to identify sedimentary components have improved, and, most importantly, it is now possible to independently date sediment deposits (see Brenner et al. 2002; Rice 1996).

Deevey and his team (Deevey et al. 1979; Rice 1996) set the stage for paleoenvironmental research in the Maya forest, and this remarkable project has continued to the present (Hodell et al. 2012; Mueller et al. 2009; Mueller et al. 2010). Deevey's research aimed at assessing the environmental impacts of Maya agriculture and urbanism left in the Petén lake sediments (Brenner et al. 2002:145). Since Holocene climate data were unknown when the initial research began, it was explicitly assumed that the tropical environment had altered little since the beginning of the Holocene, and that any changes in the record would be attributable to human impact (Rice 1996). We have little doubt that the Maya impacted their environment, and Deevey's results tell part of the story, starting with the first summary article (Deevey et al. 1979).

The Petén of Guatemala was the site of the first lake-sediment core sampling at a time when detailed radiocarbon dating was not feasible. Depositional problems affected sediment stratigraphy with variable rates of sedimentation, bioturbation, and other factors that complicate the sediment sequence and interpretations. As a result, the changes detected in the fossil pollen sequence were assumed to correspond to changes in the dated archaeological record. The sediment units were defined and linked to the archaeological chronology (Vaughan et al. 1985).

Since Deevey's work began with the assumption that changes on the landscape were due to human activity, alternative interpretations were left unexplored. Problems arose when the archaeologically linked lake-core sequences were used as a source of independent evidence to confirm the archaeological chronology. Vaughan and others (1985:75) who initially worked with the Petén data cautioned scholars, and particularly archaeologists, against tautological reconstructions of evidence without independent dating. When absolute dates became available, obvious adjustments in the chronology were necessary, allowing for more accurate analyses (Anselmetti et al. 2007; Mueller et al. 2010; Neff et al. 2006a; Wahl et al. 2006). However, despite the revisions, the original idea that any environmental change is solely attributable to human impact persists (see Dunning et al. 2012; Turner and Sabloff 2012; Webster 2002:348). The relationships between the paleoenvironmental reconstructions and ancient Maya history have only recently been subjected to scrutiny (Ford and Nigh 2009; see also Fedick 2010; McNeil 2010).

Interpreting Pollen in Maya Forest Ecology

When doubts were expressed about the ability of palynology to throw light on the history of tropical forests, the arguments pointed to the tropical pollen record as an "uninformative brew" of rare wind-pollinated species (Bush 1995:595 citing Faegri 1966). The sheer diversity of species and forest types and the proportion of unique and unknown, yet critical, species of the forest canopy (Bush 1995; Bush and Rivera 1998:389, 2001), along with a high rate of degradation under tropical conditions, seemed guaranteed to confuse the fossil pollen record (see also Bradley 1999; Morley 2000). Fossil pollen is collected from a variety of settings, most commonly from sediments of lakes and wetlands. Since these reflect a subset of the historical pollen rain, the question is: To what degree would this profile, in turn, reflect the actual composition of regional vegetation (Bush 1995; Bush and Rivera 1998, 2001)?

The vast majority of tropical woody species (98 percent) are pollinated by animals (Ollerton et al. 2011), producing small quantities of pollen dispersed over short distances, rarely traveling more than 20-40 m from the source tree (Bush and Rivera 1998). Wind-pollinated trees that distribute abundant pollen are rare. While some zoophilous trees are present in the local pollen rain, they are restricted to plants with open flower structures (Bush and Rivera 2001:360), making it difficult to infer the presence and abundance of mature canopy forest species (Bush 1995:595).

For forest types in contemporary Mesoamerican landscapes, past pollen distribution is considered representative of the patterns of today (Bush 2000; Leyden 2002). It is therefore critical to consider data from current ecological studies in interpreting fossil pollen spectra. Such studies reveal a number of problems with the methods currently used by paleoecologists and archaeologists to describe ancient landscapes (Bush and Rivera 1998; Bush 2000). Major species of the tropical forest canopy are severely underrepresented in the pollen rain and rarely appear at all in sediment records (Bush 1995; Bush and Rivera 2001). The prominent example of a wind-pollinated species is the ramon tree (*Brosimum alicastrum*), a member of the Moraceae family, which is among the most ecologically important families of the neotropical forest (Burn and Mayle 2008:187). It is well represented in the contemporary pollen rain of the Maya forest (Domínguez-Vásquez et al. 2004; Leyden 2002,), as well as in that of the Amazon (Burn and Mayle 2008, Burn et al. 2010). Ramon is an important component of the mature forest canopy, but since it is abundant in the understory as well, contemporary studies have excluded it from calculations of canopy representations of mature forest (Bush and Rivera 1998:39; see also Burn and Mayle 2008).

In pollen records for the Maya forest, the dated rise in ramon and its family Moraceae coincides with the Holocene Thermal Maximum and development of the tropical forest (Figure 3.5). A subsequent drop in abundance is associated with the onset of a general drying trend coupled with a millenium of climate chaos 4,000 years ago (Ford and Nigh 2009; Mueller et al. 2009). Ramon is tolerant to water stress in the karstic uplands of the Maya area, as witnessed today (Lambert and Arnason 1982; Puleston 1968; Schulze and Whitacre 1999:191, 283). The ramon tree is highly competitive in the well-drained uplands, where the exteme dry conditions thin out the forest (Schulze and Whitacre 1999:192-193). On lower slopes, however, where more moisture is available, ramon loses its edge and drops rapidly in dominance (Schulze and Whitacre 1999:193-194, 283-286) while other, moisture-loving dominant trees have the advantage.

Ramon is well known for its robust, highly nutritious seeds, which are used by today's Maya (Atran 1993; Flaster 2007; Maya Nut Institute 2014; Puleston 1982; Teeccino 2014) and are a favored food of many neotropical mammals (Nations and Nigh 1980). The leaves make an excellent fodder for browsers such as deer (Emery et al. 2000; Flaster 2007:29) and were used in the Petén by *chicleros*, harvesters of the chicozapote sap, for their mules and by farmers today for domestic livestock (Fairchild 1945; Schwartz 1990:137-198).[1] These properties make ramon one of the most intensively managed trees throughout the area (Peters 1983, 2000; Puleston 1968).

It is challenging to interpret landscape patterns from pollen signatures. The dominance of wind pollen in the spectra is evident in the contemporary samples as well as in fossil pollen (Bush 1995:602; Vaughan et al. 1985:76-77). Species of trees observed in the fossil pollen sequence include several species of the Moraceae family, especially ramon. Other recorded families and species include Urticales, *Byrsonima,* and Melastomataceae/Combretaceae. *Bursera* and *Cecropia* are referred to as indicators of forest disturbance. These species are, in fact, represented in all the contemporary mature forest types at Tikal (Schulze and Whitacre 1999). Further, Bush and Rivera (2001:363) note that Moraceae makes up 46 percent and *Cecropia* makes up 10 percent of the pollen rain of the current mature forests of Panama, which does not at all reflect the actual composition of the forest.

Clearly, the focus on pollen in the direct interpretation of the vegetation landscape is problematic. Weak winds and heavy rains clear pollen from the air and reduce its dispersal (Bush and Rivera 1998:350). Species that are abundant in the pollen rain, such as ramon and *Cecropia* are present in the mature canopy but can also be pioneers, exploiting forest gaps that are common in the well-drained uplands (Schulze and Whitacre 1999:240; see also Bush and Rivera 1998:389; Strauss-Debenedetti and Bazzaz 1991). Given the persistent issues surrounding the interpretation of vegetation in landscapes based on pollen in today's forest, it would follow that there are even greater ambiguities for fossil pollen in the ancient Maya forest.

Problems with Fossil Pollen

Interpretations of the lake-core pollen spectra (Brenner et al. 2002; Hodell et al. 2012; Leyden 2002) have supported the general portrait of climate trends during the late post-glacial period. As we look more deeply, however, and bring into focus the scale of human-environment dynamics in the Maya forest, uncertainties weigh more heavily. To correctly interpret the fossil record, we need a solid grasp of tropical forest ecology, especially in the context of human adaptations, which comes from current ethnobotanical and agroecological studies.

Canopy species of the tropical forest are diverse, and any given species is rare in the contemporary pollen spectra (Bush and Rivera 1998, 2001; Ford 2008; Ford and Nigh 2009), ranging from 0 to 3 percent of the *in situ* pollen rain (Bush and Rivera 1998:390). As a plant guild, canopy trees contributed about 20 percent of the trapped pollen rain in present-day forests. Yet one can expect to have from 10 to 40 percent "unknown" species in pollen from well-described forests (Bush and Rivera 2001:366). The rarity of the significant canopy trees in the pollen rain complicates the interpretation of tropical forest composition, which relies on dominant species of the understory as well as on the few heavy pollen producers of the canopy that depend on wind dispersal (Bush and Rivera 1998:391, 2001:359).

Moreover, presenting pollen profiles as simple percentages of different sample taxa assumes that the relative rise and fall of identifiable pollen reflects a variation in the type of forest cover in the pollen-shed (Brenner et al. 2002; Curtis et al. 1998; compare Figure 3.5). Work on contemporary pollen rain in the neotropics does not support this assumption (Bush 1995; Bush and Rivera 1998, 2001). One problem is that complex landscapes (Rackham 2006:79-81), like those created by the milpa cycle (see Chapter 2), do not lend themselves to descriptions with simple arboreal pollen (AP) versus non-arboreal pollen (NAP) representing the presence or absence of forest. Another problem with interpreting raw percentages in a pollen profile arises from the "indeterminable" pollen, due to post-depositional degradation, evident even in fresh samples (Bryant and Hall 1993:283). In well-described tropical forests, as with Bush and Rivera's work in Panama (1998, 2001), large proportions of the collected pollen cannot be identified (Bush and Rivera 2001), making the interpretation of relative abundance based on percentage diagrams uncertain (Bryant and Hall 1993).

The mere presence of ramon pollen is not a good signal of the overall composition of the mature forest, because the tree is a colonizer of woodland open spaces (Burn and Mayle 2008; Bush and Rivera 1998; Campbell et al. 2008). Its absence would not signal deforestation, as is often assumed in the literature on Maya paleoecology (Binford et al. 1987:121; Carrillo Bastos et al. 2010; Carrillo Bastos et al. 2012; Dunning et al. 2009:93; Rice 1996:197; Webster 2002:256). As we have seen, fluctuating percentages of the ramon pollen give an ambiguous indication of the actual arboreal composition of the landscape (Bush and Rivera 1998:389). Furthermore, as a managed tree, ramon has figured in the development of the human ecology of the forest and garden for millennia.

In other words, variation of the amount of *Brosimum*-type pollen does not translate to a proportional expansion or contraction of a forested landscape. Abundant Moraceae and *Brosimum*-type pollen can indicate more open areas cleared by drought, hurricane blow-down, and fires, where it has the competitive edge. Alternatively, it could be a result of the abandonment of buildings and public monuments allowing the expansion of *Brosimum* into new habitats of broken limestone, to which it is well adapted (Lambert and Arnason 1982). Equally, it could indicate regenerating forest gaps opened for agriculture. Drops in *Brosimum*-type Moraceae pollen may reflect its inability to compete in chaotic periods of wet and dry, as found in the millenia after 4,000 B.P., or the expansion of intensively managed domesticated orchards, where a greater variety of beneficial and useful trees would be cultivated.[2] In other words, changes in *Brosimum* pollen may actually reflect consolidation of the forest gardens, where preferred insect-pollinated species are more abundant (Campbell et al. 2006; Ford 2008). This would signal an expansion of mature forest and forest gardens rather than a loss of forest cover. It is likely that the changes in the abundance of ramon relate more to its management by the Maya than any other factor.

Many important plants that make up the diverse suite of the Maya-managed forests and gardens (Atran et al. 1999; Campbell 2007; Corzo Márquez and Schwartz 2008; Ford 2008) are invisible in the pollen record (Fedick and Islebe 2012; Ford 2008; Tables 2.1-2.4 in Chapter 2). It is possible that the ancient Maya, like their traditional descendants, favored a diversified economic forest garden that may have suppressed *Brosimum* in the pollen record. The increase of ramon at Maya sites recognized today (Lambert and Arnason 1982; Puleston 1968, 1982) may be best explained by the absence of forest garden management and by *B. alicastrum* dominance based on its pioneering phase, as in the Holocene Thermal Maximum.

Palms such as *Sabal morrisiana* (also referred to as *S. mauritiiformis*), used for roof thatch, and trees such as *Swietenia macrophylla* or mahogany, used for construction, are well-distributed plants of the humid Maya forest (Schulze and Whitacre 1999:234, 240). Even after a century of extensive exploitation by the logging industries, densities of four to eight mahogany trees per hectare are reported in the Maya forest (Patiño Valera et al. 2003). Yet these are rarely, if ever, reported in fossil pollen profiles.

Ecologists believe the distribution of mahogany today to be a direct result of the forest regeneration patterns established after abandonment of traditional Maya land use, in particular, milpa agroforestry (Snook 1998; Steinberg 2005). This widely distributed and economically important canopy tree is not, however, reflected in pollen records. Given the floral biology and reproductive strategy of mahogany, Bush and Rivera's research shows that even with the abundance of Meliaceae, pollen dispersed from trees of this family is restricted to within 5 m of an individual (Bush and Rivera 1998:388). This finding means that mahogany would be underrepresented in pollen rain, including that of fossil pollen. Contemporary studies of pollen from the Lacandon Forest confirm this deduction (Domínguez-Vázquez et al. 2004).

The evidence for reduced forest cover, starting in the Formative or Early Preclassic (from 4,000 to 3,000 years ago), consists of variations in the pollen abundance of a few specific plant taxa that represent arboreal pollen and, by extension, the forest. In many studies, the ramon tree is virtually the only representative of the forest in the pollen spectrum (e.g., Domínguez-Vászquez and Islebe 2008) and is thus used as an indicator out of necessity. The decline of ramon and similar pollen taxa in the pollen rain over time, with the proportional expansion by sun-loving non-arboreal pollen (NAP) species such as those of the Poacea family (grasses), is attributed to "widespread forest clearance." Yet grasses, while fluctuating, stay under 20 percent over the entire prehistoric period (Figure 3.5). Modern forests are assumed to have recovered as a result of depopulation and the abandonment of agriculture after the Maya collapse (Binford et al. 1987; Dull et al. 2010, Dunning et al. 2012; Peterson and Haug 2005; Turner and Sabloff 2012; Wahl et al. 2006), even though maize pollen is recorded from the Preclassic and throughout the Postclassic (Brenner et al. 2002; Domíguez-Vázquez and Islebe 2008; Islebe et al. 1996b; Mueller et al. 2010). This view rests on a tacit assumption of an inherent incompatibility between agriculture and forest cover, an assumption that is shared by many conservation biologists today (Carr et al. 2005; Green et al. 2005).

This view raises questions, however, beginning with the use of fossil pollen as evidence since its presence or absence does not necessarily reflect the composition and distribution of the tropical forest. The existing pollen record provides one line of evidence in understanding the development of the Maya forest, but it is an unreliable proxy of forest composition and extent. In the studies of these data, there is no evidence to justify the assumption that forest cover matches the percentages of indicator pollen types in sediment cores. Furthermore, the presence of arboreal and non-arboreal pollen does not necessarily equate with forest and savanna, as many assume. Tree pollen does not indicate a forest nor do herbs indicate deforestation. In a landscape mosaic, these facets are not clear cut.

Critically, pollen analyses have not acknowledged the complexity of the landscape with the diverse mixture of well-drained uplands and humid lowlands. Nor do these analyses consider the cyclic nature of land use with milpa cultivation, successional reforestation, and forest garden management. In fact, the development of the milpa forest garden cycle can readily account for the distribution of wind-pollinated taxa that create opportunities for the expansion of forbs (Ford 2008; Johnston 2003; Nigh 2008; Wilken 1987; see Figures 3.5, 3.6). Finally, no attempt is made to address the problem that more than 90 percent of the contemporary dominant forest woody trees and palm species are underrepresented in the pollen rain (Bush 1995; Bush and Rivera 2001; Ford 2008; Smithsonian Institution 2014; Turner 2001). Consequently, the current interpretations

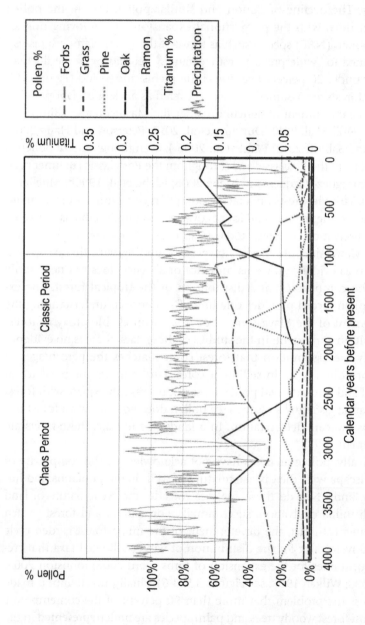

FIGURE 3.6. Precipitation and select pollen for the last 4 millennia in the Maya forest (after Brenner et al. 2002; Curtis et al. 1998; Leyden 2002). ©MesoAmerican Research Center, UICSB

of the fossil pollen record, inferring widespread deforestation from the Preclassic and "forest recovery" after the so-called collapse, are suspect (Dull et al. 2010; Mueller et al. 2010; Turner and Sabloff 2012).

Implications for the Ancient Maya Landscape

Reviewing the archaeological data in the context of our interpretations of the paleoenvironmental record demands a reconsideration of the received wisdom and conventional perspective of Maya prehistory and the historical ecology of the Maya forest. First, occupation of the Maya area dates to the original peopling of the Americas under the arid and cool conditions before the Pleistocene-Holocene transition. In other words, the earliest populations were present in the Mesoamerican Lowlands from the beginning of the great migrations to the New World. Early hunters and gatherers were present before the climate became wet and warm and the tropical woodlands became the dominant vegetation in the region. From the Early Holocene on, these ancestral populations of the Maya area dwelt intimately with the landscape at the same time as they were responding to sometimes dramatic climate variability. The Holocene Thermal Maximum from 8,000 to 4,000 years ago provided a long period of stability and time to develop knowledge of the Maya forest. For the 4,000 years of the Archaic period (Table 1.4), the ancestral Maya dwelt within, were integral to, and shaped their neotropical landscape (Lohse et al. 2006; MacNeish 1982; Rosenswig 2006a, 2006b; Rosenswig and Masson 2001; Voorhies 1998). The Maya forest is recognized today as anthropogenic in origin (Barrera-Bassols and Toledo 2005; Gómez-Pompa 2004; Gómez-Pompa and Kaus 1992, 1999; Gómez-Pompa et al. 2003; among others), a consequence of ancient human selection (Campbell et al. 2006; Ford 2008; Ross 2011; see Covich 1978:155). Archaeologists have identified the presence of the avocado, native to the Lowlands, in the Archaic (McClung de Tapia 1992). Other domesticated crops such as chile, maize, squash, and beans made up the harvest of Archaic mobile horticulturalists (Casas et al. 2007; McClung de Tapia 1992:149-151; Neff et al. 2006b; Piperno and Stothert 2003; Pohl et al. 2007; Pope et al. 2001; Smalley and Blake 2003;). This is the incipient agroecology from which the Mesoamerican and Maya milpa arose.

Major climatic extremes impacted the Maya region in the Formative or Preclassic between 4,000 and 2,000 years ago (Figure 3.6; Ford and Nigh 2014). In the face of the extremes of this chaotic period (Figures 3.2, 3.3), the Maya coped with unpredictability and no doubt struggled. Yet successes are visible by the Middle Preclassic, roughly 3,000 years ago, in

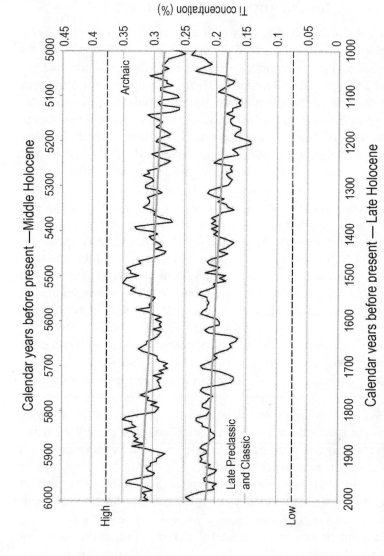

FIGURE 3.7. 1,000 years of stability showing the best-fit drying trends for two periods: the Archaic, above, and Classic, below (based on Haug et al. 2003). ©MesoAmerican Research Center, UCSB

the records of residential settlement and then public architecture, along with the regular appearance of maize in the pollen record (Pohl et al. 1996). During this period of uncertainty, early settlements appear around reliable water resources (see Gunn et al. 2014; Puleston and Puleston 1972). The water resources—areas where dependable drinking water was available in dry times and a diversity of wetland resources existed in the wet periods—must have had a long Archaic history of use.

The centuries of instability beginning around 4,000 years ago appear to have provoked dramatic changes in the environment and adjustments among the human occupants, who developed the spectacular Preclassic urban centers such as Mirador and Nakbe in northern Petén and increasingly relied on farming. The climatic challenges resulted in the creative cultural development of the Maya. We propose that this creativity was facilitated by the milpa forest garden system (Ford and Nigh 2009, 2014). We can only speculate about the nature of the inevitable defeats that indisputably occurred over the course of the erratic centuries of climate chaos. There is no doubt, however, about the ultimate achievement: Maya settlements steadily grew, and civic centers were founded. These settlements flourished and assured the prosperity of the Classic period, shaping the Maya forest up to the present.

In the Late Preclassic, around 2,400 years ago (Table 3.1), stable precipitation began with lower levels but with a consistency equivalent to the Thermal Maximum (Figure 3.7). The Classic period of stability coincides with the major settlement expansion noted throughout the region (Culbert and Rice 1990; Ford 1986; Puleston 1973; Rice 1976; Rice and Puleston 1981; among others). This pattern prevails over the entire Classic period, when the Maya civilization reached its zenith (Ford and Nigh 2014). A review of the Cariaco precipitation data (Haug et al. 2001) and its associated Petén comparison (Mueller et al. 2009; Mueller et al. 2010) reveals no other severe prehistoric precipitation fluctuations comparable to the chaotic Early and Middle Preclassic periods (Figures 1.4 and 3.2). The precipitation variation during the Classic period is minimal, comparable to that of the Holocene Thermal Maximum during the Archaic (Figure 3.7). The Classic period is largely a stable and predictable period in terms of the paleoenvironmental indicators of precipitation and pollen (Figure 3.6).

Summary

The origins of the Maya forest are linked to the challenging conditions of serious precipitation extremes of drought and deluge, under which the Maya initially established their settlements. Clearly, the Maya responded to the uncertainties of the climatic extremes with the development of a resource-management system that worked with the tropical ecology of the forest (Ford and Nigh 2009, 2014). It was a flexible system (cf. Scott 2009), amenable to varied circumstances to support the growth of the Maya hierarchy. We consider the milpa forest garden cycle to be the resource-management system that dynamically shaped the Maya forest and provided the basis to support early settlements and ultimately fueled the growth and development of the Classic Maya.

The paleoenvironment has been interpreted through a lens of negative human impacts, yet it is hard to ignore that these conditions coincide precisely with the Maya's most exuberant and prosperous development (Figure 3.6). For this period, the lake-core records show low productivity, high phosphorus loading, and low organic quality (Binford et al. 1987; reprinted in the following: Dunning et al. 2009:93; Rice 1996:197; Webster 2002:256; Wilkinson 2014:187). It is also the time of falling ramon pollen and a rise in forbs with fluctuations in grasses. Simultaneously, Maya adaptation to these environmental conditions promoted population growth and the expansion of a brilliant tropical civilization. At the close of the climatic chaos in the Preclassic period, the firmly established Maya were poised to build on their millennia of success. This position was strengthened by the stability that prevailed over the Classic period (Table 3.1; Figures 3.6, 3.7). The Maya resource system, based on the milpa forest garden cycle of the past and present, adapts to extreme conditions by moderating the impacts of deluges and managing land cover against drought. The system was resilient under conditions of change, and the climatic stability of the Classic promoted the rise of the Maya civilization.

What provoked the Classic Maya to fall? We contend that it was not an environmental collapse. The Maya forest was managed to include economically valuable and beneficial plants, not only by traditional Maya standards but also by those of today's world economy. The species recorded today confirm that the Maya had and continue to have a constructive impact on the forest.

CHAPTER 4

Maya Land Use, the Milpa, and Population in the Late Classic Period

How does the cyclic nature of the milpa forest garden play out on the Maya forest landscape? Our model reveals that, with recurring and continual investments, the cycle resiliently responds to environmental and human changes. El Pilar provides our salient example: The high residential density and population demonstrate the success of the milpa forest garden cycle. Annual fields produce ever-present wind-pollinated forbs. In our model, the proportion of land under cultivation varies based on maize yields. Whether the yields are low or high, there is always a substantial forest cover.

Introduction

How can we judge the sustainability of traditional Maya farming strategies? In the Eurocentric view, shifting landscape use is related to low-density, dispersed populations (see Boserup 1965, 1981; Van Vliet et al. 2013). But the Maya populations were undoubtedly large and dense. How did their landscape support the growth and longevity of their civilization? They relied on an intensive hand-cultivation system. We have demonstrated that the milpa forest garden cycle is just that: an intensive perennial agricultural system that evolves with investments of labor at every stage in the cycle. The Maya manage the landscape from field to forest and back again. Their cultivation of the biological capital of landscape as an asset resolves more than the immediate subsistence requirements of the family; it creates a surplus that supports the hierarchical elite administration. Within the ecosystem, the traditional milpa cycle not only manages biodiversity but also promotes water conservation, air quality, and soil fertility to avert environmental harm and respond to change. Could this intensive cultivation system support the dense populations estimated for the ancient Maya? To investigate this question we focus, as an example, on the settlement around the major center of El Pilar north of the Belize River, where significant archaeological data provide a detailed means of examining land use and population (Ford 1985, 1990, 1991a, 1992, 2004; Ford and Fedick 1992).

We examine the potentials of ancient El Pilar using the milpa forest garden model of the hand-cultivation system described in Chapter 2, bearing in mind the issues raised from the pollen data discussed in Chapter 3. El Pilar is a large, major Maya center and, as part of the greater Petén, shares a landscape of well-drained uplands and poorly drained lowlands that offer different resources for the Maya. El Pilar flourished for more than two millennia, beginning around 3,000 years ago (Ford 2004). Prosperity here, as with all the major centers of the region, was based on the management of the land for subsistence. Research conducted in 1983-84 by the Belize River Archaeological Settlement Survey (BRASS) project mapped ancient Maya settlements in transect samples and produced major data sets on settlement and environment for a 1,288-square-kilometer study area adjacent to the center (Fedick 1988, 1989, 1994, 1995; Ford 1985, 1990, 1991a, 1992). We use the El Pilar area as the basis for testing the potential of the milpa forest garden cycle to sustain the ancient Maya at the height of the Late Classic period.

Setting the Scene—Settlement and the Environment

Our view of the ancient land-use patterns at El Pilar is based on a predictive landscape model developed with the Maya Forest Geographic Information System (Ford and Clarke 2006; Ford et al. 2009) and supported with fieldwork in the greater Petén (Ford 1986; Fedick 1988). In this context, we explore the ancient settlement and population distributions guided by documented agricultural methods and strategies found in Maya ethnographies (Cowgill 1960, 1961, 1962; Eastmond and Faust 2006; Faust 2001; Ford and Nigh 2010; Harvey et al. 2008; Kolb 1985; Nations and Nigh 1980; Nigh 1999, 2008; Redfield and Villa Rojas 1962; Robin 2001; Steggerda

1941; Toledo et al. 2008; Villa Rojas 1945; Zetina G. 2007). Critical in our examination of the ancient Maya population estimates is not only the intensive level of investment in landscape management but also the importance of the nested quality of the domestic cycles of land use. The cycles of the Maya household begin with family subsistence demands, work into the annual rhythm of the wet and dry seasons, build upon the succession from field to forest and back into field, and support the growing political economy of the elite.

While all biomes of the area were utilized in one way or another, the upland hills and ridges, as well as the poorly drained lowlands and wetlands, were not equally settled, occupied, or cultivated. Archaeological settlement surveys in the Maya Lowlands have shown that the settlements generally avoided seasonal and permanent wetlands (see Fedick 1988, 1989; Ford 1981, 1986; Ford et al. 2009; Puleston 1983; Rice 1976), even though inhabitants used these areas. Similarly, natural resources were extracted from the whole area, but not all land was amenable to crop cultivation; poorly drained lands and those high in clay fall into this category (Fedick 1988, 1989, 1996a; Fedick and Ford 1990).

Beyond the monumental architecture of major centers, such as El Pilar and Tikal, are numerous small structures. Generally, as the small structures are presumed to have served domestic purposes they have been defined as ancient Maya houses. Some were permanent, others were temporary, some were large, others were small, and some were solitary and others were grouped. Yet all these structures played a role in the cycles and strategies of land use, as they do today (see Everton 2012:120; Terán and Rasmussen 1995; Toledo et al. 2008). Locations of fields and forests, like domestic sites, were not static; the landscape and its use was dynamic, ever-changing, reacting, adjusting, and responding to management by the occupants.

Population estimates are always linked to settlement patterns, and in the Maya area these patterns relate to the distribution of surface structures, as recorded by archaeologists for major civic centers and in surveys of the countryside surrounding these centers (Carr and Hazard 1961; Chase and Chase 1987, 1998, 2003; Ford 1981, 1986, 1991a, 1991b, 1992, 2004; McAnany 1993, 1995; Puleston 1973; Pyburn 1990, 1998; Rice 1976; Robin 2001, 2002, 2004, 2012; among others). Each small structure has been presumed to represent a family (see Healy et al. 2007; and Robin 2012 for most recent application). This thinking has led to estimates of inordinately high population densities (Webster 2002:264; cf. Trigger 2003:303), exceeding contemporary situations worldwide (Chase and Chase 1987, 1994, Chase et al. 2014:24; Haviland 1972). In addition, the implications of configurations of small structures and their size, groupings, and patterns tend to be discounted (cf. Levi

2002, 2003). The importance of these variations in residential or domestic architecture cannot be ignored as they affect population estimates as well as the interpretation of land use (cf. Zetina G. 2007; Zetina G. and Faust 2011).

As a proxy for population, the residential unit is the obvious and universally accepted starting point. Thus it is essential to define this unit and how it will be used to calculate population. It is our objective to make a reliable population estimate for the Late Classic El Pilar (AD 600-900) as it was the apex of the Central Lowland expansion in the region. To achieve this, we rely on a predictive model of sites for the El Pilar study area in the Late Classic period (Ford and Clarke 2015; Ford et al. 2009; Merlet 2009, 2010). Then, using this estimate, we evaluate how the landscape could have been used for milpa production, employing ethnographic examples to extrapolate the implications for ancient needs (Fox and Cook 1996).

Maya civilization developed with a reliance on farmers. That the culture grew and was sustained over 20 centuries suggests a resilient and refined agricultural system. Maize production has been identified as the core of the land-management system among Mesoamerican cultures, including the Maya (Katz et al. 1974). Thus, our population estimates for the El Pilar area, and their extrapolation for the ancient Maya region, assumes for purposes of evaluation, that the Prehispanic maize milpa system was the dominant form of production and that maize was the principal source of carbohydrate calories. As we mention elsewhere, however, the ancient Maya diet was richly varied with a wide array of fruits, vegetables, and animals (see Emery and Thornton 2008; Terán and Rasmussen 2009; White and Schwarcz 1989; Woodward 2000). We connect the traditional milpa forest garden cycle recognized today as well as historically (Atran 1999; Hernández Xolocotzi et al. 1995; Kintz 1990; Nigh 2008; Terán and Rasmussen 1995) to ancient Maya settlement patterns. Our hypothesis is that the field-to-forest cycle not only supported the maize needs of the ancient Maya populations but also conserved the forest cover in a dynamic mosaic across the region.

Defining Ancient Maya Residential Units: The Proxy for Population

Ancient structures have been routinely used as the proxy for households, providing the basis for population estimates for the ancient Maya and other civilizations; yet any estimate must be sensitive to assumptions that influence the results (see Culbert and Rice 1990; Healy et al. 2007; Robin 2012; Turner 1990). First, it is necessary to operationally define the household or residential unit. As with previous strategies, the recorded small sites of archaeological settlement survey data are the starting point for the definition of the primary residential unit (cf. Healy et al. 2007:26; Robin 2012:40-41). Our examination, however, relies additionally on ethnographic data for Maya subsistence farming and takes into account the continuity from the ethnohistorical past (Terán and Rasmussen 1995). Therefore, critical to our strategy is the consideration of the annual farming cycles recorded for the Maya, which reveal the ethnographic as well as the archaeological patterns of domestic units (Cowgill 1962; Kintz 1990; Redfield and Villa Rojas 1962; Villa Rojas 1945; Zetina G. 2007; Zetina G. and Faust 2011).

For the Maya, small structures have been analyzed individually and equally whether solitary or grouped, but they are not all the same. Groups of structures are distinct from solitary ones (Ashmore 1981), and their distribution patterns are variable and related to geography (Ford 1991b; Levi 2003; Tourtellot 1983; descriptions in Culbert and Rice 1990). All small structures may be domestic, but here we distinguish types of residential units based on surface configurations.

The archaeological issues raised about the problem of "invisible" residential remains are important (see Johnston et al. 1992; Johnston 2002; Robin 2012:40), but they elude surface accounting. We acknowledge that there may be relevant subsurface remains revealed with excavations (see Healy et al. 2007:26-27); however, they are not visible on the surface, and they cannot be counted. The quality of *visibility* makes our assessments of ancient structures consistent and comparable across all data on visible remains. The variety of the visible residential configurations provides a common comparative base. The spatial distribution of visible residential architecture is the best proxy for evaluating population and land use, conforming to the infield main residence identified in ethnographic studies (Figures 4.1, 4.2).

We define the *primary residential unit* (PRU) based on the arrangement of small, presumed domestic structures as composite groups. Traditional lowland farming households have at least two domestic structures, one for daily living and sleeping and one for the kitchen and storage (Hanks 1990:95-96; 333; Everton 2012:58). While kitchens and sleeping areas occur indoors under cover, many everyday activities take place outside, next to the domestic structures in the family patio defined by the living structures and its surroundings (cf. Everton 2012:58-60; Hanks 1990:106; 335; Robin 2002; 2012:336). This primary residential setting would be complemented with secondary domestic sites with uses closely tied to the agricultural cycle (Hanks 1990: 355; 385-386; Levi 1996). As Zetina G. notes (2007), and others have observed (Everton 2012:120; Farriss 1984; Fedick 1996a; Hanks 1990; Redfield and Villa Rojas 1962; Villa Rojas 1945), contempo-

FIGURE 4.1. *(Above and on facing page)* Maya infield house and forest garden with verdant orchard in background and drying chiles in foreground, Yucatan (Macduff Everton).

rary and historic residential patterns of Maya land use require multiple residential sites for each family (see also Zetina G. and Faust 2011). This is common among subsistence farmers worldwide. Such patterns need to be accounted for in population estimates (Zetina G. 2007).

According to the ethnographic record of Faust (1998) and Zetina G. and Faust (2011; Zetina G. 2007) and the ethnohistorical record (Farriss 1984; Redfield and Villa Rojas 1962; Steggerda 1941; Villa Rojas 1945), the annual and generational cycles of land use are complex, requiring the maintenance of multiple residential sites. There can be as many as three "houses" per family, with a principal house maintained in the community center of the village or town (Zetina G. and Faust 2011). Common experience in the field demonstrates that these primary residential units have

multiple structures, a separate kitchen, and other outbuildings and structures (cf. Hanks 1990:95-96, 106; Lopez Morales 1993:251-285; Sheets
1992; Smyth 1991; see Figure 2.2).

Main residences are used throughout the year, while secondary residences
are occupied intermittently in farming areas of the countryside (Toledo et al.
2008). Secondary outfield residences (Figure 4.3), sometimes called *rancherías*,
are associated with seasonal agricultural activities (Hanks 1990:385-386; Zetina G. 2007; Zetina G. and Faust 2011). This pattern of multiple residences has major implications for population estimates that have been largely
ignored (Everton 2012:120; Fedick 1992, 1996a; Levi 1996; Netting 1977;
Sanders 1981). In this chapter, we use only the primary residential units for
our calculation of population in the El Pilar area of the Maya Lowlands.

FIGURE 4.2. Lakantun infield house and forest garden of José Camino Viejo in 1976, Chiapas, Mexico (James D. Nations).

FIGURE 4.3. Lakantun second-year outfield milpa of José Lopez in 1976, Chiapas, Mexico (James D. Nations).

A Probability Map of Ancient Maya Settlement Patterns

Population estimates for the El Pilar area are based on the observation that ancient Maya sites are distributed with respect to geographic and environmental features: Factors such as slope, soil fertility, and drainage contribute independently to the location of all settlements but to different degrees. These degrees, or *weights*, are the basis for the use of the Weights-of-Evidence (WofE) model (Raines et al. 2000; see also Bonham-Carter 1999). Based on settlement survey data from the El Pilar area, Ford and others (2009; Merlet 2009) created and field-validated a model of Maya settlement patterns using a Geographic Information System (GIS). This validated map of the spatial distribution of ancient settlements as related to the geographic factors forms the basis of our evaluation of population and environment in the Maya forest.

It is well recognized that the archaeological record of Maya sites is incomplete, yet the location of unknown sites can be predicted with probabilistic modeling. Using Bayesian methods in the context of the GIS, known settlements and their geographic associations in the El Pilar area were converted into a site-probability map using WofE. Influential geographic factors, or themes, were classified and transformed to produce a map of expected statistical densities for each thematic factor. As each thematic map contributes proportionally to the explanatory power of the model, combined weights were calculated in the context of the GIS, producing a map that shows the expected probability of finding a settlement at a given site (Ford et al. 2009; Ford et al. 2011).

The predictive model of Maya settlement sites draws on data gathered in the Maya Forest GIS (Ford and Clarke 2006; Ford et al. 2009; Merlet 2009, 2010; Ford et al. 2011; Ford et al. 2014; Monthus 2004; Sirjean 2003). The independent settlement data are from the El Pilar area (Figure 4.4), based on the Belize River Archaeological Settlement Survey (BRASS), the El Pilar study area (Fedick 1988, 1989, 1995; Fedick and Ford 1990; Ford 1990, 1991a, 2004; Ford and Fedick 1992), and the mapped data from Barton Ramie (Willey et al. 1965). The resulting map involved extensive data correlation, model building with Bayesian predictive methods, application of the model to data from the El Pilar area, and thorough field validation with a Global Positioning System in the context of the GIS (Ford et al. 2009; Merlet 2009; Monthus 2004; Sirjean 2003).

The map identified locational probabilities for ancient settlements across the El Pilar study area (Ford and Clarke 2006; Ford and Clarke 2015; Ford et al. 2009). The predictive locations were field validated and resulted in five categories of settlement probabilities. Three major geographic variables—fertility, drainage, and slope—together influenced ancient Maya settlement preferences (cf. Bullard 1960, 1964; Fedick 1988, 1996a, 2014; Ford 1986; Isendahl

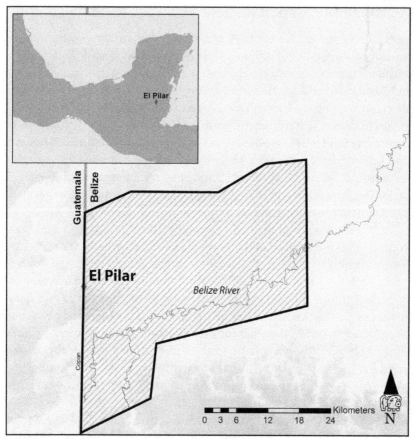

FIGURE 4.4. El Pilar study area boundaries north of the Belize River.
©MesoAmerican Research Center, UCSB

2002; Isendahl et al. 2014:46). The statistical results, with a significantly high 95 percent confidence level, were grouped to provide the basis for producing a Maya settlement-probability classification map (Figure 4.5).

Our exhaustive field validation and cross-checking have proven dependable and consistent in identifying settlements. Close-up views of distinct settlement density differences can be visualized with the BRASS/El Pilar transect data (Figures 4.6, 4.7), where settlement overlays on the probability map of the El Pilar study area reveal the relationship between the probability class and the settlement distribution. The first pair of images (Figure 4.6) shows settlement distribution in low-probability classes, while the second pair (Figure 4.7) shows the settlement distribution in high-probability classes. These variations in the settlement densities of the five defined probability classes, based on the predictive model and the probability areas, were coded for the site modeling across the area map (Figure 4.5, Merlet 2009:34).

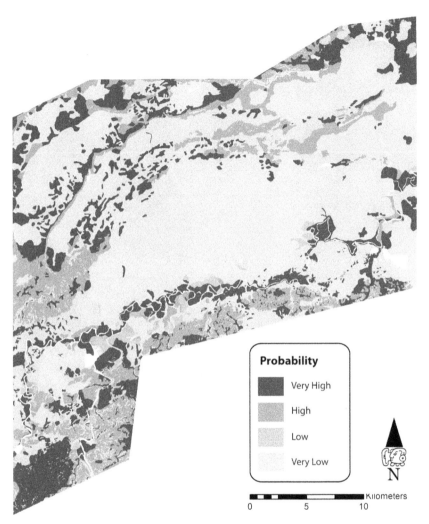

FIGURE 4.5. Maya settlement probability map for the El Pilar study area.
©MesoAmerican Research Center, UCSB

Settlement densities reflect land-use intensity. While settlements and their component residential units will not *directly* indicate agricultural patterns, among agricultural societies, farmers situate themselves with access to important resources. Thus, settlement patterns will mirror landscape investments (Basehart 1973; Brown and Podolefsky 1976; Denevan and Padoch 1988; Fedick 1988:70-72; Flannery 1976; Linares 1976; Netting 1968, 1974; Padoch 1982; Udo 1965). Location of residential sites would then reveal the farmers' needs for house construction and land use, as well

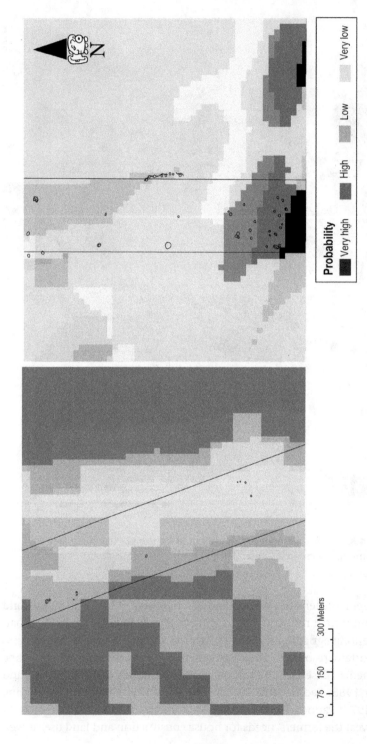

FIGURE 4.6. Low settlement probability areas for the El Pilar surveys. ©MesoAmerican Research Center, UCSB

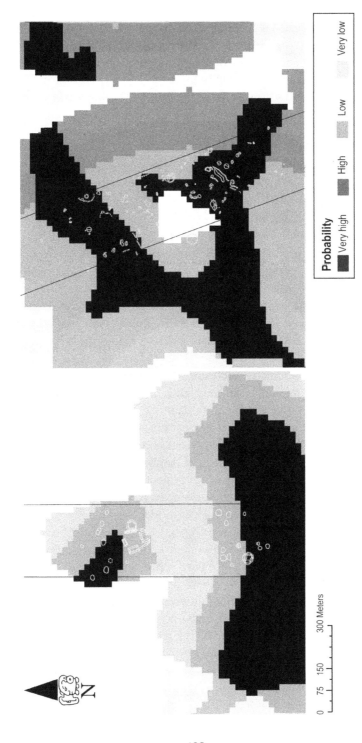

FIGURE 4.7. High settlement probability areas for the El Pilar surveys. ©MesoAmerican Research Center, UCSB

as for transport and access to centers of exchange (cf. Levi 1996). In this way, the sites indicate land use, while the number of households indicates population. Thus, the distribution and configuration of residential units in the settlement surveys provide the foundation for the development of population estimates for the El Pilar area.

Identifying the Primary Residential Unit

Evaluating residential sites in calculating population estimates is a recognized challenge for archaeology. Central to defining our use of the primary residential unit is the differentiation of groups of small structures from individual, solitary ones (Willey 1956; Ashmore 1981; Ford 1991b; Levi 2002, 2003; Robin 2012:25-26). Commonly, each defined structure, whether part of a group or not, has been used as the proxy for the population estimates (Healy et al. 2007:30; Robin 2012:28, 40-41; also see Ford 2013). This, however, discounts the variability in residential configurations, surface patterns that we can easily recognize on the archaeological landscape (Ashmore 1981; Culbert and Rice 1990; Healy et al. 2007; Levi 2003; Tourtellot 1983; Tourtellot et al. 1990:86; among others). The meaning and import of these patterns are related to land use and particularly to farming activities (Zetina G. and Faust 2011; Everton 2012:21).

A systematic approach to classifying Primary Residential Units or PRUs—based on location, structure size, residential unit composition, and labor investment in construction (from Arnold and Ford 1980; Erasmus 1965) from the El Pilar data base—was used to define the archaeological PRU.[1] Essentially, residential units that covered an average area of 290 m^2 were counted as PRU. Settlement survey data from the El Pilar area were evaluated to identify PRU and enumerated within each defined probability class based on the predictive settlement model (see Figures 4.5-4.7; based on Ford et al. 2009; 2011; Merlet 2009).

Using a GIS-based weighted random dispersal program, residential units from the survey sample were propagated across the study area according to settlement probabilities from the predictive model (Ford and Clarke 2015). The simulated model of PRU distribution using the known settlement patterns for the El Pilar area provides the basis for developing Maya population estimates for the Late Classic period. The results show how settlement and population vary across the area and provide a source for understanding the milpa forest garden landscape, a means of looking at residential densities, and a way of appreciating the mosaic of field and forest cover over the probability classes. The model for population and land use we develop has applications to the Classic period of the greater Petén Maya.

Late Classic Population Estimates for the El Pilar Area

By differentiating PRUs in the archaeological survey samples of the El Pilar area, we developed estimates of the distribution of the probable sites of the El Pilar area. Given residential site configuration, units were propagated proportionally by settlement probability class across the El Pilar study area using the GIS (Figure 4.5, Ford and Clarke 2015). This process produced a map of the residential distribution, as well as a view of the settlement concentrations in the El Pilar area (Figure 4.8).

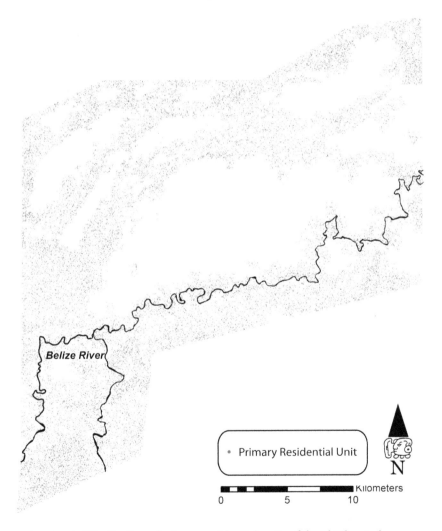

FIGURE 4.8. Distribution of primary residential units of the El Pilar study area. ©MesoAmerican Research Center, UCSB

Residential units that qualified as PRUs were counted as the proxy for ancient Maya population. To derive Late Classic populations, the total number of PRUs was reduced by the proportion of occupation of 95 percent determined for the Late Classic (Culbert and Rice 1990; Ford 1985; Ford et al. 2009:14). An average of 5.4-5.6 persons per residential unit was used (see Healy et al. 2007:31; Puleston 1973:171-189; Robin 2012:41; Turner 1990), which is considered a valid calculus for the ancient Maya "paleotechnic agrarian economy" (Turner 1990:305). We used this household range to provide estimates for the El Pilar example.

To calculate Late Classic Maya population density and distribution, we totaled the numbers of PRUs and their distribution by settlement probability class (Figures 4.5 and 4.8). These totals were multiplied by 5.4 and 5.6 persons per household respectively to derive population estimates for the El Pilar area and for each probability class, from the lowest probability class of 1 to the highest probability of 5 (Table 4.1). The El Pilar area population estimates are relatively high, with a total population that ranges from 176,077 to 182,600 persons. The distribution of this total ranges from zero occupation in the low-probability class, which represents 38 percent of the area, to 376-390 persons per square kilometer in the highest probability class, representing 20 percent of the area (Table 4.1). Based on 5.4 to 5.6 persons per PRU, the average population density for the whole El Pilar area ranges from 137 to 142 persons per square kilometer. This range is greater than some overall estimates (Turner 1990:317) but not as high as others (Chase et al. 2011:389; see also Healy 2007:33 and Robin 2012:32-33), and falls within the estimates of 100-200 persons per square kilometer published for the Late Classic period (Culbert and Rice 1990; Turner and Sabloff 2012:13,099).

How do these estimates for the Maya compare to other civilizations? Boserup (1981:9) provides a basis in her synthetic treatise on population and technology. She defines populations greater than 64 persons per square kilometer as *Dense* and populations over 256 as *Very Dense*. In her table of continental population densities based on the conditions in 1975, she notes that *Dense* and *Very Dense* categories were found only in Asia and Europe (Boserup 1981:11). Asia and Europe remain the highest in the UN summary of the world's current continental population densities (UN 2004: 62-65, see Ford and Clarke 2015).

Our estimates of population densities for the Maya are, by Boserup's standards (1981:9-11), *Dense*. When our estimates of 137-142 persons per square kilometer are compared to other ancient civilizations, they are high. For example, Boserup estimates that the Ming Dynasty of China in 1500 A.D. had an estimated population of only 64 persons per square ki-

TABLE 4.1. Probability Class, Late Classic Residential Units, and Population Distributions for the Study Area

Distributions for the Study Area						
Settlement Probability Class	Late Classic Residential Units	Area (km²)	Population	Population Density (per km²)	Percent Population	Percent Area
1	0	485	0	0	0%	38%
2	5,403	243	30,255	124	17%	19%
3	1,753	76	9,818	129	5%	6%
4	7,643	225	42,800	190	23%	18%
5	17,808	256	99,727	390	55%	20%
Total	32,607	1,284	182,600	142	100%	100%

lometer (1981:11). This estimate—for a civilization that was supporting a standing army and navy, had the ability to consolidate the Great Wall, and boasted major firepower and extensive tribute relations in the region—is less than half of our estimate for the Maya. In Boserup's estimates, pre-modern Edo Japan in 1750 A.D, under the centralized rule of the Tokugawa shoguns, had a population density of 128 persons per square kilometer, which is a little more than 90 percent of our estimate for the Maya. The densities offered by Boserup are averages for a similar patchwork landscape of full, empty, and medium-intensity occupation and are less than our calculated density for the preindustrial Stone Age agrarian Maya civilization. Our estimates, however, are not as high as some offered for the Maya area (e.g., Healy et al. 2007:33 at about 553 per square kilometer and Chase et al. 2011:389 at about 650 per square kilometer).

The high density we estimate for Late Classic El Pilar suggests an intensively used landscape. Between 176,078 and 182,600 persons are projected to have inhabited, farmed, and extracted resources from the 1,288-square-kilometer study area. Zones of the greatest density include the two highest probability classes and reached 390 persons per square kilometer. These communities were similar to those described at Chan, with sufficient land for intensive infield cultivation (Robin 2012:32; Ford 2013:111). The highest probability class supported an average of 70 PRUs per square kilometer and was distributed across zones of 0.3 to 29.7 hectares, with an average area of 20.2 hectares. The next highest probability class contained half the number of PRUs, 34 per square kilometer, making up 18 percent of the area and distributed in zones from 0.3 to 77.9 hectares, with an average area of 23.5 hectares. These highest densities, however, encompass only 20 percent of the total area and were offset by 38 percent of the area without occupation and therefore without PRUs (Table 4.1)

Such dense settlement zones incorporate 55 percent of the El Pilar population and share common landscape characteristics of fertile soil, good drainage, and moderate slope, all ideal for hand cultivation. These zones contrast with unoccupied areas, characterized by low fertility, poor drainage, and clayey soil with either too little or too much slope, problematic for hand cultivation (see details in Fedick 1988, 1989). In between these extremes are areas of moderate fertility and drainage amenable to hand cultivation and capable of supporting moderate settlement and population densities. All the settlements are distributed in a mosaic of dispersed, occupied and unoccupied zones that possess the subsistence and natural resources needed for daily life (Diemont and Martin 2009; Quintana-Ascencio et al. 1996).

The El Pilar landscape that results from this settlement pattern is complex and designed to sustain production for the estimated ancient population. Maya farming strategies recorded today, with their traditional ecological knowledge of the region, are the logical link to identifying ancient Maya land-use patterns (Terán and Rasmussen 1995). Given our discussion of the milpa forest garden cycle, the pressing question is whether the land can produce sufficient maize *and* provide ample time for the succeeding stages that build the perennial forest cover to be returned to maize cultivation. How can we visualize this system functioning on the El Pilar landscape?

Modeling Maya Population and Land Use in the El Pilar Area

By focusing on the milpa forest garden system and particularly on maize production, we can evaluate land use in relation to the population of the El Pilar area. To accomplish this, we use our estimate of the El Pilar area population to determine the annual maize requirements.

The estimate of 142 persons per square kilometer for the El Pilar study area is nearly ten times the population density of Belize and northern Guatemala today. Assuming maize is a major component of the diet, can the milpa cycle provide for the caloric and landscape needs of the estimated population, while sustaining biodiversity and the ecosystem? To answer this we employ the infield-outfield model from Maya ethnographic data to evaluate ancient El Pilar landscape dynamics under the milpa cycle (Netting 1977, 1993; Netting et al. 1989; Pyburn 1998; Sanders 1981).

Maize Calories

We calculate the energy requirements of the estimated population of 182,600 inhabitants across the El Pilar study area and assess the contribution of maize to their diet. To determine the amount of maize required to feed the Maya, we look to the literature on maize production to assess the land needs for the study area. To estimate the annual maize requirements for a population we need to make the following calculation: Daily Calories x 364.25 days x Population/Maize Calories x percent of Total Diet. Thus, we need to know the energy requisites per person, the proportion of their calories contributed by maize, and the caloric value of a kilogram of maize. We initiate the calculations for our El Pilar population with the average daily energy requirement given by the FAO: 2,100 calories per day (Anriquez et al. 2010; Basset and Winter-Nelson 2010:21; Shapouri et al. 2009). We then use 34 percent for the energy contribution of maize to the diet of preindustrial subsistence farmers in Mesoamerica.[2]

For the caloric value of the maize, Leung and Flores (1961) provide a working figure of 3,551 calories/kg. Substituting these figures in the equation, we get the following: 2,100 x 364.25 x 182,600 / 3,551 x 0.34 = 13,373,586 kg of maize per year.

We use the estimated total annual maize for the population of the El Pilar area of 13,373,586 kg per year to approximate the potential of the landscape to support the estimated population (Table 4.2). This amount is the number of kilograms required annually for the maize-field stage of the milpa forest garden cycle. The calculation must include sufficient time for the reforestation stages as well, since they maintain the ecosystem and complete the Maya diet. Can this amount of maize be produced from the El Pilar area under the milpa cycle described here? This depends on yields (Figure 4.9).

Maize Yields

To determine whether the estimated Late Classic populations of the El Pilar area were able to produce sufficient maize and have adequate land to maintain the milpa forest garden cycle, we use three case studies on traditional farming from different areas of the Maya region discussed in Chapter 2: the Petén (Cowgill 1960, 1961, 1962), the Yucatan (Redfield and Villa Rojas 1962; Steggerda 1941; Villa Rojas 1945), and the Lakantun (Diemont and Martin 2009; Nations 1979; Nations and Nigh 1980; Rätsch 1992). These studies provide the basis to evaluate ancient Maya land use at El Pilar.

The Petén Maya area reported by Cowgill (1960, 1961) is located within 100 km of El Pilar. Cowgill (1961:35) examined eight communities around Lake Petén Itzá and compiles the yield data by *cargas* of shelled

TABLE 4.2. Maize Requirement for the El Pilar Study Area

Total population of El Pilar	182,600
Energy requisite per person/day	2,100 kcal
Calculation for the population for one year	139,675,305,000 kcal
Proportion of energy consumption from maize	34%*
Energy consumption/year from maize	47,489,603,700 kcal
Energy content of maize	3,551 kcal/kg
Maize required/year for population	13,373,586 kg

* Source: Margaret E. Smith, see Note #2 for Chapter 4

maize (c.100-pound sacks, Cowgill 1960:35). She recognizes that farmers protect trees in fields (Cowgill 1961:17) and plant other crops in
their milpas (1961:21), similar to the multi-crop strategy we described
in Chapter 2. Converting her maize yields to kg per hectare results in the
production of 855 kg per hectare of maize in Petén Maya fields (Nations
and Nigh 1980). A low yield of 855 kg per hectare would require 16,642
hectares, or 20 percent of the available cultivable lands of El Pilar, to produce enough maize for the estimated El Pilar population.

Yukatekan Maya were studied in the 1930s by the Carnegie Institution of Washington and include several communities in the vicinity of
Chichen Itzá (Redfield and Villa Rojas 1962; Steggerda 1941; Villa Rojas
1945). These studies provide details on cultural traits, among them milpa production. As with Cowgill, data are reported in *cargas* per *mecate* and
for comparability are converted to kg per hectare. Yields vary from 1,144
to 1,358 kg per hectare. We use Redfield and Villa Rojas estimations as
converted by Nations and Nigh (1980) for an average maize yield as
1,144 kg per hectare. The maize product of 1,144 kg per hectare would
require 11,690 hectares, or 15 percent of the available cultivable lands of
El Pilar to produce enough maize for the estimated El Pilar population.

The Lakantun Maya of Chiapas, Mexico, represent an isolated group
that, until recently, survived within the forest with little interaction outside their communities (Nations and Nigh 1980:1; Palka 2005:1-17). In
the absence of modern influences, the Lakantun traditional environmental knowledge of the Maya forest formed the basis of their subsistence
and forest-management systems and thus provides an excellent comparison for the ancient Maya case (Nations and Nigh 1980:2; Rätsch 1992).

FIGURE 4.9. Maya farmer Marcelino Chi Pech views his maize harvest, Monte Cristo, Yucatan, Mexico (Macduff Everton).

Their intensive labor and scheduling provide insight into the potential of the milpa cycle, as we discussed in Chapter 2. Nations and Nigh (1980:10) measured Lakantun maize yield at 2,800 kg per hectare. The high field production yield of 2,800 kg per hectare would require 4,776 hectares, or 6 percent of the available cultivable lands of El Pilar, to produce enough maize for the estimated El Pilar population.

These three examples bracket traditional maize milpa yields from 855 to 2,800 kg per hectare. Each case study reports comparable strategies in plot selection, preparation, burning, and planting. Activities are managed with hand tools, skill, and labor recognized from the time of Spanish conquest up to today (Terán and Rasmussen 1995, 2009:33-40). In each case, there is evidence of multi-cropping strategies dominated by maize but including a number of distinct crops, as well as synergistic companion plants and native fruit and hardwood trees.

Crop yields of maize signal the differences in labor invested in each field (see Wilken 1971, 1987). Yields vary from the low values of the Petén, to the average values of the Yukatekan, to the high values of the Lakantun. The greater yields of the Lakantun example reflect greater investment of labor and skill in the management and maintenance of the field and the entire milpa forest garden cycle (Nations and Nigh 1980; Nigh 2008; cf. Bray 1994). This explanation conforms with our description of Lakantun practices in Chapter 2.

Turning to our ancient Maya example of the El Pilar area, we calculate that 13,373,586 kg of maize per year were required to provide enough of the crop for the estimated population (see Table 4.2). To evaluate land availability for the production of this amount of maize consistently across generations, we must determine annual requisites as well as the amount of useful land needed to ensure the complete restoration cycle from annual field to perennial forest back to field again. In other words, there must be not only sufficient cultivable lands to provide for the annual maize needs but also enough cultivable lands to cycle through the successional stages (see Table 2.1).

Maize Production and the Population of El Pilar

Prehistoric Maya cultivated by hand, as do the traditional Maya today (Terán and Rasmussen 2009; see Fedick 1988, 1989). They avoid areas that are difficult for hand cultivation, including clayey and poorly drained areas, preferring the well-drained limestone soil known as mollisols or redzinas (Fedick 1989, 1992; Fedick and Ford 1990). The amount of maize grown in the home-garden infield and diverse zones of the outfields changes with family size, land-use history, and climate uncertainties. (see Zetina G. and Faust 2011). Of course, there were areas of more and less intense use, dependent upon settlement and population density, and our probability model of Maya sites speaks to this variable. Indeed, nearly 38 percent of the area was unoccupied and thus extensively used, while 20 percent of the area was occupied by the majority (55 percent) of the settlement (see Table 4.1).

FIGURE 4.10. Zacarias Quixchan in front of his stored maize, Petén, Guatemala (Macduff Everton).

The three case studies provide examples of the range of land use employed by the Maya. The Petén case demonstrates low yields of maize, the Yukatekan case average yields, while the Lakantun case is an example of the upper range of high yields. Intensification of land use increases the relative productivity of the cultivated landscape, where greater investment of labor, skill, and scheduling improves yields.

To determine whether the El Pilar landscape could produce sufficient maize for the population, we apportion the maize-production areas according to the infield-outfield model of subsistence farmers as applied to the Maya. The infield home gardens are fixed plots for cultivation and storage (Figure 4.10), and the maize contribution is calculated as constant. The outfield is the dynamic variable of the agricultural cycle dependent upon maize yield. For the infield maize contribution we used our extrapolated number of PRUs and the size range of infield cultivation that averages 0.4 hectares (Figure 2.2; Fedick 1992; Lope-Alzina and Howard 2012:25; Netting 1965:424, 1974:253). For the outfield we included all hand-cultivable land area, as defined by Fedick (1988:394-395, 1992), excluding settlements and infield areas. The outfield landscape is thus a fixed area of 1,288 square km, more than half falling within Fedick's "hand-cultivable" classification.

Ethnographic cases of the Maya suggest that approximately 30 percent of home cultivation was dedicated to maize (Everton 2012:57-72; Lopez Morales 1993:222). While the actual cultivation area changed, maize was consistently maintained in the infield area (Corzo Márquez and Schwartz 2008; Schwartz and Corzo Márquez 2015). Based on the estimated number of residential units (32,607, see Table 4.1), we calculate the fixed total for infield home-garden maize production for all households in the El Pilar study area to be 39 square km (Table 4.3).

The area needed for outfield maize necessarily varies according to yield. For lower yields, more outfield land is required in maize production at one point in time, while higher yields mean less outfield land is needed. However, more area devoted to maize production means that the milpa forest garden cycle has to be shorter, leaving less time for reforestation. Is there sufficient land at the lowest yields to allow a minimum managed reforestation cycle to be completed? This is a critical question.

Traditional farmers plant maize for about four consecutive years in the same place (Cowgill 1961; Steggerda 1941; Villa Rojas 1945). The period between maize plantings, the so-called period of rest or abandonment, is now recognized by agroecologists as the object of ongoing permanent plant and land management (Nigh 2008; Terán and Rasmussen 1994; Terán et al. 1998; Wilken 1987; see also Brookfield 2001). It hardly represents rest or abandonment—intensive and permanent investment in the regenerative stages is crucial to land management, which emphasizes soil fertility, water conservation, and biodiversity (see Chapter 2). Thus, the whole cycle is completed only with managed reforestation stages that extend for at least 10-12 years, making for a minimum of a 16- to18-year total cycle (Levy Tacher and Aguirre Rivera 2005; Diemont et al. 2006). We will use a 16-year-cycle as the baseline in our examination of the El Pilar study area.

Using the GIS data from the probability map (Figure 4.2), along with the land-use qualities for the El Pilar area defined by Fedick (1988, 1989, 1992), we exclude soil classes with severe limitations for hand cultivation (Fedick 1992:92), such as those that are too clayey and subject to inundation in the wet season. Of the total study area of 1,288 square km, we calculate the land available for hand cultivation at 734 square km, or

TABLE 4.3. Infield Home Garden Maize Production in the Maya Lowlands

Base for Calculated Land Use/Home Gardens	Factors
Home garden area per residential unit	4000 m²
Percent of maize infield garden	30%
Infield area for orchard garden	2800 m²
Infield area for maize per residential unit	1200 m²
Total area of home garden for study area	130 km²
Total area of maize infield for study area	39 km²

about 57 percent of the total, with another 5 percent for the Maya architectural space. The areas with limitations, 38 percent or 480 square km of the study area, were not included as cultivable. These areas, which are not used for either settlement or milpa, would have been managed for natural resources, such as flora and fauna, as well as geological materials such as clay and chert.

To evaluate whether the El Pilar area has sufficient land to cover the maize requirement for the estimated Late Classic population, we measure the cultivated area and the variable yields from the ethnographic cases to inform our infield/outfield maize milpa-cycle calculation. The three traditional Maya maize yields used to assess land capacity of the El Pilar study area are:

Low Yields: 855 kg per hectare

Average Yields: 1,144 kg per hectare

High Yields: 2,800 kg per hectare

The annual yields from each case are applied to both constant home infield and variable outfield maize production, approximating the annual needs of a family (Stuart 1990:138). As a basis for sustainability, a minimum 16-year cycle must be fulfilled. The entire milpa forest garden cycle is composed of four years of maize production followed by a minimum of 12 years of reforestation.

Our calculations are revealing. First, all three yields provide sufficient maize production to support the requirement of the estimated El Pilar population (Table 4.4). Importantly, the land-use requirements for the

TABLE 4.4. Maize Yields for the El Pilar Population under Different Production Regimes

Yield and Location	Yield kg/ha	Total Land Needed for Maize (km²)	Infield/ Outfield Maize/Cycle In Years	Milpa/ Managed Succession In Years	Area for Long-Term Forest Management (km²)
Low Yield Petén Itzá	855 kg	156 sq km	39/117 sq. km	4/16 yrs	134 sq km
Average Yield Yukatan	1144 kg	117 sq km	39/78 sq km	4/27 yrs	292 sq km
High Yield Lakantun	2800 kg	48 sq km	39/9 sq km	4/275 yrs	569 sq km

entire cycle meet and exceed the 12-year minimum required for reforestation. Since the variation in maize yields relates directly to the field management and investments in the general form of labor (Boserup 1965), ever-greater maize yields could only be accomplished by increasing investments of knowledge, skill, labor, and scheduling (see Stone et al. 1990; compare Fukuoka 1978).

Based on low and average yields, where the case studies have historical continuity in one place, the projected agricultural cycles mirror family cycles of 20-31 years and supply only 25-33 percent of their maize needs from the home infield (see Table 4.4). Based on the high-yield case, where production strategies were developed to support an entire family in place, the intensive infield could provide as much as 81 percent of the maize needs of the estimated El Pilar population (see Table 4.4), requiring little use of outfield lands. These yields, based on traditional case studies, demonstrate the capacity of the milpa forest garden to provide for the maize needs as well as to maintain land cover and resources in a dynamic system of land rotation. This system shows the flexibility and productivity of Maya agriculture.

The data reveal the vibrant mosaic landscape that is the milpa forest garden. It is remarkable that, in each case, our calculations of the requirements for maize show an allowance for long-term forest management within the preferred hand-cultivated areas and beyond the unoccupied poorly drained lowlands and wetlands (Table 4.4). The allowances are significant. In the low-yield case, 10 percent of the upland landscape could be reserved for long-term management and still produce sufficient maize for the estimated El Pilar population. In the average-yield case, 18 percent could be reserved, and in the high-yield case as much as 40 percent could be reserved for long-term management in the well-drained uplands.

It is also noteworthy, in terms of forest cover, that in the example of the El Pilar study area nearly two fifths of the area is outside of agricultural pursuits (Table 4.1). These uncultivated and unoccupied areas—the poorly drained lowlands and wetlands that are typical across the Maya region (Dunning et al. 2002)—would be naturally forested and under management as well. At a minimum, half of the El Pilar landscape could have been dedicated to natural resource management for firewood, diverse hardwoods, and fruit trees (Ferrand et al. 2012), production palms, and specific woods such as logwood from the seasonal wetlands (e.g., Lentz and Hockaday 2009).

In summary, the nature of the milpa forest garden cycle is dependent on labor and skill, without which the time-honored strategies could not endure (Terán and Rasmussen 1995). The labor intensification that made this complex system possible, as illustrated in the ethnographic cases, would leave no visible archaeological traces. The intensive and permanent Maya agricultural system does not require terraces (but compare Robin 2012), and the fields are rainfall dependent (Whitmore and Turner 2005:165). With little irrigation, terraces, or drainage, but with an investment of labor, skill, and scheduling, the Maya were able to create the intensive milpa forest garden cycle and domesticate an entire landscape, thus, belying the assumption that intensification must involve engineering landscape (Terrell et al. 2003; Terrell and Hart 2008).

Discussion

Research on the agroecology of the Maya has revealed that sun-loving plants that are interpreted as weeds (forbs and grasses), as well as the coppiced stumps of shrubs and trees, grow among the crops of the hand-cultivated milpa (Everton 2012:66, 256; Ford et al. 2012; Kellman and Adams 1970; Quintana-Ascencio et al. 1996). This approach hastens the growth of land cover and reforestation as the system cycles through the successional phases (Karthik et al. 2009:378). Furthermore, farmers upgrade that natural process by selecting for desirable plants and those that improve soil productivity (Table 2.2; Diemont et al. 2006; Nigh and Diemont 2013), creating the forest garden (Ford and Nigh 2009; Levy Tacher and Aguirre Rivera 2005; Nigh 2008; Terán and Rasmussen 1994).

Case studies of the contemporary Maya milpa yields represent a continuum of field investments from the low yields of the Petén to the high yields of the Lakantun. All prove the value of the traditional Maya system. Our inquiry shows that maize yields from the traditional milpa forest garden cycle, far from being environmentally destructive, meet the basic human dietary requirements and have the potential to generate managed forests that fit well into the landscape of the region.

These traditional Maya farming strategies are viable and account for the persistence and endurance of the Maya in the face of adversity into the 21st century (Atran 1999; Camacho 2011; Faust 2001; Van Vliet et al. 2013; Zetina G. and Faust 2011 cf. McElwee 2009; Nikolic et al. 2008; Siebert et al. 2014; Seibert and Belsky 2014). Ancient settlements and centers such as Tikal and El Pilar, which developed over "hand-cultivable" millennia under elite administration, are achievements that were managed under conditions of prosperity, where the dominant mode of production was the milpa forest garden. The ancient subsistence economy supported these settlements, and the traditional practices of the Maya today offer an obvious and practical link. Not just the language of the Maya hieroglyphs (Macri and Ford 1997) but also the fundamental subsistence system links the past to the present Maya. This view of settlement patterns demonstrates that their traditional farming also works effectively on the ancient landscape.

It has been argued that ancient Maya left an enduring impression on their forest (Campbell et al. 2006; Fedick 1996b; Gómez-Pompa and Kaus 1990; Ross 2008). Major centers such as El Pilar, the foundations of residential units, and the patterns of their locations are direct evidence of this impact. Though the relationship between the Maya of the past and the present has been debated, links have been clearly established between the language and calendar (cf. Freidel et al. 1993; Kennett et al. 2010; Macri and Ford 1997) and the resources and conservation of the forest (Atran 1993; Rätsch 1992). Our results forge an additional link with the traditional Maya subsistence system.

CHAPTER 5

The Forested Landscape
of the Maya

For the Maya, it was not enough to satisfy the needs for maize. The forest cover was also essential to supply natural resources, conserve water, enhance biodiversity, and replenish the soil. Their practice of reforestation is evident with pioneering trees heralding healthy forest regeneration. Today, the dominant palms and fruit trees of the tall canopy forest are as diverse as they are valuable. Yet, because these are pollinated by birds, bees, and bats—as in the past—they have gone undetected in fossil lake pollen. Moreover, not all hardwoods are found in the well-drained uplands where the ancient Maya lived: Trees valued for fruit, gum, and construction are abundant in the uninhabited wetlands, alerting us to the importance of the entire landscape to this people.

Introduction

The assumption that ancient Maya deforested their land rides on the notion that agricultural practice and forest cover are incompatible. Yet, as we have demonstrated, the milpa cycle does not involve deforestation. Indeed, cultivation and forest coexist as critical components of an agroforestry sequence that continually converts land from one type of cover to another. Now the question is: What was the proportion of land with forest cover

Anabel Ford and Ronald Nigh, "The Forested Landscape of the Maya" in *The Maya Forest Garden: Eight Millennia of Sustainable Cultivation of the Tropical Woodlands*, pp. 125-153. © 2015 Left Coast Press, Inc. All rights reserved.

and what kinds of natural resources were available in the forest, together with their milpa forest garden cycle?

In this chapter we describe the Late Classic forested landscape using the UCSB (University of California, Santa Barbara) Maya Forest GIS database for the El Pilar area (Ford et al. 2014). Our model of the land-use mosaic draws on ethnographic examples of the multi-crop maize field and habitat data for the contemporary forests described for Tikal by Schulze and Whitacre (1999). We compare ancient settlement patterns to Maya forest habitats with an eye to tree classifications, fossil pollen record, and animals. To build a picture of forest cover for the three maize yield levels, we expand on the land-use design we developed for the field component of the milpa cycle of the well-drained uplands to include the range of habitats discussed by Schulze and Whitacre (1999).

Based on ethnographic examples, we can estimate the stages of managed succession that represent the cyclic milpa forest garden (Table 2.1). These stages are comparable to those named and described in great detail by contemporary Maya farmers (Diemont and Martin 2009; Nigh 2008; Toledo et al. 2008; cf. Chazdon 2014). For our examples, we divide the agricultural cycle into three main periods, beginning with annual multi-cropping fields, which create discontinuous gaps over the landscape. These gaps prevail on average for four years before transforming into the perennial system, as maize production lessens and forest building begins. In this chapter, we use an agricultural cycle of 20 years (the low maize yield model from Chapter 4), which allows for 16 years of perennial growth. Of those, the first eight years are focused on the early stages of succession—the critical planting, selection, and expansion of woody shrubs and trees. This is succeeded by eight years of mature forest to close the canopy and complete the cycle. After 16 years, the reestablished mature forest is at a point when it can be harvested and converted into a new maize field to continue the cyclic process.

Ancient Maya settlements are concentrated in the well-drained uplands, on the ridges and hills typical of the Maya region. This leaves large expanses of managed lowland and wetland forests, in addition to the managed forests of the uplands. Such forested areas provided natural resources—fruit trees and production palms, as well as habitat for wildlife. The kaleidoscope of landscapes underscores the historical ecological integration of fields and forests that emerged around 8,000 years ago. Given our understanding of the nature of the Late Classic El Pilar landscape (Table 4.1) and the land-use requirements for the milpa cycle (Table 4.4), as presented in Chapter 4, we can now consider the varying proportions of different forested habitats in relation to the whole. This will provide a synchronic snapshot of the human-environment relationship at the height of the Late Classic period. What would the ancient Maya landscape mosaic have looked like? Evidence comes from the native forest today, the paleoenvironmental data, and the impact of ancient settlement and land use related to the milpa forest garden cycle. We consider each of the data sets in turn to build our picture.

The Maya Forest Today

Clues to the range of resources available to the ancient Maya are found in the environment today (Gómez-Pompa et al. 2003; Wilken 1971, 1987). Botanists and agroecologists acknowledge the economic value of today's forest (Ankli et al. 1999; Arvigo and Balick 1993; Atran et al. 1999, 2004; Balick 2000; Barrera Vásquez et al. 1977; Roys 1976; Schlesinger 2001; Torre-Cuadros and Islebe 2003). The dry upland forest maintains an oligarchic and homogeneous quality, dominated by plants beneficial to humans (Campbell et al. 2006; Ross 2008). Given that the forest and the ancestral Maya have cohabited for at least eight millennia, it is helpful to review the vegetation types these people managed and conserved.

We use the classification of Tikal tree communities assembled by Schulze and Whitacre (1999). These authors studied forest composition with respect to topographic and soil variation, significant variables that contribute to ancient settlement patterns (Fedick and Ford 1990; Ford 1986; Ford et al. 2009). Schulze and Whitacre conclude that environmental factors *rather than historical events* are responsible for the vegetation patterns, which must have been established in the Holocene Thermal Maximum (Nesheim et al. 2010). Yet the historical forest ecology has included humans from the outset. Maya settlements, for example, strongly favor well-drained areas, which are associated with certain types of vegetation (Campbell et al. 2006; Ford 1986; Ross 2008). Furthermore, field crops require a neutral pH and low clay content; that also imposed limits on areas suitable for maize and other crops. We can associate the forest types discussed by Schulze and Whitacre (1999:191-203) with the ancient habitation areas (all dry upland forests) and areas without habitation (the poorly drained lowlands and wetland forests). We therefore assume that degree and density of ancient occupation had an impact on forest extent and, to some degree, its composition.

Inhabited Dry Uplands Areas

The Tikal forest types typical of the greater Petén and the Maya area in general are characterized by four well-drained woodland communities, named by Schulze and Whitacre (1999:186,191-197): Dry Upland, Upland Standard, Mesic Upland, and Hillbase (Table 5.1). These forest types are similar to Lundell's (1937) vegetation classifications and match general environmental data used by Ford (1981, 1986, 2003a) and Fedick (1988). As a group, the uplands share many characteristics, particularly shallow rocky limestone earth and good drainage, giving a basic pH quality to the soil.

Dry Uplands feature the major dominant trees of the Maya forest (Campbell et al. 2006), and the soil, as described by Schulze and Whitacre (1999), is friable and well drained, with low clay and high rock content indices (Table 5.1). This environment favors species with spreading root systems, such as ramon (*Brosimum alicastrum*), which is indeed abundant here (Schulze and Whitacre 1999:191-196), indicating a drought tolerance that is needed in the annual dry season.

Long considered an important economic tree for the ancient Maya (Fairchild 1945; Puleston 1982), ramon is relatively dense in all the upland areas (Table 5.1), with an average of 477 trees per square kilometer overall. Notably ramon is most abundant today where ancient settlement was most dense as well. As ancient settlements expanded, there would have been competition for space between the residential units and the trees, which certainly would have included ramon, known to be part of home gardens.

Upland forests span the topographic gradient of the hills and ridges (Schulze and Whitacre 1999:191-197, 232-247) and are composed of common tree communities (Schulze and Whitacre 1999:176) that were useful to the Maya in areas of long-term management (Ross 2008). The tops of hills and ridges cover an estimated 20 percent of the forest at El Pilar, where dry conditions make palms rare in the understory. Yet significant numbers of zapotillo (*Pouteria reticulata*), ramon (*Brosimum alicastrum*), guaya (*Talisia oliviformis*), and to a much lesser extent mamey (*Pouteria sapota*) and chicozapote (*Manilkara zapota*) are present.

The slopes of the Upland Standard rolling hills cover about 18 percent of the area of El Pilar, and the trees present are zapotillo, ramon, chicozapote, and mamey. Ramon drops off noticeably, but there is an increase in important understory plants, which include palms, particularly escoba (*Cryosophila stauracantha*), used for brooms and the extraction of salt, as well as the shrub cordoncillo (*Piper aduncum*), which has medicinal properties (Balick et al. 2000:53).

On the moister lower slopes, the Mesic Uplands make up only 5 percent of the El Pilar area. These forests show a major decrease in ramon and chicozapote. The understory composition also changes with additional moisture; the shrub cordoncillo becomes rare, while escoba palms predominate. At the bottom of the hills and ridges, Hillbase forests occur in a narrow zone with comparable upland trees but a lower canopy (Schulze and Whitacre 1999:195-197). Cohune palm (*Attalea cohune*) forests occur in unique de-

TABLE 5.1. Characterization of Ancient Settlement and Environment of Upland Forests for the El Pilar Study Area (62% of area)

Forest Type	Percentage of El Pilar Area	Residential Unit Density (per km²)	Soil Depth	Clay Content* (index 1-10)	Rock Content * (index 1-10)	Ramon Density** (plot/km²)
Dry Upland	20%	70	40.7 cm	4.1	3	3.50/875
Upland Standard	18%	35	45.4 cm	4.9	2.2	2.32/580
Mesic Upland	6%	23	53.5 cm	5.8	2.0	1.13/248
Hillbase	18%	22	105.3 cm	9.0	0.3	1.16/205
Total Uplands	62%	38	61.2 cm	5.9	1.9	2.03/477

Based on Schulze and Whitacre 1999:190, 250 * 1999:240**

pressions at Hillbase-Sabal transitions. Friable soil differentiates these depressions from the compact clay lowland and wetland depressions. Stands of *Attalea* of the Amazon, called babassu, are considered an artifact of human-environment interaction and are called the subsidy from nature because they provide for so many needs (Anderson et al. 1991). All *Attalea* uses noted by Anderson and his colleagues (1991) are recognized by the traditional Maya.

The mature upland canopy of today's forest consists of tall stands of diverse trees reaching from 18 to 22 m in height. *Cecropia peltata* occurs in the gaps, and its presence indicates the dynamic qualities of the forest. The composition of canopy and understory species provides a clue to ancient Maya management (Campbell et al. 2006; Ross 2011; Ross and Rangel 2011).

Uninhabited Lowlands and Wetlands Areas

Schulze and Whitacre describe four poorly drained lowland and wetland forest types (Schulze and Whitacre 1999:197-203): Sabal, Transitional, Tall and Low Scrub, and Mesic Bajo (Table 5.2). These swamp groups differ from upland groups but share many soil characteristics: The soil is deep, uniformly clayey, and without rock. We know from Cowgill's work that these swamp areas are very acidic (Cowgill 1960; Cowgill and Hutchinson 1963). Deficient drainage means there is standing water in the wet season, but plants exhibit moisture stress in the dry season.

TABLE 5.2. Characterization of Uninhabited Lowland Forest
Environments of the El Pilar Study Area (38% of area)

Forest Type	Residential Unit Density (per km²)	Soil Depth (in cm)	Clay Content* (index 1-10)	Rock Content * (index 1-10)	Ramon Density** (plot/km²)
Sabal	0	145	10	0	1.44/360
Transitional	0	145	10	0	0/0
Tall & Low Scrub	0	145	10	0	0/0
Mesic Bajo	0	145	10	0	0.23/58
Total Lowlands (32%)	0	145	10	0	0.42/104

Based on Schulze and Whitacre 1999:190, 250* 1999:240**

The pioneering tree *Cecropia peltata* occurs in most areas with the exception of the scrub forests. Ramon, on the other hand is absent, except in the Sabal forests and on rare occasions in Mesic Bajos (Table 5.2). Of significant interest for the ancient Maya, mahogany is abundant in these lowlands, as is chicozapote, with twice as much mahogany and considerably more chicozapote in the lowlands compared to upland forests (Figure 5.1). Conspicuous are the palms that provide household products, such as the escoba palm, and those that are used for construction, such as the guano palm. They are particularly abundant in the uninhabited Sabal and Transitional forests (Figure 5.2) and are maintained in homes in the Yucatan (Alayon-Gamboa and Gurri-Garcia 2008; Anderson 1996; Caballero 1992; Correa-Navarro 1997; de Clerk and Negreros-Castillo 2000; Fairchild 1945; de Miguel 2000; Gómez-Pompa et al. 1987; Lope-Alzina and Howard 2012; Rico Gray et al. 1990; Smith and Cameron 1977).

Comparing inhabited uplands to uninhabited lowlands and wetlands reveals an inverse relationship between rock content and clay content, and between rock content and soil depth (Figure 5.3). In these terms, the distinctions between the upland forest types and the lowland and wetland forest types are dramatic. It is obvious that ancient habitation favored shallow, low-clay, rocky soils of the kind most desirable for farming and housing.

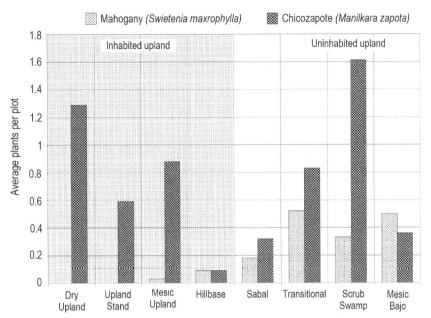

FIGURE 5.1. Distribution of mahogany and chicozapote trees by forest types (based on Schulze and Whitacre 1999). ©MesoAmerican Research Center, UCSB

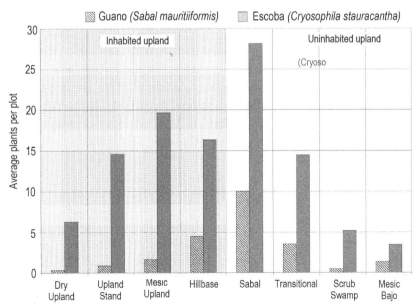

FIGURE 5.2. Distribution of guano and escoba palms by forest types (based on Schulze and Whitacre 1999). ©MesoAmerican Research Center, UCSB

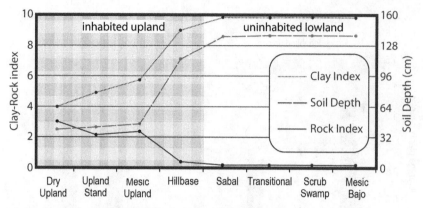

FIGURE 5.3. Clay and rock indices with soil depth by forest types (based on Schulze and Whitacre 1999). ©MesoAmerican Research Center, UCSB

Forest Overview

In sum, the contemporary Maya forests provide a basis for considering Maya historical ecology. Residential sites, home-garden preferences, and the milpa cycle all would have impacted forest types, specifically in the upland forest types, where the population would prefer useful and beneficial plants. Where the influence of occupation was peripheral, however, in the lowland and wetland forests, human influences would have been light. Yet it is still possible to recognize important resources. These include materials for construction, items for household use, as well as edible, medicinal, and other utilitarian plants (Hernández Xolocotzi et al.1995:274, 459). There is a considerable variety of economic trees to be found in uninhabited areas, compared with inhabited areas (Figure 5.4). In some cases, specific trees prefer the conditions of the uninhabited area, like the guano palm, used for roof thatching, and the multiple-use chicozapote.

Ramon, a dominant forest tree today and relatively abundant in the Schulze and Whitacre (1999) samples, is concentrated in the uplands, accounting for four out of every five recorded examples. Archaeological surveys document an average of 70 residential units per square kilometer in an area where 875 ramon per square kilometer exist today. However, ramon is not the most abundant tree of the well-drained uplands; zapotillo is consistently more abundant in all upland contexts and tolerates poorly drained areas as well. It is, nevertheless, absent in the pollen profiles.

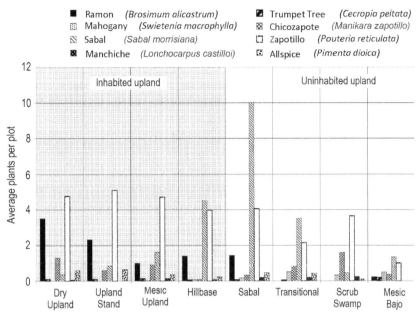

FIGURE 5.4. Select economic trees by forest types (based on Schulze and Whitacre 1999). ©MesoAmerican Research Center, UCSB

Cecropia, a tenacious pioneer of open gaps in forests and regenerating milpas, exists in almost every habitat except the scrub swamps (Figure 5.4). Far from being an indicator of deforestation, *Cecropia* is a critical succession species in all forest types (Bush and Rivera 1998). It is a well-known food source for a wide variety of mammals and birds that serve to spread its seeds (Medellin and Gaona 1999). Densities range from 14 per square kilometer in poorly drained areas to 24 per square kilometer in the mature forests of the dry uplands.

Hardwoods are a significant component of all forest types, and assumptions that hardwood species are restricted to the uplands (e.g., Lentz and Hockaday 2009) are not substantiated (Schulze and Whitacre 1999). In fact, chicozapote and mahogany are abundant in the poorly drained lowlands (see Figure 5.1), as are the valued hardwoods Santa Maria (*Calophyllum brasiliense*) and manchiche (*Lonchocarpus castilloi*). Managed lowlands and wetlands hold many other resources as well. These areas feature palms (as evident in Figure 5.2) and provide significant assets for local inhabitants. Thus the mosaic of land use by the ancient Maya, as with present-day Maya management, exposes the extensive natural forest resource potential.

Paleoenvironmental Pollen Data

Fossil pollen data provide significant insight into the Maya forest, but as the record is largely limited to the wind-pollinated plants, these data represent only a small subset of flowering plants in the world: 10 percent of all flowering plants (Machtmes 2011; Ollerton et al. 2011; Smithsonian Institution 2014), 8 percent of the edible plants (Fedick and Islebe 2012), and only 2 percent of all plants in tropical latitudes (Turner 2001). The paucity of wind-borne plants in the tropics frustrates efforts to identify refugia, areas where tropical plants survived the ice ages (Kellman and Tackaberry 1997:18). When we consider what the record holds, we are fortunate that the megathermal taxa are distinct and that the palynologist can identify the temperate-tropical transitions in the early Holocene, some 8,000 years ago. Yet the shift from a temperate to a tropical context is striking with the rise of the *Brosimum*-type Moraceae pollen in the lake-core records. The presence of *Brosimum* pollen, presumed to be *B. alicastrum* (Leyden 2002; Piperno 2006), is considered key to the change from a cool, dry climate to a warm, wet climate; this shift marks the dawn of the tropical Maya (Figure 3.4).

While ramon must have been dominant throughout the ancient Maya forest, its soil requirements and its competition would have restricted it primarily to the well-drained limestone upland hills and ridges of the area, where the trees are today (cf. Tables 5.1 and 5.2; Lambert and Arnason 1982; Schulze and Whitacre 1999:191). The plants of the poorly drained lowlands, however, are distinct, as can be seen in the recent pollen studies at Aguada Zacatal and Laguna Yaloch (Wahl et al. 2007; Wahl et al. 2013). In these humid lowland and wetland locations, species such as *Cladium* sp. and *Bucida burseras*, representing lowland forests as characterized by Schulze and Whitacre (1999:231-247), appear during the Maya expansion.

Ramon pollen and its fluctuations through prehistory have been the source of much speculation. It is the only wind-pollinated species among the dominant upland mature forests (Campbell et al. 2006; Ford 2008). Furthermore, since it is abundant in the mature forest and the understory of the uplands, as noted by Bush and Rivera (1998), it is a poor indicator of the mature forest canopy. Bush and Rivera consider ramon an aggressive pioneer of the forest gaps. Clearly ramon, as a megathermal plant, demonstrates the major environmental shift from temperate to tropical ecology in the Early Holocene. It is not, however, the best indicator of the composition of the mature forest, since birds, bees, and bats are largely responsible for pollination of tropical forest plants. What is more, it is intensively managed for food and forage in the area today; fluctuations in the presence of ramon pollen will more likely reflect human intentions rather than natural processes.

As a pioneer and a canopy tree, ramon was well positioned to dominate the emergent Holocene tropical forest ecosystem. Its expansion is understandable, given its affinity to rocky limestone soil (Lambert and Arnason 1982). Yet, as human selection in the forest began, it is equally logical that other forest trees would begin to play more important roles in the historical ecology of the area (Schele and Freidel 1990; Schele and Mathews 1998:119-123). Consequently, ramon would be only one of many economically important trees in the repertoire of the forest gardener, and would play a smaller role in a fully managed Classic Maya forest than in the Archaic Early Holocene forest (see Lope-Alzina and Howard 2012).

Given the wind-pollination bias in the palynological record, it is little wonder that there is an increase in wind-pollinated forbs in lake sediments with the initial settlement and expansion of the ancestral Maya across the region more than 3,000 years ago (see Figure 3.5). Sun-loving species that characterize open fields and residential sites increase and then remain stable during the development of Maya civilization (A.D. 250-900). This is also when maize becomes significant in the record (Mueller et al. 2009; Wahl et al. 2013). Wind-pollinated forbs of the milpa field are represented within the profiles (e.g., Asteraceae, Chenopodiaceae/ Amaranthaceae), indicating widespread investment in the milpa cycle. While field crops are signaled by maize in the pollen record, it is worthwhile noting that most field plants are not wind pollinated; these include *Capsicum* spp., *Cnidoscolus aconitifolius*, *Curcubita* spp., *Phaseolus* spp., *Xanthosoma* spp., *Lagenaria* spp., among others (see Appendix A). Fedick and Islebe (2012) report that only 20 percent of 500 identified and named edible plants rely on wind for pollination. Trees common in gardens and fields that are not wind pollinated include *Persea americana, Theobroma cacao, Chryso-phyllum cainito, Cedrela odorata, Ceiba pentandra, Acrocomia mexicana, Attalea cohune, Psidium guajava, Talisia oliviformis, Sabal morrisiana, Byrsonima crassi-folia, Pimenta dioica, Cordia dodecandra,* and *Manilkara zapota* (Cowgill 1961; Lundell 1933; see Table 2.2 and Appendix B).

Poaceae (grass) pollen, assumed to indicate "widespread forest clearance," maintains a constant level, rarely exceeding 15 percent in the pollen profile (Figures 3.4 and 3.5). It may simply indicate gaps in the forest, gaps that would reflect expanded ancient settlements (cf. Rackham 2006:79-81). After all, grasses native to the Maya and Mesoamerican forests have long coexisted as part of the natural succession process, ready to colonize gap openings created by tree falls, hurricane damage, and, of course, houses and fields.[1]

Cecropia, a wind-borne species ubiquitous in the pollen record (see Figure 5.4) and linked with the deforestation hypothesis, has a persistent presence in the mature forests of the dry uplands and wet lowlands of the forest today (Schulze and Whitacre 1999:240-241). Its heavy pollen rarely travels more than 60 m (Piperno 2011:202). Rather than being associated with deforestation, however, *Cecropia,* like grasses, take advantage of forest gaps that are part of the dynamics of the region. As the multi-crop maize field gives way to succession, *Cecropia* is a common component of reforestation and is an important food source for many animals (Medellin and Gaona 1999). Thus any increase in *Cecropia* in the record would be anticipated as part of the development process of Maya settlement and the agricultural cycle.

Wind-pollinated forbs and grasses remain stable through most of the prehistoric periods of Maya occupation. As the Maya extend their reach, forb pollen rises, but grasses maintain a low profile. The major changes can be seen when the civic architecture is left unattended after the Classic period, leading to the rise in ramon and the drop in forbs. Ramon's requisites are precisely suited to the abandoned temples, palaces, walls, and terraces. While today the co-occurrence of ramon and high-density ancient residential and monumental architecture has long been recognized (Appendix B; Lambert and Arnason 1982; Puleston 1968, 1982: Schulze and Whitacre 1999:191), the overwhelming conclusion is that historic factors are not as relevant as the biological demands of the plant. This is yet another indication of how closely the ancient agricultural system was enmeshed in the forest ecology. As the infrastructure was left unattended, the pioneering plant communities derived from those selected and cultivated by the Maya would expand into the collapsing limestone architecture and develop into the "feral" forests we see today.

Diversity in the Milpa Cycle

The diverse, resilient, and flexible milpa cycle has endured the long test of time (Figure 2.3). It is practiced in all terrains, habitats, and climates of Mesoamerica, proving its suitability across the region (Wilken 1987; see also Scott 2009; Van Vliet 2013). The practice depends on individual skill, knowledge of cultivated plots, investment in cultivated resources, and scheduling of tasks. Selected sites are cleared, planted, cultivated, maintained, managed, and reaped by hand. Typically, undesirable plants are cut for mulch, leaving the material in the field to decompose and add organic materials to the soil (Everton 2012:17). In the dry season, many plants, regardless of type, are left standing as cover to minimize water loss, a critical aspect of management where woody plants are left to grow and contribute to field composition.

Water management is essential not just for everyday needs but also for the produce of the milpa forest garden. For this, land cover is indispensable, especially during the annual dry season. Porous limestone desiccates when cleared, so the use of cover crops, the encouragement of trees and shrubs, and the management of the perennial components of the milpa cycle are crucial. Indeed, the integration of perennial trees and shrubs provide critical shade needed to control moisture in the maize field. Traditional farming practices today control evapotranspiration by leaving sprouting trees that can be eliminated once the wet season begins.

Fields exposed to the sun are crowded with cultigens, volunteers, and beneficial and protected plants (Ford et al. 2012; Kellman and Adams 1970), including many of the grasses and forbs recognized in the lake cores (Binford et al. 1987; Brenner et al. 2002; Curtis et al. 1998; Deevey et al. 1979; Hillesheim et al. 2005; Hodell et al. 2008; Islebe et al. 1996b; Leyden 2002; Mueller et al. 2009; Rice 1996; Rosenmeier et al. 2002; Rue 1989; Vaughan et al. 1985; Wahl et al. 2006, 2007). Many forbs classified as weeds (Steggerda 1941:99-107) are actually valuable plants allowed to grow in the cultivated fields. Some are medicinal and edible (Roys 1976), others attract beneficial insects in order to increase the harvest of maize or beans (Gliessman 1998), and still others attract birds and insects critical for fruit pollination, such as the midge that pollinates the cacao tree (*Theobroma cacao*). Wind-pollinated forbs found in the fields and recognized in the pollen cores include the families Amaranthaceae, Asteraceae, Cyperaceae, Euphorbiaceae, Melastomataceae, Poaceae, and Urticaceae, not to mention *Zea mays* (maize).

Diversity is the strength of the milpa forest garden cycle. Farmers protect themselves from unpredictability in weather patterns and plant diseases that lead to crop failures by investing in a variety of field crops and by varying the locations for them. They take precautions in selecting fields, establishing them in different habitats and taking advantage of differing water regimes: Steep plots promote good drainage, an advantage in seasons with too much precipitation, while flat plots capture water in dry spells. In addition, farmers combine plants to match field conditions for moisture and soil. As the diverse plots cycle from field to forest, the forest changes accordingly.

As with forest succession (Chazdon 2014; Packham et al. 1992), the milpa cycle starts with the field gap, moves into the stage of building perennials, and culminates in the mature closed-canopy forest, eventually returning to maize fields (Everton 2012:16-18). The improvement of perennial woody shrubs and trees is a significant component of the cycle, creating an ever more domesticated landscape (Johnston 2003; Terrell et al. 2003; Terrell and Hart 2008).

As the cycle involves management, selection, and planting at every stage, the process directs the building and succession process and hastens mature perennial forest phases (Terán and Rasmussen 2009:47-49). Traditional Maya farmers maintain perennial forest reserves in order to have access to specific natural resources: products used in the household (Ford 2008). Certain construction materials would not be available without the shade of the mature forest. Binding vines, for example, used for structural supports, and certain palms such as bayal (*Desmoncus orthacanthos*), used for basketry and furnishings, occur only in the shade of the mature forest. Thus, construction materials for civic enterprises and houses, including perishable materials for domestic products used by the Maya, depend on these woodland reserves.

The creation of this diversified landscape, with open field gaps, reforested plots, and mature closed-canopy forest, results in prolonged economic stability and reveals the sophistication of the milpa cycle. The complexity of the few wind-pollinated plants is consistent with the paleoenvironmental data on pollen as well as with that of the forest today. But wind pollination does not characterize the complete composite forest or garden environments (cf. Rackman 2006:79). Zoophilous canopy species are constantly underrepresented in modern pollen rain (Bush and Rivera 1998) and, predictably, absent from the fossil pollen sequence as well. Given the dynamic field and forest conversion process, we can expect a stable presence of forbs and grasses with plants initiating the reforestation phases. The forest is a biodiversity hot spot (TNC 2014), and the traditional forest gardens today are considered the most diverse in the world (Campbell 2007); however, the majority of these species are invisible in the pollen rain.

Landscape Complexity: The El Pilar Model

The El Pilar landscape model shows how the milpa cycle has the potential to provide a sufficient supply of maize for the ancient population even at its apogee in the Classic period, without removing vast tracts of woodlands. While we have demonstrated that the maize component of the cycle meets the caloric requirement for the estimated population of the El Pilar area, in this chapter we illustrate that this provision can occur without "widespread deforestation."

Assumptions about the nature of the ancient Maya forest have not taken into account the full diversity of plants that was available. Recent research at Chan (Robin 2012) demonstrates a considerable variety of available trees as well as crops, based on direct archaeological evidence from middens spanning all occupations at the site. Faunal analyses of the Petexbatun area in the southwest Petén (Emery 2004, 2010) provide a complex series of data showing that the use of animals was constant over the course of the Maya development.

Results from Chan and Petexbatun also point to a stable landscape throughout the Preclassic and Classic periods, supporting a diverse matrix of productive crops and natural resources while providing adequate animal habitat. This is consistent with the stable pollen record of minimal grasses, ample forbs, and low *Brosimum*-type Moraceae. Within this stable landscape, the Maya acquired the basics of everyday life. They needed construction materials for pole-and-thatch building—lumber, wood poles, binding vines, and palm thatch; they needed supplies for the production of baskets, bags, containers, stuffing, and fiber; and they harvested plants for medicines and poisons, food and beverages, fuel, oil, tanning, fumigants, and for ritual (Everton 2012:66; Ford 2008). And, to maintain stability, they had to manage soil fertility, understand the water cycle, and protect habitats for plant and animal biodiversity, all skills practiced in the milpa cycle we have detailed from the ethnographic record (Chapter 2).

The archaeological model of the forest in the Late Classic period is based on calculations of maize production presented in Chapter 4, where a continuum of low, average, and high yields corresponds to increasing investments in the management of the cycle process. The investments are, in Boserup's terms, that of labor, but in the Maya case we also recognize scheduling (Stone et al. 1990) and skill as significant factors (compare Bray 1986). This is along the lines of Scarborough's concept of "labor-tasking" (2003:13-16; see also Scarborough and Burnside 2010). The greater labor investment in maize yields provided for greater proportions of mature upland forests dedicated to long-term management and greater diversity of the perennials in the milpa cycle. In addition, we must consider the lowlands and wetland forests that, while not used for residential or agricultural purposes, provided other vital resources. The varied nature of the well-drained uplands, coupled with the vibrant resources of the lowlands and wetlands, based on the research of Schulze and Whitacre (1999) at Tikal, satisfied the diverse natural resource needs of the ancient Maya subsistence and political economies and assured their endurance over time. The description of the Tikal forests provides the method for evaluating the assets of the perennial forest components of El Pilar and by extension the region as a whole, thus giving us a picture of the landscape created by the ancient milpa cycle and the natural resources it made available.

Inhabited Managed Uplands

The topographic gradient of upland forest types around Tikal corresponds to the El Pilar area, as well as the Maya area as a whole (Fedick and Ford 1990). While it has been well documented that topographic and soil characteristics of the uplands are largely responsible for the current distribution of certain trees, such as ramon, these areas are the same ones preferred by the ancient Maya for farming (compare Tables 5.1 and 5.2). As espoused by Netting (Netting 1977; Netting et al. 1989; Pyburn 1998), the intensive infields and cycled outfields created the landscape that fostered the development of the Maya and resulted in their forest today.

As the majority of the Maya were farmers, the intensively cultivated uplands, characterized by friable, basic pH, and low-clay soil, reflect the human imprint. In the El Pilar model, 62 percent of the study area of 1,288 square km is classified as uplands by Schulze and Whitacre (1999). These are the hand-cultivable areas (Fedick and Ford 1990) that supported dense human occupation in the past (Table 5.1). Settlement density is relatively high overall, averaging 25 residential units per square kilometer, and ranging from 22 to 70 based on the five probability classes of the predictive model (Table 4.1).

This density of occupation implies a well-developed and intense land-use system over many years (Hernández Xolocotzi 1985; Terán and Rasmussen 1995). Residential units and their potential infield-outfield areas were calculated for each settlement probability class, as defined in Chapter 4 and in relationship to the available area (Figures 5.5 and 5.6). Based on our research (Ford 1981, 1986, 1991b; Ford et al. 2009), the five settlement probability classes match the greater Petén forest types detailed by Schulze and Whitacre (1999; Tables 5.1 and 5.2) and form the basis of the settlement and environment picture discussed in this chapter.

With each land-use example, the cycles occur at different intervals (Figures 5.5 and 5.6). The low-yield example with a 20-year cycle provides a complex agricultural matrix with 20 percent of the uplands in open multi-crop maize fields at any one time, while the remainder is divided according to the stages of succession. The land under the most extensive use for fields includes space for long-term upland forest reserved as woodlands outside of the cyclic cultivation requirements. In the average yield example of a 31-

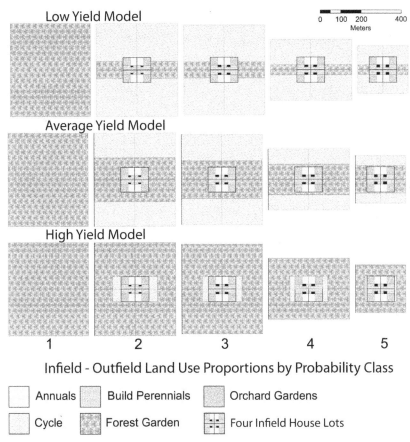

FIGURE 5.5. Residential land use for maize production models per four house lots by probability class. ©MesoAmerican Research Center, UCSB

year cycle, 13 percent of the uplands are dedicated to open maize polyculture at any one time within a cycling agricultural matrix where 87 percent of the uplands are in the stages of succession and forest cover. The high-yield example with an estimated 1 percent of the lands in open polyculture maize fields at any one time provides for 99 percent of the cultivatable upland landscape matrix under succession and mature forest cover. It is clear that the extent of upland forest varies according to requirements for maize productivity. These data demonstrate that a large proportion of inhabited uplands maintain plant cover, and, given the dynamic quality of the milpa cycle, these lands are most often in forest stages.

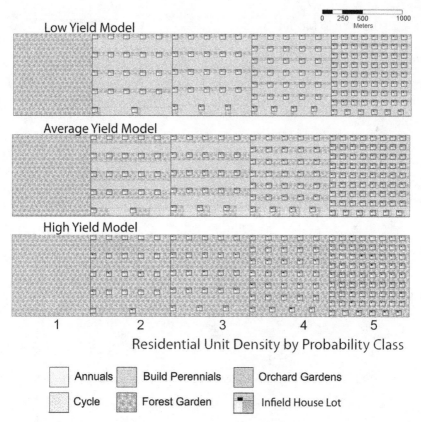

FIGURE 5.6. Residential house lot density per square kilometer for maize production models by probability class. ©MesoAmerican Research Center, UCSB

Long-Term Managed Upland Forests

As we have seen, the well-drained uplands provide a variety of resources in the field-to-forest cycle. Understanding the proportions of open field gaps, woody plant building, and closed-canopy mature forests of today helps reveal the Maya forest landscape story.

Beneficial and useful plants are dominant in the Maya forest (Campbell et al. 2006; Gómez-Pompa and Kaus 1990; Ross 2008, 2011; Ross and Rangel 2011). The trees and palms that characterize the dry uplands today would have formed the basic upland reserves. Common trees favoring dry conditions, tolerant of the vagaries of annual drought and adapted to limestone bedrock, would be zapotillo, ramon, guayaba, mamey, and chicozapote. Less prominent species would include allspice, copal, manchiche, manax, redwood, and malerio, as well as some cedar and jobo. All these plants are recorded in traditional Maya forest gardens (Appendix B, see also Maya Forest Gardeners 2015).

Palms play a significant role in tropical forest life (cf. Beckerman 1977), making up a major proportion of tropical forests, and are prominent in the dry upland forests. Escoba, guano, corozo, and pacaya figure as useful plants and are abundant in the forest. Vines, used for everything from basket making to construction, are a critical resource for household livelihoods and occur in varying proportions. In all, the Maya emphasize a diversity of important canopy trees and productive palms, but without canopy shade, a number of noteworthy understory plants would not thrive.

Long-Term Managed Lowlands and Wetlands

For the study area of El Pilar, 38 percent, or 485 square km, are uninhabited because they are not well drained, are inappropriate for hand cultivations, and are ill suited for houses. The major distinction between the soils of the upland forests and those of the lowlands and wetlands is the lack of limestone and high clay content (see Figure 5.3), which creates a very intractable medium for hand cultivation (Fedick 1988, 1989). The poorly drained forests are seasonally inundated, and palms, which prefer humid areas, are abundant there. For example, the Sabal forest types exhibit very high quantities of palms, dominated by the guano palm, for which it is named, as well as the escoba palm (Figure 5.2). While palms dominate these areas and their transitions, however, many of the common plants of the Maya forest are also present (Figure 5.4).

The wetlands provide unique plants with specialty uses, such as epiphytes, used for ornamentals (for example, Bromeliaceae and Orchidaea), the logwood or tinto tree (*Haematoxylum campechianum*), used for dye and lintels at Tikal (Lentz and Hockaday 2009; Orrego Corzo and Larios Villalta 1983), and the pukte (*Bucida buceras*), used in tanning and construction. Vines occur twice as frequently in the wetlands compared with the uplands (Schulze and Whitacre 1999:189). Wetland forest types are thus significant for plant cover, resources, and materials, and for habitat for animals. Management of the resources of these forests played a part in the land-use practices of the Maya, as noted by Lentz and Hockaday (2009). Clearly, the poorly drained lowland and wetland forest types reveal a varied treasure of natural resources, including fruit, wood, and household products.

The Managed Mosaic

Twenty years ago, Scott Fedick edited a volume that anticipates our examination on the managed mosaic here (Fedick 1996b). Using the El Pilar
model for ancient Maya land use, we can assess the proportions of the
open field to closed forest created by an active milpa forest garden cycle.
Archaeological data for population estimates of El Pilar (Chapter 4) approximate the requisites for fields, while the Tikal data of Schulze and
Whitacre (1999) will provide the basis for forest cover. By generalizing
the balance between the settled well-drained upland forest resources and
the managed poorly drained lowland and wetlands resources, we can
derive proportional values and determine the availability of agricultural
and managed forest resources within specific habitats. Thus, we arrive
at the combination of plant and animal resources that underwrote the
prosperity of the ancient Maya.

In terms of areas and their associated forest types, these resources are
not distributed in a single space; they occur in small and large patches
throughout the region, depending on drainage, bedrock, and landforms.
Populations residing in the upland forests would never be far from wetlands; forest reserves would be distributed in different sectors within the
uplands, managed for such objectives as construction, beehives (Kintz
1990; Terán and Rasmussen 2009), or fruit and scattered in areas of historical ecological preference (Atran 1999). Moreover, the diversity of land
cover, from open residential to forested woodlands, provided animal habitat that conforms to the archaeological record (Emery 2007; Emery and
Brown 2012; Emery and Thornton 2008, 2012).

The value of the milpa forest garden is in the reliability of the cycle.
The dynamic quality of this perennial and intensive agricultural system
promotes the development of new forest compositions, tailored to the
changing needs of the households and responding to the complexity of
the landscape. While our examples for the El Pilar area present a static
picture for the population of the Late Classic, the reality changes over time,
interacting with annual rainfall, interdecadal climate variations, and the
varying needs of the domestic cycle.

Using the El Pilar landscape distributions, we can calculate the forest
cover based on maize yields of open fields. We have a continuum that
brackets production of maize from a low yield of 855 kg per hectare to an
average of 1,144 kg per hectare and a high of 2,800 kg per hectare. Land-
use requirements to meet the maize needs of the estimated El Pilar population (186,200 people, see Chapter 4) are greater for lower maize yields and
less for higher yields. Our question now is: Based on the lands required to

produce enough maize and to complete the milpa cycle, what is the proportion of the different land cover types for each yield level?

The calculation of forested lands takes into account the model of Maya settlement for the El Pilar study area discussed in Chapter 4, starting with the land cover data we derived for the milpa cycle model. To appreciate the forest environments of Late Classic Maya, we use the proportions of long-term uplands plus the lowlands and wetlands as the main forested areas. These forests would also provide for the animal habitat (Emery 2010; Emery et al. 2000; Emery and Thornton 2008, 2012, 2014; Emery and Brown 2012; Foster et al. 2009; Kintz 1990; Medellin 1991, 1994a, 1994b; Medellin and Equihua 1998; Ortega and Arias Reyes 2008; Repussard et al. 2014).

Our calculations begin with the diverse infield home gardens that, in each example, are equivalent for all households. As with the calculation of the land requisites for the agricultural fields, the variable is the changing maize yields that impact the proportions of reforested uplands and available area for long-term upland forest management. Since the milpa cycle provides for a four-year maize field, followed by eight years of reforestation and culminating with another eight years of mature forest, it is the forest area more than 20 years old that increases the extent of mature forest. Thus, the estimated proportions of forest cover vary according to the area of residential unit infields, outfield cycles, managed stages of reforestation, and mature forest corresponding to Schulze and Whitacre's (1999) forest types.

The complex landscape mosaic for each example provides for considerable areas with land cover when combining all forest types, including maturing forests within the milpa cycle and the long-term managed forests, as well as forested lowlands and wetlands. Upland areas dedicated to long-term managed forests in the El Pilar case vary by maize yields: Low yield provides for 11 percent of land cover in the forest; average yield, 22 percent; and high yield, 43 percent (Table 5.3).

It is the milpa cycle that brings the intricacy to the system. In each case, the multi-crop maize fields require only a small proportion of the total land base, but the overall land requirements for the cycle make the difference. The residential infields take 3 percent of the total landscape. Add to this the outfields that compose 12 percent for the low-yield example, 9 percent for the average yield example, and 4 percent for the high-yield example. The total proportion of land in open fields at any one time combines the infield and outfield and ranges from the largest area at 15 percent for low yields (3 plus 12 percent) to 12 percent for average yields (3 plus 9 percent) and to just 7 percent for high yields (3 plus 4 percent; Table 5.3).

TABLE 5.3. Maize Yields and Land-Use Models for El Pilar*

Maize Yield	Upland Maize Infield	Upland Maize Outfield	Upland 8-yr Building Cycle	Upland 8-yr Mature Cycle	Upland Developed > 20 yr	Upland Long-Term	Lowland Forest	Total Area
Low Yield 855 kg/ha	3%	12%	18%	18%	0%	11%	38%	100%
Average Yield 1144 kg/ha	3%	9%	9%	9%	10%	22%	38%	100%
High Yield 2800 kg/ha	3%	4%	0.5%	0.5%	11%	43%	38%	100%

* Figures in round numbers

The estimates of land cover for the Maya forest in the Late Classic period are expressed in Table 5.3 and in pie charts (Figures 5.7, 5.8, and 5.9). In round figures, the low-yield example provides for 29 percent of the area in mature and developed upland forest at any one time; the average-yield example, 42 percent; and the high-yield example, 56 percent. To these proportions we add the lowland and wetland forest types, making up 38 percent in each case. The resulting totals for forest cover are remarkable, even for low maize yields. In every case the *majority* of the landscape supports valuable woodlands (Figure 5.10). In the low-yield example, where the milpa cycle encompasses 20 years, there would be at least 66 percent of the area in forest cover between the well-drained upland reserves and the lowland and wetland forest types. This proportion increases to 80 percent for the average-yield example and to 94 percent for the high-yield example.

What is immediately obvious in the calculations is that there is significant forest cover and a minimal amount in open fields at any one time. The application of the milpa cycle throughout the forest produces a diverse, variable, and largely woodland landscape. Infields, composed of fields and orchard gardens, are associated with permanent residential units, spread in varying densities across the uplands. Outfields are found in the interstices of the uplands linked to the location of the permanent residences. Forest reserves dispersed in the uplands and uninhabited lowlands and wetlands would have been managed to take advantage of the different forest types we have described for Tikal.

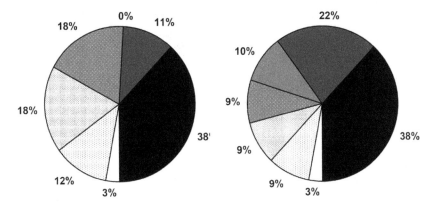

FIGURE 5.7. Low yield maize model. ©MesoAmerican Research Center, UCSB

FIGURE 5.8. Average yield maize model. ©MesoAmerican Research Center, UCSB

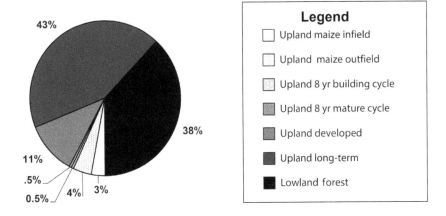

FIGURE 5.9. High yield maize model. ©MesoAmerican Research Center, UCSB

FIGURE 5.10. *(Above and on facing page)* The Maya forest garden cycle creates valuable woodlands with managed succession, Petén, Guatemala (Macduff Everton).

Historical Ecology of the Maya Forest

Viewed from a historical ecological perspective, the Maya forest is influenced by the selective forces exerted by the prehistoric inhabitants across eight millennia. Useful and beneficial plants found today in the forest and the gardens are those that could survive the intentional and selective land-use cycle and those that were purposely encouraged by the ancient Maya and their predecessors. Debates as to the potential of the tropical forest to sustain urban life center around the balance between agricultural demands for fields and the value of forest cover, natural resources, and ecological services (Meggers 1954; Hirshberg et al. 1957). Doubts as to the potential of the traditional milpa system to support the growth and development of

the Maya have loomed without testing, and the idea that milpa swidden would destroy the forest has been a foregone conclusion (Gómez-Pompa and Kaus 1992; McNeil 2012).

Given that maize is the foundation of Mesoamerican and Maya land use, the geography of the El Pilar area serves as a vital example to appreciate the distribution of resources and to provide a basis for interpreting the historical ecology here. Our calculations reveal that there would have been not only a wide variety of resources but also a complex range of habitats flourishing in the region during the Late Classic period. Furthermore, the milpa cycle would have developed these habitats in ways useful and beneficial to the inhabitants. Sufficient grain in the form of maize cannot account for all household needs. Domestic products, home construction, and balanced nutrition require a landscape replete with the varied seasonal resources for daily living. For example, within the forest garden, there are fruit and nut trees and production palms, in addition to field vegetables, which supply important sources of food (Lentz et al. 2012; Wyatt 2012). The value of trees in the home garden and managed forests is exemplified by the fruit trees featured as the "orchard of ancestors" on Pakal's tomb at Palenque, which shows carvings of the avocado, cacao, mamey, nance, and guayaba (Schele and Mathews 1998:119-120). All of these fruit trees are common and valued in traditional gardens and the forest today.

We have affirmed that in the milpa forest garden cycle the more intensive the skill investment is, the greater the open-field productivity and the larger the area of forest cover. The diversity of land cover, from residential zones to mature forest, makes available habitats for animals that richly augment the Maya diet. Indeed, research has shown that the use of animals in the diet was habitual, dependable, and consistent (Emery 2004, 2010; Emery and Thornton 2008, 2012, 2014; Greenberg 1992; White and Schwarcz 1989). Faunal analyses from the region demonstrate that animals used by the Maya inhabited the environment everywhere from field to forest (Emery and Thornton 2008). Additionally, the diversity of species remained stable over the Classic period with no change over time in subsistence habits in the Petexbatun area or in the land cover (Emery 2004, 2010:269-272; erroneously reported in Turner and Sabloff 2012:13910), a conclusion that accords well with our model Maya landscape.

Interestingly, the evidence for habitat use for animal procurement extends from residential areas to agricultural fields, secondary forests, and mature forest (Emery and Thornton 2008, 2012, 2014), a mosaic that corresponds to the qualities of the milpa cycle. In our examination of the El Pilar model, mature forest makes up the greater proportion of the total landscape (Figures 5.7-5.9). The data on animal use, however, present a distinct preference for hunting in fields and secondary forest habitats (Arias Reyes 1995a; Everton 2012:76; Greenberg 1992; Kintz 1990; Hernández Xolocotzi et al.1995:63-64). The infield home garden, the multi-crop maize outfield, and the initial succession restoration areas are precisely those that farmers most frequent in their daily work schedule and would thus provide opportunity for hunting (Anderson 2005; Linares 1976; Ortega and Arias Reyes 2008; Romero-Balderas et al. 2006; Terán and Rasmussen 2009:309-321) with more intensive attention at harvest time (Everton 2012:76).

Understanding the milpa cycle and resource management at the landscape level provides insight into how the ancient and current traditional Maya developed their home economy (Gliessman et al. 1981). The milpa forest garden cycle can meet the maize requirements of the estimated large populations of the Late Classic period. The cycle also provides the land cover needed to manage soil fertility, the water cycle, and tropical biodiversity while building a forest that benefits the inhabitants. The diverse environments, particularly secondary vegetation, also supported habitats from which animals were hunted (Emery and Brown 2012; Jacke and Toensmeier 2005).

If we conceptualize a pollen record created by the landscape of the milpa forest garden cycle, we can see it is congruent with the actual fossil pollen record described in the literature (for example, Binford 1987; Hillesheim et al. 2005; Hodell et al. 2008; Mueller et al. 2009; Wahl et al. 2007). New archaeobotanical and zooarchaeological materials from ancient sites are also consistent with the landscape we envision from these data (Emery and Thornton 2012; Robin 2012). With the establishment of settlements across well-drained uplands, infield home gardens and cycling outfield maize-polyculture would naturally increase the presence of forbs, just as we see for the Classic period. The majority of native grasses are not wind pollinated. Maize is the principal grass that relies on wind pollination. Indeed, an examination of the pollen for the Classic period shows no significant change in the proportions of grasses from earlier periods (Figure 3.4).

The expansion of permanent residences would affect farming settlements concentrated in well-drained uplands, favored by specific trees, especially the zapotillo and ramon. Zapotillo is insect pollinated (Ford 2008:188) and not detected in pollen sequences, but ramon is wind pollinated and is part of the fossil pollen sequence. Both are part of the Maya home gardens, and ramon's presence in pollen sequences changes with the development of ancient settlements. Importantly, when change occurred 4,000 years ago during climate chaos, new vegetation patterns stabilized across the Classic, particularly of forb and ramon pollen. Animal use was similarly stable (Emery 2004, 2010; Emery and Thornton 2008). After the so-called Terminal Classic, when Maya temples and palaces of the regional centers were no longer maintained, the collapsed architecture provided a new niche for pioneering plants, such as ramon, which ultimately shaded out forbs and grasses. Interestingly, the presence of forbs continued until the conquest 500 years ago (See Figure 3.4). This supports the implication that the milpa forest garden cycle persisted until the shock of the Spanish conquest and the impositions it wrought on the traditional subsistence system (Roys 1952).

Woodland management in the context of the milpa cycle has historical ecological roots in the Maya forest (Atran 1993; Toledo 1990; cf. Conklin 1957). Botanists and agroecologists recognize the inherent values of the economic species of the forest that make up cultivated trees (Appendix B) and reserves of today's forest gardeners (Figure 5.11). Some, like tinto,

FIGURE 5.11. *(Above and on facing page)* Zacarias Quixchan in his reserve with his mahogany, Petén, Guatemala (Macduff Everton).

allspice, mahogany, and chicozapote, have played major roles on the world stage (Schwartz 1990). In fact, trees were so important to the Maya that they were hailed as ancestors (Schele and Mathews 1998:122), and even today the ceiba, *Ceiba pentandra,* is considered sacred. In sum, the complex and intentional relationship of the Maya and their woodland environment was founded on the essential contributions of the flexible and resilient milpa forest garden.

CHAPTER 6

Maya Restoration Agriculture as Conservation for the Twenty-first Century

Our exploration leaves no doubt regarding the role of the ancient Maya in enriching the composition of the forest, one that today is recognized for its economic values and biodiversity. But the traditional Maya milpa we have described has been commodified and marginalized. Currently, the twin conservation and development schemes for the region compel the exclusion of people from the forest and the expansion of industrial farming strategies, both guaranteed to destroy the forest cover. Without understanding the value of the milpa forest garden cycle and the knowledge of traditional smallholder farmers, conservation designs for the future will fail and we will lose the Maya forest and the knowledge of its stewards, the Maya people.

A Co-Creative Landscape

Indigenous farming systems that develop with efforts invested in hand tools and within the context of the natural setting create an entirely anthropogenic landscape. That this is true of the Maya and their forest is not debated, but the scope and depth of this co-creativity has not been explored before now. The economic values of the forest and the distribution of ancient sites across the region speak directly to the importance of the integrated human-environment relationship. Our analyses of the nature of the milpa forest garden, our discussion of the qualities of the pollen record, and our presentation of the model landscape have detailed the cyclical impacts and expanded appreciation of the influence of the Maya on their forest, past and present. Now, however, we are facing catastrophic human impacts to the Maya forest. The introduction of cattle and the plow and, along with them, of exotic and invasive grasses, has transformed the forest cover that is so vital to the milpa forest garden cycle (Gómez-Pompa and Kaus 1999). Today, introduced ecological imperialist strategies have arrested the natural cycle of succession, not just in the Maya forest but also around the tropical world (Chazdon 2014; Dean 2013; McElwee 2009; Nikolic et al. 2008; Siebert and Belsky 2014; Siebert and Belsky 2012). The potential for the contemporary Maya to influence the conservation of the forest into the future rests on, first, recognizing their contribution to restoration agriculture and, second, including them in the process before it is too late (Diemont et al. 2011).

We have shown that strategic management of the landscape, beginning with the forest and the purposeful selection of land for the agricultural fields, the careful protection of trees in the fields, and the investment in the development of the perennial phases of the agricultural cycle—all absent in Western development schemes—results in the human plant preferences of the Maya forest. We have also demonstrated how Maya land-use strategies can support the high population densities proposed for prehistoric occupations as well as how the land-use system has directed the makeup of the forest by managing plant succession over generations, centuries, and millennia. Maya land use and management produced the lasting patterns of plant and associated animal communities that persist today. The indigenous techniques of felling, cutting, pruning, coppicing, and pollarding perennial shrubs and trees within a cycle of complex dispersed annual fields built a resilient forest. Not only was there a preference for specific fruitful perennials, the Maya also encouraged regenerating and resprouting after "slash-and-burn" practices that we prefer to call "select and grow." This is the serial progression that made the Maya forest a garden.

Based on our research, analyses, and modeling of Maya land use, we have demonstrated that the forest was intentionally shaped by human ecology, creating one of the most diverse anthropogenic landscapes in the world. Today the Maya forest is a conservation hot spot (Cincotta et al. 2000; Mittermeier et al. 2000). Its legacy lives on. Studies of the home gardens show that they are among the most biodiverse domestic systems in the world (Campbell 2007).

Our research leaves no room for doubt. The traditional Maya farming system recorded today—the complex agroforestry polyculture milpa we describe in Chapter 2 and its application to the example of the El Pilar landscape of the Late Classic in Chapters 4 and 5—indeed reflects the sustainable agricultural strategies of the people who lived in the forest for 8,000 years. We have probed the signatures of this system with multiple lines of evidence: the contemporary strategies, the paleoecology, the settlement patterns, and the forest composition.

No single line of evidence is sufficient. For example, the pollen data have been interpreted as a direct snapshot of the actual landscape at any point in time, when they are a picture *only* of wind-borne pollen. Nevertheless, we understand the potentials of the data sets, and we have used their multidimensional qualities to create a new vision of Maya human ecology, one that matches the ascendency of the Classic period political system as well as its demise, and that accounts for the ethnohistorical observations at the time of the conquest. The milpa forest garden subsidized the growth and development of Maya civilization that climaxed between A.D. 500 and 900. The same system underwent changes with the ebbs and flows of the hierarchy, yet it supported the ecological continuity recognized by agroecologists and economic botanists of the region today. The adaptive strategies the Maya experimented with, learned, and developed were recorded by the Spanish in the 1500s. Because of this flexibility, the system perseveres today through the practices of tenacious traditionalists who, unappreciated for their sophistication, are vanishing.

Ancient Maya Historical Ecology: Rethinking Assumptions

A major motivation for investigating Maya prehistory is to draw lessons from the past that are relevant to the condition of our own civilization (see Diamond 2005, 2012; Redman 1999; Wilk 2013). This exercise is a legitimate use of scholarly knowledge, yet we must be cautious lest the filter of our own concerns distorts our view of the Maya and hides some of the insights that we are seeking. Though we have emphasized the environmental aspects of Maya prehistory, we are actually arguing against an overly deterministic environmental view. The volume on the Maya Terminal Classic by Demarest and others (2004) bears ample witness to both the complexities of the collapse of the Classic Maya and the importance of the sociopolitical system in the sometimes dramatic events that centered in the Maya Lowlands around the 10th century A.D.

To recap the human-environmental back story, we can see that the cultural developments of Mesoamerica and the Maya area were related to major climate changes. The paleoecological data have given us ample verification of a major regional climatic shift at the end of the Pleistocene some 10,000 to 12,000 years ago, creating the conditions for the emergence of Lowland Mesoamerican ecological culture. An examination of regional data on precipitation provides evidence of significant climate shifts that accompanied this process. After the warming of the early Holocene came a period of climatic stability during the Holocene Thermal Maximum that coincided with the Archaic occupation in the New World. This was followed by extreme climatic variability, beginning about 4,000 years ago, representing an important challenge to the inhabitants of the Maya forest (Ford and Nigh 2014), not to mention the whole forest environment. The immediate human response to this uncertainty was the initial development of settled farming communities, and later, with population growth, of hierarchical organization and urban civilization. These considerations compel a revision of tenaciously held views of Maya forest prehistory.

Turning to the local data of the Petén area of the Maya forest, pollen analysis confirms the major climatic transition at the end of the last ice age. But it cannot bring into focus the land-cover changes that had a bearing on human settlement, agricultural activity, and adaptive forest management. While archaeological data suggest that Maya occupation of the forest gradually intensified over several millennia from the Early Preclassic, no evidence indicates that human activity was the significant force in driving vegetation change, soil erosion, or local climate change over the course of prehistory. Yet the early changes wrought by human influence on the forest, while subtle, were enduring.

The argument presented in this book leads to the following four related hypotheses that are anchored in our interpretation of available archaeological, ethnographic, ecological, and paleoecological data:

1. Maya agricultural intensification was a 4,000-year process of adaptation to gradual climatic drying, punctuated by periods of marked climate instability and alternation between extreme dry and wet conditions. Around 4,000 years ago, increased El Niño Southern Oscillation was reflected in regional climate extremes that catalyzed the human development of water control, intensive agriculture, and the urbanization in the Maya forest. Climate extremes induced the inhabitants of the forest to seek stability. This resulted in the establishment of Preclassic settlements around reliable water resources, giving rise to the economic and political formations associated with urbanism and Classic civilization.

2. Throughout the Preclassic, the Maya were challenged by periodic climate extremes and probably famine, while populations steadily grew and important cities—El Mirador, Cerros, Tikal, and El Pilar—waxed and waned at different times. Where elite traditions proved unsustainable, they were abandoned, especially beginning in the tenth century. There was no overpopulation or destruction of forest resources. Populations moved, particularly as a consequence of elite military adventures, but no general dramatic demographic collapse took place in the region until the sixteenth century.

3. Beginning in the Archaic, sophisticated Maya agroforestry led to a diversified forest garden landscape, characterized by graded stages of use and directed regeneration. These stages are invisible in the pollen record, which reduces the interpretation to arboreal and non-arboreal landscapes. This leads to an erroneous proposal of deforestation, based on the presence or absence of a limited set of taxa. The use of *Brosimum*-type Moraceae pollen as an indicator of the extent of mature forest cover must be reconsidered. Essential indicators show that the Maya lived and farmed in the forest, transforming it into a dynamic and domesticated landscape mosaic.

4. Maya smallholders, employing techniques of the high-performance milpa and related agroforestry, created the forest garden. This process began in the forest before the Preclassic and continued during the long transition to settled farming communities. Even with the rise of urban centers, dispersed populations dwelled in the forest and were integral to sustainable and reliable land use. We envision a "galactic" form of urbanism similar to that described for prehistoric Angkor of Southeast Asia or the Amazon of South America. When political crises struck Classic Maya society, the population largely retired to the forest garden, leaving elite centers abandoned. Depopulation after the Spanish conquest resulted in the contemporary feral forest, where floral composition and abundances are still demonstrably influenced by past selection for species of interest to humans. This reflects the imprint of Maya smallholders who lived by constructing forest gardens wherever they could.

Current interpretations of ancient Maya agriculture express a Eurocentric perspective that has been blind to the cultural legacy of the Maya forest. Our review of the evidence supports the hypothesis that the Maya forest ecosystems are essentially anthropogenic, the result of millennia of selective management. The Maya honed smallholder skills and knowledge over 8,000 years of continuous habitation in intimate contact with the neotropical woodlands. Far from threatening their tropical habitat, the skills and practices of the traditional Maya today provide valuable options for the conservation of the region and the survival of the forest and its people. It is the rapid disappearance of traditional forest gardeners—with their store of traditional ecological knowledge—that most threatens the Maya forest as we know it.

The Post-Colonial Milpa and Anticommodity Production

Globally today, small farmers, those who work less than half the croplands and produce at least 70 percent of our food worldwide, are no longer at the hub of food-system decision making (ETC Group 2009:1). The commodity market and financial corporations drive production, without regard for the interests of producers and consumers. The persistence of the traditional Maya milpa (Hernández Xolocotzi et al. 1995:75; Terán and Rasmussen 2008:133-134), as well as other indigenous production systems around the world (La Via Campesina 2014), has become a form of opposition in response to globalization (Barkin 2002; see also Scott 2009). The aim of this movement is to position people who produce and consume food at the center of food systems. For Mesoamerica, this involves the culture of maize:

> From the data available about maize production and other fieldwork experiences in [Mesoamerica], it is clear that rural communities are actively involved in a complex process to construct their own social and productive alternatives to respond to the challenges of globalization.... [T]he persistence...can best be interpreted not simply as a subjective reaction to a desire to preserve peasant traditions, but rather as a part of a collective search for mechanisms to reduce their vulnerability to many of the negative impacts of international economic integration. The rural communities are implementing their own strategies...to diversify their regional economics, to make rural society more viable, [involving] a broad range of specific productive and cultural projects that offer vivid testimony to the depths of the commitment of many "poorer" economic groups to protect their unique societies in the face of a global process of economic and social consolidation and integration. (Barkin 2002:10)

Despite the efforts of thousands of farmers, and the fact that the majority of land in the Maya area is still planted in maize, the milpa system faces considerable challenges today. Where milpa is still practiced, it persists in the face of centuries of official hostility and accusations of backwardness

(Hernández Xolocotzi et al. 1995:565-566; 598-599). Though we lack exact statistics, most researchers note the gradual loss of species diversity in the contemporary milpa (Boege 2008). Some small farmers have accepted the advice of government technicians (see de Schlippe 1956:ix-x) and are gradually abandoning multi-cropping, packing more maize plants per unit area and tending toward maize monoculture.

The milpa has also lost much of its role as the central organizing principle of the Maya families' productive activity (Corzo Márquez and Schwartz 2008). As we have described, milpa was the crucial element of an agroecosystem that included the milpa field, maize-centered polyculture, and protected reforested woodlands, orchards, and house gardens. Often a genetically impoverished maize field is all that remains today of this once-diverse agroecology. The contemporary de-intensified conventional milpa of landless marginalized families only partially reflects the original system (compare Conklin 1957), but it is a defensive thrust to conserve seed and provide fresh corn and other products for domestic consumption.

Farming techniques have also changed under the influence of Western funded development projects. Chemical fertilizers have sometimes been incorporated, and burning has been greatly suppressed by pressures from conservation-minded officials. Fire had been judiciously used and, if properly managed, brings many benefits to the swidden farmer (Nigh and Diemont 2013). The suppression of fire, which has been among the most negative ecological effects of these external pressures, changes the ecology of the milpa-forest cycle. This has been recognized in other regions, such as the Northeast of the United States, where oak woodlands are being replaced by pine.

Official hostility to milpa in the Maya region is not the first instance of the marginalization of smallholders. It is described by Ivan Illich (1981) as the war on subsistence, and Polanyi, referring to enclosure in sixteenth-century England, states:

> The war on cottages, the absorption of cottage gardens and grounds, the confiscation of rights in the commons deprived cottage industry of its two mainstays: family earnings and agricultural background. As long as domestic industry was supplemented by the facilities and amenities of a garden plot, a scrap of land, or grazing rights, the dependence of the laborer on money earnings was not absolute; the potato plot or "stubbing geese," a cow or even an ass in the common made all the difference; and family earnings acted as a kind of unemployment insurance. *The rationalization of agriculture inevitably uprooted the laborer and undermined his social security.* (Polanyi 2001[1944]; emphasis ours)

The issues affecting agricultural sustainability are not solely or even principally technological (Cleveland 2013). There are significant social and political values as well. Milpa, the primary production system of Maya agroforestry, is technically very similar today to what is reconstructed for the Prehispanic period (see Terán and Rasmussen 1995). It is the social and political context of Maya society that has been transformed in the 500 years since the conquest. The major difference resides in the overall value that social and political systems provide to the farming sector of society. In the Classic period, the elite administration was dependent on dispersed smallholders to underwrite the growing civic infrastructure. This changed under, first, the European colonial regimes and, later, the national administrations.

As we have attested, the elite class of the ancient Maya necessarily valued and encouraged milpa as the basis of social stability and growth. This is not the case today for the Maya or for any indigenous production system (compare Vietnam: McElwee 2009; Nikolic 2008; Sowervine 2004). The ancient Maya elite accepted and worked with the implications of the milpa forest garden with its dispersed settlement pattern. The centrifugal pattern preferred by milpa farmers made the art of governing a challenge (see Scott 1998, 2009). Yet the success of the Prehispanic elite was contingent on a system that demanded population dispersal into the prime farming zones. There was no alternative.

From the time of the Spanish policies of *reducción* (Farriss 1992; Schwartz 1990) to modern development projects in the tropical rainforest (Nations 2006; Nations et al. 1999; Primack et al. 1998), the post-colonial authorities have tried to concentrate populations in controlled centers recognized by the state (cf. Scott 1998). This increasing emphasis on centralization is directly related to a decrease in the value of traditional milpa production (Figure 6.1).

In stark contrast to its preeminent role in the economy of Prehispanic Maya society, the milpa forest garden of today is denigrated as inefficient by governments. Yet adaptable and flexible Mesoamerican maize continues to be produced as an indigenous product for local consumption by the Maya. Furthermore, maize, established throughout the world by the seventeenth century by means of the Columbian exchange, prospers in the most diverse environments and features prominently in international commodity exchange (Warman 2003). With distinct virtues over other grains, maize offers reliable yields, high nutritional value, and simplicity of cultivation. Maize today feeds a multitude of smallholders worldwide (Scott 2009:201-205).

FIGURE 6.1. Crowded *ciudades rurales* (top) with no garden vs. traditional house (bottom) with forest garden (www.liderazgojoven.com and Macduff Everton).

The success of growing maize and other Mesoamerican crops in dispersed plots has been transformed into an act of resistance, even of "escape agriculture" as described by Scott (2009: 187-231). Maat (2015) defines as anticommodities those major commodity crops, like maize or rice, that are produced in smallholdings and intended for local use. These crops oppose monocrop plantations intended for global commodity markets.

Anticommodities have arisen in the shadow of commodity production and the industrial strategies that invade livelihoods and local markets. Perceived by the market as insignificant because of uncertain or undefined economic value, anticommodity production occurs at sites that are local, indigenous, small, fragmented, and scattered on the margins of commodity monoculture (Maat 2015). Though not valued by the dominant political economy, anticommodity production is often vital to the survival of the rural population who are the source of cheap labor for commercial agricultural sectors.

Maize, which began in a smallholder system in ancient Mesoamerica, is now produced worldwide as a major commodity (Warman 2003) and increasingly in highly technological industrial monoculture (Sweeney et al. 2013; cf. Cleveland 2013). In this new context, milpa has taken on the role of an anticommodity. The milpa forest garden persists in provisioning the family. Thus, maize from a milpa field is not a commodity, even though it may be, in part, locally commercialized.

It would be misleading, however, to perceive anticommodity production purely as a subsistence activity devoted to support the farming household. We should not ignore its commercial importance at the household and local level. Smallholders deliberately create surplus crops for trade in local or regional markets. Thus, maize, like rice (Bray 2015; Maat 2015), can be a commodity or an anticommodity, depending on the biological, material, and social context of its production.

The varieties planted, the technology employed, the purpose to which the product is to be put, and even the economic rationale applied to production decisions distinguish commodity maize from anticommodity maize:

> The essential difference between present-day and pre-Colonial milpa can be explained by different social relations of production. In pre-Conquest society, all land was dedicated to [the milpa forest garden system], and since it was communal, there was better access to new, fertile land. Logically, the ruling class supported the milpa system, which was then the *only* system, and this invariably resulted in higher production. The milpa of today, though structurally similar, is only a vague shadow of yesterday's well-functioning system.... This is due to the fact that the governing class,

since the Conquest, has done all it could to eradicate the "inefficient" milpa system, and to substitute it with an "efficient" type of mono-crop cultivation. (Terán and Rasmussen 1995: 378)

The process referred to by Terán and Rasmussen is reminiscent of the dislocating effects of the expansion of commodity production and the global capitalist economy. The variations in intensity, diversity, and productivity of the traditional milpa, illustrated particularly in the case of the Lakantun but others as well, contrast with the conventional milpa found in much of Mesoamerica and the Maya area today. The conventional milpa system is largely shaped by contemporary challenges of land tenure and off-farm labor demands (e.g., Daniels et al. 2008; Parsons et al. 2009). Alejandro Nadal states:

> Today, with economic pressure from all sides...producers are shifting towards a distorted version of the traditional *milpa*. The reason for this is that yields appear to increase, although not enough to reduce the plight of producers' households. In this transformation, monoculture cultivation becomes the main feature of the production system, agro-chemical inputs develop into a necessity, and the old method based on agro-diversity starts to break apart. (cited in Wise 2007:9)

Of course, even distorted forms under extreme conditions demonstrate the milpa agroecosystem's resilience. The ideological campaign by governments, development agencies, and conservationists against milpa agroforestry reveals a profound ignorance of the nature of the high-performance milpa (cf. de Schlippe 1956). The promotion of "modern" methods such as the use of fertilizers and herbicides, undermines traditional practices, reducing the agrobiodiversity that would enrich the diet and converting the milpa into a toxic area where the Maya family can no longer safely work. Maya farmers have been admonished over the last 500 years that their slash-and-burn cultivation is primitive, and policy makers from the outset have consistently attempted to "sedentize" the milpa to end the cycle. They fail to understand the importance of the cycling of fields to woodlands in a sustainable regime that maintains fertility and biodiversity.

Focusing exclusively on maize as "the staple grain," authorities have considered the milpa to have low productivity. They ignore or discount the wide variety of food and materials that are produced continuously from the system as a whole (cf. Bray 1994). This sustainability is, indeed, achieved through simple, low-input technology. Despite the subordinate role of the milpa forest garden in the contemporary commodity economy, its traditional forms endure and are structurally similar to their historic versions, demonstrating the importance, flexibility, and resilience of this indigenous production system in the Maya forest.

The diversification of food production by farmers is not only a move in defense of food sovereignty, but as Maat (2015) points out, it is also key to the overall commodity production within a capitalist economy. Only diversity of seed stock can protect us from destructive monocultures (Turrent et al. 2012; Wise 2010). Anticommodities can be seen as a strategic move against the war on the subsistence economy (cf. Polanyi 2001[1944]), at the same time providing meals for millions.

Future of the Maya Milpa

The environmental impacts of industrial agriculture are significant (Nadal and Wise 2004; Weis 2010). Conservationists are concerned about the loss of biodiversity, including agrobiodiversity, as well as damage to the pollination, soil formation, and biogeochemical cycles that sustain fertility. Use of chemicals and a heavy dependence on fossil fuels results in greenhouse gas emissions. Finally, and critically, the industrial commodity food system has resulted in the displacement of small farmers, primarily due to large government subsidies to commercial commodity farmers, which smallholders do not receive (Roberts 2008; Weis 2010).

The current universal faith in the efficiency and low cost of the industrial food system appears, in the light of recent research, to be misplaced (Cleveland 2013). The perceived benefits of modern technology in agriculture and food production are deceptive and fraught with a number of biophysical contradictions that bring their sustainability into question (Weis 2010). Upon careful reflection, these contradictions lead us to propose the strategies of the milpa technology as reliable solutions for feeding the growing twenty-first-century world population (e.g., Wilson 2002).

The hidden costs of industrial agriculture are not included in the usual economic calculations of efficiency. These costs are paid by society at large by the effects on health and welfare (Weis 2010) and include obesity, cardiovascular disease, and diabetes (for example, Ames 2006; Reaven 2005). Other costs are more direct and may affect the productivity of systems as well as food quality and nutrition (Benbrook et al. 2008; Halwell 2007). Contamination is a threat to human and environmental health. Ironically, a significant percentage of the nitrogen fertilizer applied on industrial monocrops is emitted or leached into the air or groundwater, creating serious pollution problems (e.g. Carberry et al. 2013). Pesticides and farm waste can further contribute to pollution.

Moreover, increased soil erosion and compaction are provoked by cultivation with heavy machinery, the use of intensive monocultures, the depletion of soil organic matter, and the salinization of water and soil from irrigation and mineral fertilizers (Montgomery 2007a, 2007b; Scholes and Scholes 2013). Irrigation also causes overexploitation of aquifers and, in coastal areas, the infiltration of seawater into fresh groundwater. These factors indicate that current forms of industrial agriculture are unsustainable.

If we take these real human and ecological costs into account and systematically compare them to the intensive Maya milpa, we find that milpa is neither primitive nor unproductive and is positive for human health and the environment. Food produced by the milpa is of high quality, as it is based on the natural fertility maintained in the forest garden cycle, where regenerated woodlands continually restore minerals and organic matter. High biodiversity assures that pesticides are unnecessary and all wastes are recycled in the field. Water is managed by the conservation of vegetation and by the infiltration of rainwater stored in the soil. A healthy and natural relationship is fostered for animals that are attracted to the secondary vegetation of the milpa forest garden, resulting in a kind of semi-domestication based on the landscape. Dependence on fossil fuel is nonexistent, and, far from contributing to greenhouse gas emissions, the Maya milpa creates a long-term store of carbon in the soil (Nigh and Diemont 2013).

Significantly, the milpa and its diversity provide a livelihood for farm families and a food surplus for local markets. Small farmers supply the majority of the world's food on a fraction of the land surface (FAO 2014a). There is little doubt that they represent a far greater potential for increasing food production through indigenous agroecological methods than industrial agriculture, which is reaching limits in many dimensions and threatening world food security (Altieri and Toledo 2011; Cleveland 2013; IFAD 2014; Turrent et al. 2012).

Indigenous food production is based on critical local environmental knowledge that can help sustain the world's growing food needs. The Maya milpa forest garden has been commonly assumed to be destructive of natural resources. Considering our research presented here, this view is completely misinformed. Millennia of experimentation and decades of empirical research demonstrate the sophisticated flexibility of the milpa forest garden in the tropical ecological setting.

Yet milpa agroforestry seems to violate the master narrative of our times: the incessant march of progress from hunter-gatherer to complex sedentary agriculture (Johnson and Earle 1987; Scott 2009:187-190; Service 1962, 1975). The Eurocentric vision assumes that Western civilization is the pinnacle of human progress (Crosby 1986) and that disappearing cultures can only aspire to emulate it (Diamond 2012; Wilk 2013). Not only in the popular mind, but also in the view of scientists, politicians, and technicians, it is capitalist industrial agriculture that is the unquestioned standard of production; all previously existing forms are, in this view, ready to be replaced.

We must vindicate the milpa forest garden and similarly sophisticated systems of human ecology that are native to their place. Their intricacy, subtlety, and contribution to our environmental balances are critical to our future. Recognizing the complexity of traditional agroecology (Martínez and Rosset 2010; Vandermeer and Perfecto 2013), a number of organizations are growing to defend small-scale sustainable agriculture, like La Via Campesina (LVC 2014). This is particularly important for the tropics, which represent one of our last terrestrial frontiers (Altieri 1995, 2002; Altieri and Toledo 2011). Addressing the developed world's need for expansion coupled with the concern for biodiversity, we see scholars trying to influence policy makers to favor the smallholder (Chazdon et al. 2009). They have identified individual methods and their applications, for example, in the case of live fences of the tropics. More farmers mean more living fences and, with them, more birds and more regenerating forests.

There is also a growing interest in responsible tourism where travelers desire to understand local environmental issues, wish to make a contribution to local well-being, and are interested in participating in community activities. In the Maya area, culture and nature are major factors in the development of tour destinations. One such place is the El Pilar Archaeological Reserve for Maya Flora and Fauna (Figure 6.2), centered around the ancient city of El Pilar (Figures 6.3, 6.4). The protected area is open to visitors, featuring *Archaeology Under the Canopy* (Exploring Solutions Past 2014) and the Maya house and forest garden (MesoAmerican Research Center 2014). Situated on the troubled border of Belize and Guatemala, the major Maya site and its surrounding forest are shared by the two nations across a single cultural and natural resource area, the Maya forest. Formally registered in both countries in 1998 and developed with an adaptive management framework (CONAP 2004; IA 2006; MARC 2014), the 2,000-hectare reserve has protected the cultural and natural resources of the site, and since the establishment of the boundaries, life has returned to the forest (Figures 6.3, 6.5-6.7). At El Pilar, the Maya forest is recognized as a creation of the ancient Maya and connected to traditional farmers in the surrounding area (Ford 2010, 2011a, 2011b; Ford et al. 2005; Ford and Havrda 2006; Ford and Knapp 2011; Ford and Nigh 2009). The landscape becomes part of the visitor experience and is linked to community forest gardens nearby, with the aim of recognizing master forest gardeners and elevating the importance of the milpa forest garden in forest conservation today (Ford and Ellis 2013; Ford et al. 2005; see also McAnany and Parks 2012; Stump 2013).

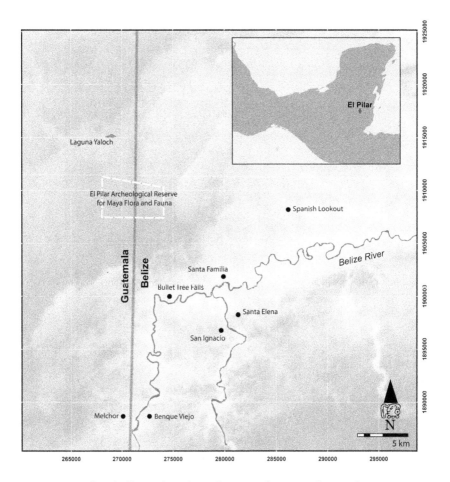

FIGURE 6.2. The El Pilar Archaeological Reserve for Maya Flora and Fauna bridges the international border of Belize and Guatemala. ©MesoAmerican Research Center, UCSB

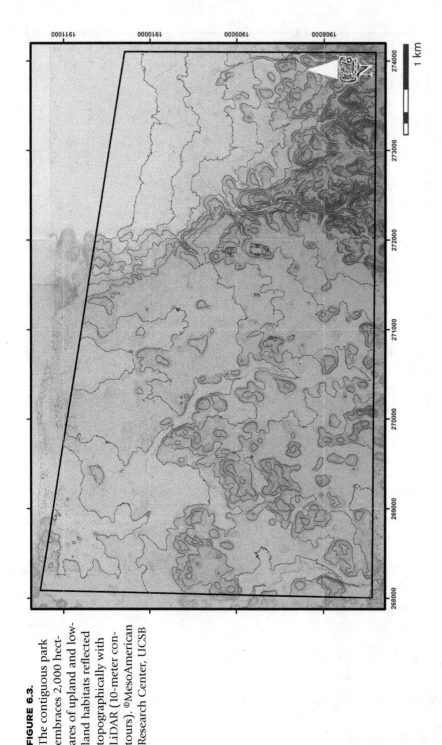

FIGURE 6.3.
The contiguous park embraces 2,000 hectares of upland and lowland habitats reflected topographically with LiDAR (10-meter contours). ©MesoAmerican Research Center, UCSB

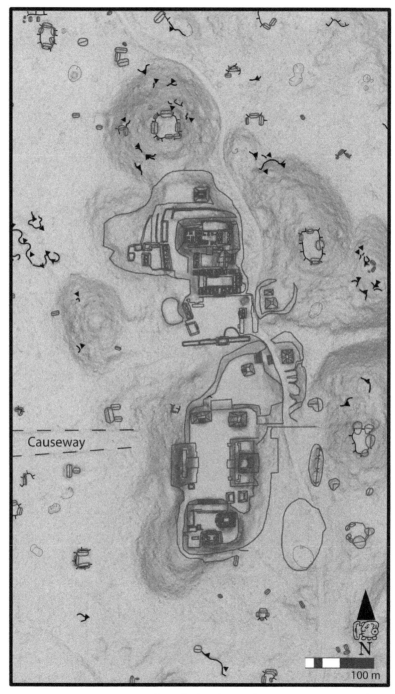

FIGURE 6.4. LiDAR topographic relief with a traditional map overlay of the Maya city of El Pilar. ©MesoAmerican Research Center, UCSB

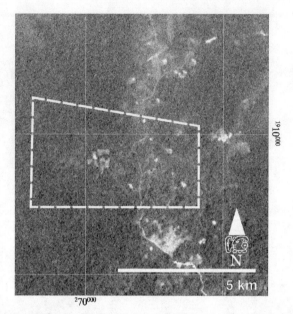

FIGURE 6.5. 1994 *Landsat 5* view of the El Pilar Archaeological Reserve before establishment of the protected area boundaries. ©MesoAmerican Research Center, UCSB

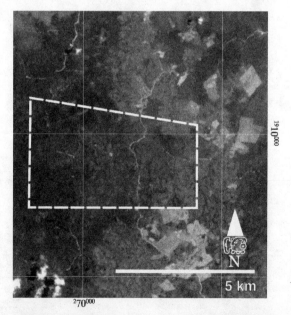

FIGURE 6.6. 2003 *Landsat 7* view of the El Pilar Archaeological Reserve after the 1998 protected area declaration in Belize and Guatemala. ©MesoAmerican Research Center, UCSB

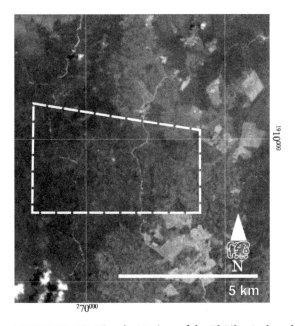

FIGURE 6.7. 2014 *Landsat 8* view of the El Pilar Archaeological Reserve showing forest integrity inside and increased forest fragmentation outside the reserve. ©MesoAmerican Research Center, UCSB

Yet the future of milpa in the twenty-first century is unclear. Though some form of milpa is still the most widespread type of farming in the Maya area, it is only one of many other systems. These include industrial livestock operations, conventional monocropping, commercial citrus orchards, and recently commercial African palms, as well as vegetable truck farms and specialty cropping with organic cacao, vanilla, and coffee (see Palerm 1967). These systems can benefit from the traditional knowledge of the milpa and the forest garden cycle. Soil management, water conservation, erosion controls, ecological restoration, and biodiversity maintenance are all highly relevant to the food crisis. These secrets need to be understood, encouraged, and developed.

Traditional indigenous farmers and smallholders are able to support themselves and provide quality products for local markets. Promoting modernization displays a pitiful lack of knowledge of the value of the Maya traditions, an understanding long held by agroecologists and economic botanists (Hernández Xolocotzi et al. 1995:598-599). As ecological imperialism gains momentum and consumer commodity markets ignore answers found in local knowledge, the challenges to the preservation of sustainable systems only grow. The greatest threat to the future of life is the loss of traditional ecological knowledge, of which the milpa forest garden is one of our most significant examples.

In its high-performance mode, the Maya milpa is a form of restoration agriculture as defined by Shepard (2013:223, 273). Each cycle of production results in abundant products for family subsistence, trade, and tribute. The system also prevents erosion and compaction, increases soil fertility, and builds long-term carbon reserves in the soil and in enriched woodland vegetation. A dialogue of scientific and traditional farmer knowledge is desperately needed to construct productive conservation landscapes for the future of the tropics worldwide (cf. Cleveland 2013).

Maya Forest Conservation

Contemporary conservation practices for tropical forests have relied upon the Western approach: removing the human element from the equation. Yet ecological and botanical research on the Maya forest reveals a variegated garden dominated by plants of economic value that are highly dependent on human interaction.

What are the consequences for Maya forest conservation and the world at large to cast aside the values of the traditional land use? Satellite views of the region demonstrate all too clearly the trajectory of increasing population growth with the expansion of pastures and plowed fields (Figures 6.8-6.10). Expanding Western systems of pasture and plow are eliminating the biodiversity of the forest (TNC 2014). Recognizing the importance of community participation in conservation is a good beginning, but it must incorporate the grand experiment of 8,000 years in the Maya forest. While the traditional farmers manage the forest as their garden, the tragedy of the commons prevails on behalf of shortsighted gain (Hardin 1968). The nurtured trees that produce fruits for all are cut down to make way for development (see Schwartz and Corzo Márquez 2015). The importance of indigenous ecological knowledge cannot be ignored. This accumulated knowledge of the landscape is what makes the Maya forest. Conservation without the ingenuity of the Maya forest gardeners will eradicate the values that underwrote the Maya civilization.

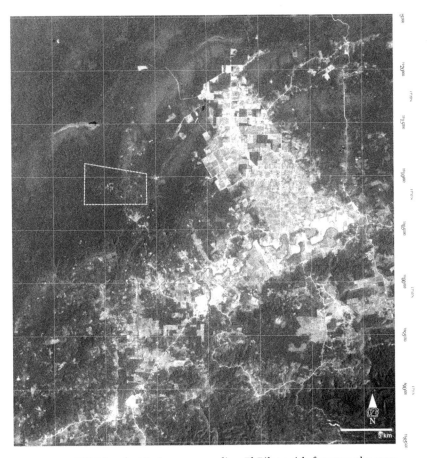

FIGURE 6.8. 1994 *Landsat 5* view surrounding El Pilar, with forest to the west in the Maya Biosphere Reserve, Petén Guatemala, and cleared areas of pasture and plow to the east in Spanish Lookout, Cayo Belize. ©MesoAmerican Research Center, UCSB

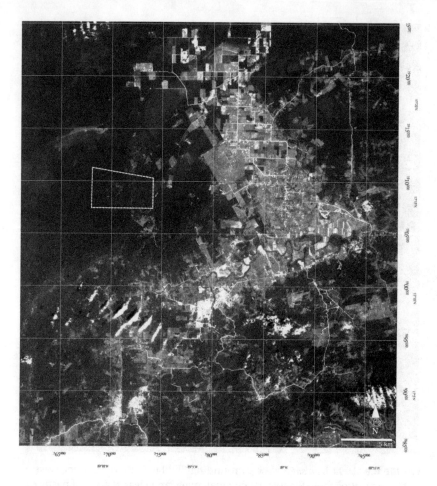

FIGURE 6.9. 2003 *Landsat 7* view surrounding El Pilar, with forest to the west and north of Melchor, Petén Guatemala, and expanded pasture and plow to the east in Spanish Lookout, Cayo Belize. ©MesoAmerican Research Center, UCSB

FIGURE 6.10. 2014 *Landsat 8* view surrounding El Pilar, with forest and new agricultural expansion to the west in Melchor, Petén Guatemala, and further expansion of pasture and plow to the east in Spanish Lookout, Cayo Belize. ©MesoAmerican Research Center, UCSB

APPENDIX A

Basket of Mesoamerican Cultivated Plants

Binomial	English	Spanish	Mayan	Uses
Acalypha arvensis Poepp.	cancer herb, cat tail, field copperleaf	hierba de cancer	mis xiv	medicine
Agave fourcroydes Lem.	sisal plant	henequén, agave	kih, kí	fiber
Amaranthus caudatus L.	tassel flower	ataco	huautli	herb
Amaranthus dubius Mart. ex Thell.	amaranth	quelite	kiltosh	food, condiment
Amaranthus spp.	amaranth	amor seco, bledo	xtess	ceremonial
Ananas comosus Merr	pineapple	piña	p'ach	food
Anthurium schlechtendalii Kunth	pheasant's tail	cola de faisan	bobtun, tye-pe, xiv-tun-ich, xiv-yak-tun-ich	medicine
Aphelandra scabra (Vahl) Sm. in Rees	indian head	anal grande, cabeza de indio	anal, anal-chae	ornamental
Arachis hypogaea L.	peanut	cacahuate	kakawat	food
Aristolochia maxima Jacq.	Florida dutchman's pipe	canastilla	wako aak'	medicine

Binomial	English	Spanish	Mayan	Uses
Arthrostemma ciliatum Pav. Ed D. Don	pinkfringe	pin-win	top-tuk	ornamental
Asclepias curassavica L.	bloodflower	gato, hoja de veneno	chushu-yu-shi, cuchilli-xiv, ka-ki-at'sum	medicine
Bauhinia herrerae (Britton & Rose) Standl. & Steyerm	cowfoot, cowhoof	guaco	ki-bix, malo kibish	medicine
Belotia mexicana (DC.) K. Schum		capulin blanco	tao, tow	construction, fertilizer
Bixa orellana L.	annato	achiote	ki'wil, k'uxub	food, condiment
Caesalpinia pulcherrima (L.) Swartz	peacock flower	cabello de angel	chak sikin	ceremonial, medicine, ornamental
Calathea lutea (Aubl.) Schult	Havana cigar	platanillo	moxan	thatching, wrapping
Canna sp. L.	canna lily	canna	sak wowoh	food
Carica papaya L.	papaya	papaya	p'ut	food, medicine
Capsicum annuum L.	hot pepper	chile	ik	condiment
Capsicum chinense Jacq.	habanero pepper	chile habanero	kat ik	condiment
Capsicum frutescens L.	cayenne	chile del monte	maxik, ik	condiment
Cestrum nocturnum Ruiz and Pavon	night-blooming jasmine	huele de noche	ak'ab yon	food, ornamental, medicine
Chenopodium abrosioides L.	wormseed	epazote	k'oxex	herb, medicine
Cnidoscolus chayamansa Mc Vaugh	tree spinach	chaya, chaya mansa	chaay, chayok	food
Cnidoscolus aconitifolius (Mill.) I.M. Johnson	wild chaya	chaya silvestre	ch'inch'in chay, saj, tsaaj	food, medicine

Binomial	English	Spanish	Mayan	Uses
Combretum fruticosum (Loefl.) Stuntz	monkey brush, yellow brush	flor de cepillo	xtabeché, xkanché	food
Crescentia alata Kunth	calabash	jícara pequeña	wasluch	utensil, medicine, food
Crescentia cujete L.	calabash	jícaro	luuch	utensil, medicine, food
Crotalaria cajanifolia Kunth	chipilin	frijolillo	yaax ooch, sat'ooch	food, condiment
Crotalaria longirostrata	chipilin	chipilín	chepil ix	food, condiment
Croton draco Schltdl.	dragon's blood	sangre de dragón	chucum	medicine
Cucurbita argyrosperma Pang.	cushaw pumpkin	pipián silvestre	xka o xtoo'p	food
Cucurbita moschata (Lam.) Poir	butternut	calabaza grande	xnuk k'uum	food
Cucurbita pepo L.	field pumpkin, winter squash	calabaza dzol, calabacin	ds'ol, k'um	food
Cucurbita spp.	squash	calabaza	xtoob, k'um, ts'ol, poir	food
Cydista aequinoctialis L.	garlic vine		axux ak'	condiment
Dahlia sp. Cav.	dahlia	dahlia	ch'oliw	ceremonial, condiment, ornamental
Duranta repens L.	bluesky flower	velo de novia	xcambocoché	food
Echites yucatanensis Millsp. ex Standl.		loroco de zope, cruz-ojo	kalis aak'	medicine
Eryngium foetidum L.	Mexican coriander	culantu	remax	condiment, medicine
Euphorbia pulcherrima Willd. ex Klotzsch	poinsettia	noche buena	iik'il che'	ceremonial, condiment, ornamental

Binomial	English	Spanish	Mayan	Uses
Gonolobus sp. Michx.		cuchamper	loch' op	fiber, food
Gossypium spp. L.	cotton	algodón	jtaman, piits'	fiber, food, medicine
Hamelia patens Jacq.	Mexican firebrush	sanalotodo	ixcanan	medicine
Hybanthus yucatanensis Millsp.		cilantrillo	sakbakil kaan	condiment, medicine
Hylocereus undatus (Haworth) Britton & Rose	strawberry pear, dragon fruit	pitahaya roja	wob, chakam	food
Indigofera suffruticosa Miller	Guatemalan indigo	añil chiquito	ch'ooj	condiment, medicine, pigment
Ipomoea batatas (L.) Lam.	sweet potato	camote	is, sac, kam, morado	food
Lagenaria siceraria (Molina) Standley	bottle gourd	bule, guaje	leek, chuu	utensil
Lantana camara L.	wild sage	palabra de caballero	petekin, ikilhaxin	herb
Lycopersicon esculentum Mill.	tomato	tomate	p'ak	food
Malpighia glabra L.	wild crepe myrtle	pico de paloma	kib che, chi'	food
Manihot esculenta Crantz	manioc	yuca	ts'lim	food
Melothria pendula L.	watermelon rat, guadalupe cucumber	melón de ratón	sandia stulub, sandia tuul	food
Mimosa pudica L.	sensitive plant, twelve o'clock plant	dormilona	guara kish	medicine
Mirabilis jalapa L.	four-o'clock flower	maravilla	tutsuy xiw	ornamental
Neurolaena lobata (L.) Cass.	jackass bitters	trespuntas, mando de lagarto	kayabim, k'an-mank	medicine

Binomial	English	Spanish	Mayan	Uses
Nicotiana tabacum L.	tobacco	tobaco	k'utz	medicine
Nopalea cocheneillifera L.	prickly pear	nopal	tsakam	food, medicine
Pachyrhizus erosus L.	jicama, yam bean	jícama	ch'ikam, suri	food
Parmentiera aculeata K.	cucumber tree	cuajilote	kaat	
Passiflora coriacea Juss.	wild sweet calabash, bat leaved passion flower	ala de murciélago	maak xikin soots'	food
Passiflora edulis Sims	passion fruit	granadilla	chun ak'	food
Petiveria alliacea L.	anamu	zonillo	oay-che	repellent, medicine
Petrea volubilis L.	queen's wreath, purple wreath	machiguá	thathub	ornamental, medicine
Phaseolus coccineus L.	scarlet runner bean	ayocote	botil	food, ornamental
Phaseolus lunatus L.	lima bean	comba, frijol lima	ibes	food
Phaseolus vulgaris L.	common bean	frijol	xmehenbuul, tsamá, bu'ul	food
Phyllanthus acidus (L.) Skeels	otaheite gooseberry	ciruela costeña	po'ok	food
Piper aduncum L.	matico	matico	pu-chúch	medicine
Piper auritum H.B & K.	bullhoof, cowfoot, mexican pepperleaf	hoja santa, santa maria	Mak'olan, xmak'ulan	condiment
Piper marginatum Jacq.	marigold pepper, cake bush	cordoncillo	ya'ax pe'ejel che	medicine
Pithecellobium sp.	black beads	tucuy	chukum	construction
Plumeria rubra L.	frangipani	flor de mayo	nicté	ceremonial, condiment, ornamental

Binomial	English	Spanish	Mayan	Uses
Portulaca pilosa L.	pink purslane	verdolaga peluda	tsayoch	ornamental, medicine
Priva lappulacea (L.) Pers.	cats tongue	hierba del cancer, masote	tzayuntzay	medicine
Pyllanthus liebmannianus Müll. Arg.	Florida leafflower	hierba de ojo	piix t'oom	medicine
Rivina humilis L.	pigeon berry	coqueta, coralillo, hierba mora, tomatillo	k'uxu'ub xiix	colorant
Sagittaria lancifolia L.	duck potato	lirio	cere	food
Salvia coccinea Buc'hoz ex Etl.	sage	clavel	chatepec	herb
Sechium edule (Jacq.) Swarts	squash	chayote	k'iix pach k'uum, p'ix	food
Sida acuta L.f.	broomweed	escoba, escobilla	chichibe, mes-bel	utensil
Sida glabra Mill.	smooth fanpetals	malva	chichibe	ornamental
Solanum americanum Mill.	edible nightshade	yerba mora	ix ch'a yuk	food
Solanum rudepannum Dunal	orangeberry	hierba san cayetano	ts'ay ooch	food
Stachytarpheta cayennensis (Rich.) Vahl	blue vervain, wild verbena	verbena	cot-a-cam	medicine
Tagetes erecta L.	marigold	flor de muerto	ixtupu	ceremonial
Tecoma stans (L.) Juss. ex Kunth	yellow trumpet bush	sauco amarillo	xk'anlol	condiment, medicine
Tradescantia spathacea Sw.	moses in the boat	maguey sylvestre	chatsum	herb
Urera baccifera (L.) Gaudich.	cow-itch	ortiga	laal	food, medicine

Binomial	English	Spanish	Mayan	Uses
Vanilla planifolia Jacks. ex Andrews	vanilla	vainilla	t'sil	condiment
Vigna unguiculata L.	cowpea	chícharo tropical	xpelón	food
Vitis tiliifolia Humb. & Bonpl. ex Schult	wild grape	uva de monte	xta'kanil	food
Wedelia acapulcensis Kunth	creeping oxeyes	cutumbuy	sajum	medicine
Xanthosoma yucatanense Engl.	malanga	malanga	makal, x-makal	food, ornamental
Yucca gigantea Lem	yucca	yucca	isote	food
Zea mays L.	maize	maíz	ixim, nal	food, ceremonial

APPENDIX B

Favored Trees

Family	Species	Habit	Maya Common Names	Spanish Common Names	English Common Names
Fabaceae	*Acacia angustissima* (Mill.) Kuntze	shrub or tree	kan te' mo'	guajillo, cantemó	prairie acacia
Fabaceae	*Acacia collinsii* Saff.	shrub or tree	subin	cuernero	bullhorn acacia
Fabaceae	*Acacia cornigera* L. Wild	shrub or tree	liscanal, zubin, huascanal	cornezuelo	bullhorn wattle, cockspur
Fabaceae	*Acacia Glomerosa* Benth.	tree	pal'liro, salam	espino de san pedro, palo de zorro	bastard prickly yellow, white tamarind
Fabaceae	*Acacia pennatula* (Schltdl. & Cham.) Benth	tree	ke-ich-che	tepame	feather acacia
Fabaceae	*Acaciella angustissima*	shrub	waaxim		prairie acacia

Family	Species	Habit	Maya Common Names	Spanish Common Names	English Common Names
Cactaceae	*Acanthocereus pentagonus* (L.) Britton & Rose	cactus	tsakam, nuum tsutsuy	organo-alado de Pitaya	triangle cactus
Arecaceae	*Acoelorraphe wrightii* (Griseb. & H.Wendl.) H.Wendl. ex Becc.	palm	casiste, chi-it, papta, taciste	palma, prementa, primenta	palmetto, honduras pimienta
Fabaceae	*Acosmium panamense* (Benth.) Yakovlev	tree	ka che	samcuy, bálsamo	billy webb
Arecaceae	*Acrocomia aculeata* (Jacq.) Lodd. ex Mart	palm	coyol, cocoyol, istuk, suppa	coyol	grugru
Euphorbiaceae	*Adelia barbinervis* Schlecht. & Cham.	shrub or tree	pak'aal che', sak oox		teenek
Adiantaceae	*Adiantum tenerum* Sw.	fern	ok-pick-ek-chi-chan, roc-che-cwan	helecho, espuma, palo negro	maiden-hair fern, black stick
Rubiaceae	*Alseis yucatanensis* Standley	tree	cacao-che, ison, zon, haas'che, ts'om	tabaquillo, mamey silvestre	wild mamey
Picramniaceae	*Alvaradoa amorphoides* Liebm.	shrub or tree	xbesinic-ché, bel-ciniché	corticuero	mexican alvaradoa
Ulmaceae	*Ampelocera hottlei* (Standl.)	tree	luin, sitz muk	cuerillo	female bullhoof
Anacardiaceae	*Anacardium occidentale* L.	tree	tupi acajú	marañon	cashew

Family	Species	Habit	Maya Common Names	Spanish Common Names	English Common Names
Annonaceae	*Annona cherimola* Mill.	tree	ek'mul, op, oop, pox, poox, ts'almuuy, ts'armuy	cherimoya	custard apple
Annonaceae	*Annona diversifolia* Saff.	tree	takob	guanabana	
Annonaceae	*Annona muricata* L.	tree	p'op'osh, tak'ob, tak'op, tak'oop, takob	guanabana	spiny custard apple
Annonaceae	*Annona purpurea* Moc. & Sessé ex Dunal	tree	chak oop, pool boox, poox, oop che'hun, oop tsiimin	soncoya	wood-pecker's or horse annona, wild annona, cowsap
Annonaceae	*Annona reticulata* L.	tree	oop, tsulipox, k'an oop, ya'ax oop, pox, ts'ulimuy, ts'uli poox	annona blanca, annona colorado, annona del monte	custard apple
Annonaceae	*Annona* spp.	tree	oop	annona	golden sugar apple
Annonaceae	*Annona squamosa* L.	tree	ts'almuy, tsalmuy, dzalmuy	saramoyo	sweet sop, sugar apple
Apocynacaea	*Aspidosperma cruentum* Woodson	tree	sa'-yuk	malerio, chichique, bayo	milady, my lady, red malady
Apocynacaea	*Aspidosperma megalocarpon* Muell. Arg	tree	peechmaax	malerio, fustan de vieja, chiquique blanco	mylady, white mylady

Family	Species	Habit	Maya Common Names	Spanish Common Names	English Common Names
Arecaceae	*Astrocaryum mexicanum* Liebm. ex Mart.	palm	tuk-'u, ak-té, ak-t, chapay,	lancetilla, pacaya, cocoyol	chocho palm, chapay
Anacardiaceae	*Astronium graveolens* Jacq.	tree	kulimche	jobillo, palo mulato	glassy wood
Arecaceae	*Attalea cohune* Mart.	palm	tutz, manaca	corozo	cohune
Asteraceae	*Baccharis trinervis* (Lam.) Pers.	shrub	sisk'uts	romerillo	
Fabaceae	*Balizia leucocalyx* (Britton & Rose) Barneby & J.W.	tree		jesmo	wild tamarind
Fabaceae	*Bauhinia divaricata* L.	shrub or tree	tsulubtok	pata de vaca	pom pom orchid tree
Fabaceae	*Bauhinia jenningsii* P. Wilson	shrub or tree	chand-zulutok, cocohoof, dsuruktok, ts'ulubtok	lengua de vaca	cow tongue, snake plant
Tiliaceae	*Belotia mexicana* Schum.	tree	tao	corcho colorado	
Boraginaceae	*Bourreria oxyphylla* Standl.	tree	chi-che, cacuche, sac-pa, sac-bay-eck, ter-ech-mas	roble blanco, laurel, lima del monte, palo de nance	strong-back
Boraginaceae	*Bourreria pulchra* (Millsp.)	tree	bakal bo'		

Family	Species	Habit	Maya Common Names	Spanish Common Names	English Common Names
Moraceae	*Brosimum alicastrum* Sw.	tree	masicaran, ox, ujushte, hach osh	capomo, copomo, macica, ramón, ramón blanco, ramón	breadnut, ramon nut
Moraceae	*Brosimum guianense* (Aubl.) Huber	tree	ba'am bax	ramón silvestre o cimarrón	wild or mountain breadnut
Combretaceae	*Bucida buceras* L.	tree	pukte	cacho de toro	bullet tree
Burseraceae	*Bursera penicillata* (DC.) Engl.	tree		torote copol, aceitillo	indian lavender
Malpighiaceae	*Byrsonima crassifolia* Rich ex Kunth	tree	ch·, chì, sacpan, zacpan, shinich	nance, nanci, nonce	golden spoon
Fabaceae	*Caesalpinia gaumeri* Greenm.	tree	kitin che	quebra hacha, rudo del monte, chaparral	axe master, bastard logwood, peccary wood, peacock flower
Fabaceae	*Caesalpinia pulcherrima* (L.) Sw.	shrub or tree	zink-in	cansic	bird of paradise
Fabaceae	*Caesalpinia yucatanensis* Greenm.	tree	Taa k'in che	caramayo	bastard billy webb
Verbenaceae	*Callicarpa acuminata* Kunth	shrub or tree	puk'in		Mexican beauty-berry, black beauty-berry

Family	Species	Habit	Maya Common Names	Spanish Common Names	English Common Names
Calophyllaceae	*Calophyllum brasiliense* Cambess.	tree	baba	barí, Santa Maria	Santa Maria
Caricaceae	*Carica papaya* L.	shrub or tree	p'ut	papaya	papaya, manbird papaya
Salicaceae	*Casearia nitida* Jacq.	shrub or tree	ximche, xmaben-che	chamiso, chilillo	smooth honeytree
Fabaceae	*Casimiroa edulis* La Llave & Lex.	tree	yuy	matasano	white zapote
Fabaceae	*Cassia atomaria* L.	shrub or tree	xtu-habin		yellow candle wood
Moraceae	*Cassia grandis* L. f.	tree	bookut, bukut	carao	stinky toe
Moraceae	*Castilla elastica* Sessé	tree	hule, kiikche, kikiche, kukche, yaxha	hule	wild rubber
Urticaceae	*Cecropia obtusifolia* Bertol.	tree	k'axix-kooch, kooche	guarumo	trumpet
Urticaceae	*Cecropia peltata* L.	tree	a'kl, ixcoch, cho-otz, k'och	yagrumo	trumpet tree, shield-leaf pump-wood
Meliaceae	*Cedrela odorata* L.	tree	kulché	cedro	Mexican cedar
Malvaceae	*Ceiba pentandra* (L.) Gaertn.	tree	yaxche	ceiba	ceiba, kapok
Cannabaceae	*Celtis iguanaea* (Jacq.) Sarg.	shrub or tree	zidz-muc	garabato	iguana hackberry

Family	Species	Habit	Maya Common Names	Spanish Common Names	English Common Names
Arecaceae	Chamaedorea pinnatifrons (Jacq.) Oerst.	palm	chib, chem-chem, xate, xal-a-cam	pacaya, guaya de cerro	San Pablo palm
Arecaceae	Chamaedorea seifrizii Burret	palm	xate	palmera bambu	bamboo palm, reed palm
Moraceae	Chlorophora tinctoria L. Gaud.	tree	kanklisché	mora amarilla	fustic tree
Clusiaceae	Chrysophyllum cainito Brandegee ex Standl.	tree	zikay, chiceh	caimito	wild star apple
Clusiaceae	Clusia flava Jacq.	shrub or tree	chuunup, k'an chuunup	matapalo, memelita	strangler fig
Euphorbiaceae	Cnidoscolus chayamansa McVaugh	shrub or tree	tza	chaya	chaya, tree spinach
Polygonaceae	Coccoloba belizensis Standl.	shrub or tree	bob	uva montes, papaturro	wood grape
Polygonaceae	Coccoloba uvifera L.	shrub or tree	niiché	uva	sea grape
Arecaceae	Coccothrinax readii H.J. Quero	palm	náaj k'aax	miraguano	Mexican silver palm
Fabaceae	Cojoba arborea (L.) Urb.	tree		algarrobo	Bahaman sibucú
Combretaceae	Conocarpus erectus L.	tree	k'anche	botoncillo, mangle prieto	button-wood
Boraginaceae	Cordia alliodora (Ruiz & Pav.) Oken	tree	bohun	laurel	Spanish elm

Family	Species	Habit	Maya Common Names	Spanish Common Names	English Common Names
Boraginaceae	*Cordia bicolor* A. DC.	tree	bohun	sombra de ternero, nopo blanco	
Boraginaceae	*Cordia dodecandra* DC.	tree	chack opte	ziricote	siricote, orange cordia
Boraginaceae	*Cordia gerascanthus* L.	tree	bochom, bojunche	laurel negro, barillo	
Chryso-balanaceae	*Couepia polyandra* (Kunth) Rose	tree	us piib	guayabito de tinta	baboon cup, baboon cap, monkey cap
Bigoniaceae	*Crescentia cujete* L.	tree	hom, huaz	jícara	calabash, savannah calabash, wild calabash
Euphorbiaceae	*Croton niveus* Jacq.	shrub or tree	copalché	uvitas	white stock
Arecaceae	*Cryosophila stauracantha* Heynh. R.J.Evans	palm	kuum, akuum, mis	escoba	silver thatch
Akaniaceae	*Cupania belizensis* Hook	shrub or tree	chac pom	copal colorado, palo de carbon	grande betty, red copal
Annonaceae	*Cymbo-petalum mayanum* Lundell	tree	muc	candelero, guanabo	falsa annona
Fabaceae	*Dalbergia glabra* (Mill.) Standl.	shrub or tree	ahmuk', kibix		logwood brush

Family	Species	Habit	Maya Common Names	Spanish Common Names	English Common Names
Araliaceae	*Dendropanax arboreus* L.	tree	sac-chacah, tziub	mano de leon	lion's hand, angelica tree
Arecaceae	*Desmoncus orthacanthos* Mart.	palm	bayal	ballal	basket tie-tie
Fabaceae	*Dialium guianeense* Willd.	tree	we'ech	guapaque	velvet tamarind
Ebenaceae	*Diospyros anisandra* S.F. Blake	tree	x-gagalche, ka-kal-che, kakal che', pisit, uchulche, xnob che'	ébano	cala-mander wood
Ebenaceae	*Diospyros cuneata* Standl.	tree	ka-kal-che, siliil, sibil, uchul che', uchiche'	pepenance	
Ebenaceae	*Diospyros digyna* Jacq.	tree	uch'	zapote negro	black zapote
Fabaceae	*Diphysa carthaginensis* Benth. & Oerst.	shrub or tree	susuck, tsutsuc	brasilillo	rue, wild ruda
Asparagaceae	*Dracaena americana* Donn. Sm.	tree	tuét	isote, isote del monte	dragon tree
Boraginaceae	*Ehretia tinifolia* L.	shrub or tree	bek	roble, arrayan, manbimbo	cherry ehretia
Fabaceae	*Enterolobium cyclocarpum* (Jacq.) Griseb.	tree	pich, tubroos, petz'k'in	guanacaste, parota	ear-tree, monkey-soap

Family	Species	Habit	Maya Common Names	Spanish Common Names	English Common Names
Fabaceae	Erythrina standleyana Krukoff	tree	chacmolche	pito, colorin	coama wood, tiger wood
Myrtaceae	Eugenia ibarrae Lundell.	shrub or tree	chilon-che	guayabillo	
Moraceae	Ficus cotinifolia Kunth	tree	koopo' chit, xkoopo	amate negro	
Moraceae	Ficus maxima Mill.	tree	amate	higuero	wild fig
Rubiaceae	Genipa americana L.	tree	huito	jagua, genipapo, huito	genipap
Fabaceae	Gliricidia sepium (Jacq.) Kunth ex Walp.	tree	hotz	madre de cacao	quick stick
Malvaceae	Gossypium hirsutum L.	tree	taman	algodón	cotton
Meliaceae	Guarea glabra Vahl	tree	bul-ba	cedrillo, cramante	wild orange, pink mahogany
Annonaceae	Guatteria anomala R.E. Fries	tree	guela dauguixi, ek'bache	corcho negro, zopo	black balche
Malvaceae	Guazuma ulmifolia Lam.	tree	pixoy, op chuhum	cualote, tapaculo	West Indian elm, guacima
Rubiaceae	Guettarda combsii Urb.	shrub or tree	tastab	arepa, verde lucero, manzanillo	glassy wood, glossy wood, green star, velvetseed

Family	Species	Habit	Maya Common Names	Spanish Common Names	English Common Names
Polygonaceae	*Gymnopodium floribundum* Rolfe	shrub or tree	ts'iits'il che	tzitzilché	bastard logwood
Fabaceae	*Haematoxylum campechianum* L.	tree	ek	palo de tinta, palo de campeche	logwood, dye wood
Rubiaceae	*Hamelia patens* Jacq.	shrub or tree	ixcanan, axcanan, canaan, chactoc, x-kanan, klaush	corallillo, sanalo-todo, arbusto de color escarlata, indios	red pollyhead, firebush, scarlet bush
Malvaceae	*Hampea stipitata* S. Watson	tree	ts'uk tok	majagua	
Fabaceae	*Harvardia albicans* (Kunth.) Britton & Rose	tree	chucum		
Olacaceae	*Heisteria media* S.F. Blake	shrub or tree	silion	copalche macho, nance cimarron	wild cinnamon
Malvaceae	*Heliocarpus americanus* L.	tree	chai	majaguillo, majagua	broadleaf, moho
Chrysobalanaceae	*Hirtella racemosa* Lam.	shrub or tree	chilimis, luyamche	grenada, palo de escoba	blossom berry, wild pigeon plum
Lamiaceae	*Hyptis verticillata* Jacq.	shrub or tree	shkot kwai	san martin, hoja de martin	john charles
Fabaceae	*Inga jinicuil*	tree	bitz	jinicuil	shimbillo, jinicui

Family	Species	Habit	Maya Common Names	Spanish Common Names	English Common Names
Euphorbiaceae	*Jacaratia mexicana* A. DC.	tree	k'umché	bonete	
Euphorbiaceae	*Jatropha curcas* L.	shrub or tree	sikir te	tuerca de barbados	barbados nut, purging nut, physic nut
Euphorbiaceae	*Jatropha guameri* Greenm.	shrub or tree	chipche, pomolche	piñon	hazel nut, wild physic nut
Asteraceae	*Koanophyllon albicaule* Sch. Bip. ex Klatt	shrub or tree	socha, xolexnuc	cordoncillo negro	black piper
Asteraceae	*Lasianthaea fruticosa* (L.) K.M.Becker	shrub or tree	ish-ta, shti-pe, zta-ach	margarita del monte	margarita
Fabaceae	*Leucaena leucocephala* (Lam.) de Wit.	tree	guaxin	guaje	white leadtree, white popinac
Chryobal-anaceae	*Licania platypus* (Hemsley) Fritsch	tree	succotz, sunco, urraco, sakatz	sonzapote	monkey apple, sansa-pote, meson-sapote
Fabaceae	*Lonchocarpus castilloi* Kunth	tree	manchich	manchiche	black cabbage bark
Fabaceae	*Lonchocarpus minimiflorus* Donn. Sm.	tree	manchich	palo de guzano	white cabbage bark
	Lonchocarpus yucatanensis Pittier	tree	ya'ax xu'ul		lumber, honey, medicine

Family	Species	Habit	Maya Common Names	Spanish Common Names	English Common Names
Malvaceae	*Luehea speciosa* Willd.	tree	k'an kaat	tepecacao	luchea
Fabaceae	*Lysiloma auritum* (Schltdl.) Benth	tree	tsu	tamborcillo, palo de sangre, quebracho	bastard mahogany
Fabaceae	*Lysiloma latisiliquum* (L.) Benth.	tree	tzalam, chalan, salam	salom	rain tree, false tamarind
Rubiaceae	*Machaonia lIndeniana* Baill.	shrub or tree	k'uch'eel, k'an pok'ool che', tank'an che'		
Annonaceae	*Malmea depressa* (Baill.) R.E. Fr.	tree	elemuil, eremuel, eremuilitz-imul, x-ele-muy	sufrekaya, sufricaya	wild coffee, che-che, chief of herbs, lance-wood
Malpighiaceae	*Malpighia glabra* L.	shrub or tree	simche	cicerola	acerola, barbados cherry, manza-nita, wild crape-myrtle
Sapotaceae	*Manilkara zapota* (L.) P. Royen	tree	hach ya	chico zapote, sapote, zapote, zapotillo, zapote	red sapodilla, sapodilla
Phyllanthacese	*Margarita nobilis* L.f.	shrub or tree	ininche	mato palo, ramon macho	more, bastard madre cacao, bastard hogberry

Family	Species	Habit	Maya Common Names	Spanish Common Names	English Common Names
Sapindaceae	*Melicoccus bijugatus* Jacq.	tree	genip	limoncillo	spanish lime
Anacardiaceae	*Metopium brownei* Jacq. Urb.	tree	chechem, chen-chen	chechem negro	black poison wood, Honduras walnut
Muntingiaceae	*Muntingia calabura* L.	tree	pujam, pujan, pujan	cacaniqua, nigua, capulin blanco	capulin, jamaica-cherry tree, panama-berry, strawberry tree
Lauraceae	*Myroxylon balsamum* L.	tree	na-ba	balsam	balsam
Polygonaceae	*Neomill-spaughia emarginata* (H. Gross) S.F. Blake	shrub or tree	sakitsa		
Bombacaceae	*Ochroma pyramidale* Cav. ex Lam. Urb.	tree	polak, puh,chujum	corcho	balsa
Araliaceae	*Oreopanax obtusifolius* L.O. Williams	tree	chac mo'ol chich	mano de leon	
Malvaceae	*Pachira aquatica* Aubl.	tree	uacut, kubuh	santo domingo, zapote bobo	provision bark/tree, water sapote
Bignoniaceae	*Parmentiera aculeata* (Kunth) Seem.	tree	kat, k'at	cuajilote, pepino de arbol silvestre, caiba	candle tree, cow okra, wild okra
Lauraceae	*Persea americana* Mill.	tree	on	aguacate	avocado

Family	Species	Habit	Maya Common Names	Spanish Common Names	English Common Names
Phyllanthaceae	*Phyllanthus glaucescens* Kunth	monkey rattle	pitaya	piix t'oon	food
Myrtaceae	*Pimenta dioica* Lindl.	tree	naba-cuc	pimienta, pimienta gorda	allspice
Fabaceae	*Piscidia piscipula* (L.) Sarg.	tree	tiaxib	jabin, palo de gusano	Jamaica dogwood, fishfuddle
Fabaceae	*Pisonia aculeata* L.	shrub or tree	beeb	coma de uña	tiger nail embra, pull back and hold
Fabaceae	*Pithecellobium dulce* (Roxb.) Benth.	shrub or tree	piliil, ts'iuche	chiminango	madras thorn, monkeypod
Fabaceae	*Pithecellobium mangense* (Jacq.) J.F. Macbr.	shrub or tree	ts'aslam, xiaxek		catsclaw
Salicaceae	*Pleuranthodendron lindenii* (Tunis) Sleumer	tree	iximche	maicillo	
Apocynaceae	*Plumeria alba* L.	tree	sak nicte		frangipani
Apocynaceae	*Plumeria rubra* L.	tree	cacaloxochitl	flor de mayo, zopilote	mayflower, Spanish jasmine, frangipani
Asteraceae	*Podachaenium eminens* (Lag.) Sch.Bip	herb	k'ibok		giant tree daisy

Family	Species	Habit	Maya Common Names	Spanish Common Names	English Common Names
Sapotaceae	*Pouteria campechiana* Baehni	tree	k'aniste', k'aaniste', k'anaste', chak ya', ot ya	zapotillo rojo, sapotillo, canistel, mamey ciruela	yellow sapote, egg fruit
Sapotaceae	*Pouteria hypoglauca* Standl.	tree	chooch, choch	zapote amarillo, matasano	cinnamon apple
Sapotaceae	*Pouteria reticulata* (Engl.) Eyma	tree	chacal-haaz	zapote negro, zapotillo	wild cherry
Sapotaceae	*Pouteria sapota* (Jacq.) H.E.Moore & Stearn	tree	saltule, ha'as	zapote grande, mamey zapote	mame, mammee, sapote, mamey
Burseraceae	*Protium copal* Burm.F.	tree	pom, copal che, pomte, hach pom	copal	copal
Bombacaceae	*Pseudobombax ellipticum* (Kunth) Dugand	tree	chak kuyché, kuy ché	amapola/clavellina	shaving brush tree
Moraceae	*Pseudolmedia oxyphillaria* J.D. Smith	tree	manax, tzotzash	manax	wild cherry
Myrtaceae	*Psidium guajava* L.	shrub or tree	coloc, heliche, pata, pat, pa-taih, piche, pichi, pichik, pur	guayaba	apple guava
Fabaceae	*Pterocarpus rohrii* Vahl.	tree	hu lu	palo de sangre, sangre de chuco	bloodtree, mountain kaway, dog's blood

Family	Species	Habit	Maya Common Names	Spanish Common Names	English Common Names
Bombaceae	*Quararibea funebris* (La Llave) Pittier	tree	cacahuax-ochitl, mahas	flor de cacao, rosita de cacao	funeral tree
Fagaceae	*Quercus oleoides* Schltdl. & Cham	tree	beek	encino, roble encino	oak
Aceraceae	*Roystonea regia* (Kunth) O.F.Cook	palm		palma real	royal palm
Arecaceae	*Sabal mauritiiformis* Bartlett	palm	sha-an	botan, guano, guanu	bay leaf, sabal, bay leaf palm
Arecaceae	*Sabal mexicana* Mart.	palm	sha-an	huano de sombrero, guano	bay leaf, unspined salt palm
Arecaceae	*Sabal morrisiana* Bartlett	palm	sha-an	guano, botan	bay palm
Sapindaceae	*Sapindus saponaria* L.	tree	siijum, zubul	jaboncillo, amole	soap seed, soap berry, soap tree, mountain cherry
Euphorbiaceae	*Sapium lateriflorum* Hemsl.	tree	bobtob, u'cunte	palo de leche	
Fabaceae	*Schizolobium parahyba* (Vell.) S.F.Blake	tree	petskin	guapuruvú	Brazilian firetree, tower tree
Fabaceae	*Sebastiana tuerckheimiana* Lundell	tree	o iki-che	chechem blanco, reventadillo	poison-wood, white poison-wood

Family	Species	Habit	Maya Common Names	Spanish Common Names	English Common Names
Fabaceae	*Senna racemosa* (Mill.) H.S.Irwin & Barneby	shrub or tree	kan lool, kan jabin	cante	
Sapotaceae	*Sideroxylon foetidissimum* Jacq.	tree	subul	caracolillo, tortugo amarillo	mastic, false mastic
Simaroubaceae	*Simarouba glauca* DC	tree	pa sac, xpazakil	aceituno, negrito	dysentry bark, paradise tree
Rubiaceae	*Simira salvadorensis* (Standley) Steyerm.	tree	sac te m'ooc, chakax, chakte kok	palo colorado, puntero, nazareno	redwood, high ridge redwood
Anacardiaceae	*Spondias mombin* L.	tree	k'aan abal, k'iinil, k'inil abal, xk'iinil, jujuub, jobo, kanabal, pok , k'inim	ciruela cochino, jocote, jobo	hogplum, wild tree plum
Anacardiaceae	*Spondias purpurea* L.	shrub or tree	abal ak, chak abal, chi' abal, abal, abil (Peten), abal-ac	jocote	summer plum, plum, may plum, red hogplum
Anacardiaceae	*Spondias radlkoferi* Donn. Sm.	tree	hobo, ho-bo, hu-hu, pook, rum-p'ok	ciruela amarilla, jobo, jocote jobo	hogplum, wild plum
Fabaceae	*Stemmadenia donnell-smithii* (Rose) Woodson	shrub or tree	chakl	cojoton, cojones de burro, huevo de caballo	horse tone, horse's balls
Malvaceae	*Sterculia apetala* (Jacq.) Karst.	tree	anis	castaño tropical, camoruco, bellota	Panama tree

Family	Species	Habit	Maya Common Names	Spanish Common Names	English Common Names
Fabaceae	*Swartzia cubensis* (Britton & Wilson) Standl.	tree	kat'alox	llora sangre, sangre de toro, corazon azul	Mexican ebony
Meliaceae	*Swietenia macrophylla* King	tree	chacalte, punab, sutz'uch, punah	caoba	broken ridge mahogany, mahogany
Bignoniaceae	*Tabebuia guayacan_* (Seem.) Hemsl.	tree	hahauche	araguaney, guayacán	yellow may-flower, trumpet tree
Bigoniaceae	*Tabebuia rosea* DC.	tree	hokab, shna'-corts	maculiz	may-flower, may bush
Apocynaceae	*Tabernae-montana alba* Mill.	shrub or tree	chakilikin, ton-cha, ton-chi, ton-samin	cojeton, cojon de perro, huevo de chucho	white milk-wood
Sapindaceae	*Talisia oliviformis* Radlk.	tree	wayah, uayum	cotoperiz, guaya	kinep
Combretaceae	*Terminalia amazonia* (J. F. Gmel.) Exell	tree	canxun	guayabo	nargosta, pine ridge bully tree
Euphorbiaceae	*Tetrochidium rotundatum* Standl.	shrub	mumuche		small leaf tetrochid-ium
Malvaceae	*Theobroma cacao* L.	tree	kawkaw	arbol de cacao	cacao, chocolate tree
Apocynaceae	*Thevetia peruviana* (Pers.) K. Schum.	shrub or tree	tze-puí	palo de suerte	good luck tree

Family	Species	Habit	Maya Common Names	Spanish Common Names	English Common Names
Sapindaceae	*Thouinia paucidentata* Radlk. Ex Millsp.	tree	dzol, canchunub	hueso de tigre	fewden-tate thouinia
Arecaceae	*Thrinax radiata* Lodd. ex Schult. & Schult.f.	palm	chit	palmetto	florida thatch, jamaican thatch
Meliaceae	*Trichilia havanensis* Jacq.	shrub or tree	cot-a-cam, camacolal, xtyay-ach-bak-shel	limoncillo, palo de cuchara	spoon tree, bastard time
Meliaceae	*Trichilia hirta* L.	shrub or tree	choben-che	acahuite, palo de son, sombra de carneiro	red cedar, broom-stick
Malvaceae	*Tricho-spermum grewiifolium* (A. Rich.) Kosterm.	shrub or tree	capulin chai, cha-hib	lagroso, macapal, algodon-cillo	balsa wood, narrow-leaf, moho
Malvaceae	*Tricho-spermum mexicanum* (DC.) Baill.	tree	taw	corcho colorado	
Moraceae	*Trophis racemosa* (L.) Urb.	shrub or tree	sac oox	eldorado, ramon blanco, waya del monte	female white ramon, white breadnut, wild waya
Urticaceae	*Urera caracasana* (Jacq.) Gaudich. ex Griseb.	shrub or tree	laal	ortiga de arbol, chichicaste, migirillo	flame-berry

Family	Species	Habit	Common Names Mayan	Common Names Spanish	Common Names English
Verbenaceae	*Vitex gaumeri* Greenm.	tree	yaxnik, sak-u-sol, yax nik ux pe	flor azul, arbol murcielago	fiddle-wood, walking lady
Salicaceae	*Zuelania guidonia* (Sw.) Britton & Millsp.	shrub or tree	chu-ya-ak, tamay, tamai	paragua, moroco	drunken bayman wood, water wood, umbrella

NOTES

INTRODUCTION

1. We are using the indigenous Maya orthography used by Hofling (2004).
2. Alfonso Tzul, a retired extension officer of the Belize Ministry of Agriculture, contends that he has never seen a traditional milpa with erosion and never seen a plowed field without.

CHAPTER 1

1. By European filter, we are referring to the interpretation of the world from the point of view of the dominant Western pedogogy, also called ecological imperialism (Crosby 1986).
2. This scenario is not unlike Detroit, where today more than 50 major private buildings, including banks, offices, theaters, and hotels, as well as many public buildings, such as libraries, schools, and even the central railroad station, have been abandoned. Some have been demolished for gardens.

CHAPTER 2

1. Amaranth was known to be an important grain at contact but was suppressed by the Spanish. It is presently receiving renewed attention (Early 1992; NRC 1984).
2. Dunning et al. (2012) use the word *Kax* in the title of their article, not *K'ax* with the glottal stop. We understand the Yukatek word for chicken is *Kax,* and the word for forest to be *K'ax.*
3. It is interesting to note that the majority of the weeds that Steggerda (1941) records as invasive in the milpa were documented as useful plants by Roys (1976). Both researchers were working at the same time with the Carnegie Institution of Washington.

CHAPTER 3

1. Leonardo Obando kept a grove of ramon that he personally planted to feed his livestock over the annual dry period. His ramon grove was inspired by a farmer workshop of the 1980s and has served his animals well. Obando, a remarkable forest gardener who also cultivated flowering plants for his bees, died in October 2014.
2. Ramon is found in home garden studies of the Yucatan averaging 58-72 percent of gardens surveyed by Alayon-Gamboa and Guri-Garcia 2008; Caballero 1992; Correa-Navarro 1997; Cuanalo de la Cerda and Guerra Mukul 2008; Garcia de Miguel 2000; Lope-Alzina and Howard 2012; Rico-Gray et al. 1990. When ramon is present in gardens today, there may be as many as two to four trees, used mainly in the dry season for animal fodder.

CHAPTER 4

1. Defining the Primary Residential Unit (PRU): Small structures are accepted as representing domestic and residential use, yet it is clear that not all small structures are equal in a Maya house (Arnold and Ford 1980; Ford 1991b; Robin 2012:26; Tourtellot 1983; see Wauchope 1938). To incorporate the use of multiple residences into our view of the Late Classic Maya population distribution, an assessment of primary and secondary residential units was developed that counted only criteria of the PRUs for population estimates (Ford and Clarke 2015). Following the ethnographic descriptions of Maya residential units, PRUs are defined as large single structures and groups of structures (not unlike Tourtellot et al. 1990:85-86), while the remaining individual and isolated small structures were defined as secondary residential units (SRUs).

    Only defined PRUs were counted for the population estimates. In addition, we adopt the position of continuous occupation that Robin (2012:41) advocates for our evaluation of Late Classic Maya of El Pilar. As detailed by Tourtellot et al. (1990:90), by the Late Classic, the Maya were well established with little evidence of mobility.

    The defined PRUs include formal and informal groups of structures with an average of 2.5 structures per unit, an average unit diagonal of greater than 24 m, and an average area of about 290 square meters, as calculated by the GIS. While designated PRUs composed 41 percent of all residential units of the surveys, they covered 73 percent of the surface area devoted to residential architecture and represented 50 percent of the units within preferred settlement areas. The remaining domestic sites were small individual structures. These SRUs are about one-third the size of the PRUs, with an average structure diagonal of about 9 meters, and are isolated from the groups. In the high-density settlement areas, these small structures were located at a distance of greater than 20 m from PRUs, and in low-density areas they are more than 500 m from any other units. Composing 59 percent of all units of the study area, but as minor components of the domestic scene, SRUs have a total surface area of only 27 percent of residential architecture yet make up 72 percent of the units in low-density areas. In consideration of the land-use intensity, both PRU and SRU need to be taken into account. For our calculation of population, we depend on the PRU so as not to overestimate ancient Maya populations.

2. Source: 1998 email communication with Anabel Ford on the proportion of maize in the diet of traditional pre-WWII Mesoamerican and Central American farmers, from Margaret E. Smith, specialist in maize adaptation at Cornell University, College of Agriculture and Life Science (plbrgen.cals.cornell.edu/people/margaret-e-smith).

CHAPTER 5

1. From Colin Young, Chief Executive Officer, Belize Ministry of Energy, Science & Technology and Public Utilities. As an ecologist with specialty in ethnobotany, Young argues that the wind-borne grasses and forbs dominate natural and human-created field and home garden gaps.

REFERENCES

Adams, R.E.W.
1986 Archaeologists Explore Guatemala's Lost City of the Maya: Rio Azul. *National Geographic* 169(4):420-451.

Aimers, James and David Hodell
2011 Societal Collapse: Drought and the Maya. *Nature* 479:44-45.

Aimers, James and Gyles Iannone
2014 The Dynamics of Ancient Maya Development History. In *The Great Maya Droughts in Cultural Context: Case Studies in Resilience and Vulnerability*, edited by G. Iannone, pp. 21-49. University Press of Colorado, Boulder, Colorado.

Alayon-Gamboa, Jose A. and Francisco D. Guri-Garcia
2008 Home Garden Production and Energetic Sustainability in Calakmul, Campeche, México. *Human Ecology* 36(3):395-407.

Alcorn, Janis
1990 Indigenous Agroforestry Systems in the Latin American Tropics. In *Agroecology and Small Farm Development*, edited by M. A. Altieri and S. B. Hecht, pp. 203–213. CRC Press, Boca Raton, Florida.

Alexander, Rani T.
2006 Maya Settlement Shifts and Agrarian Ecology in Yucatán. *Journal of Anthropological Research* 62:449-470.

Altieri, Miguel A.
1995 *Agroecology: The Science of Sustainable Agriculture*. Westville Press, Boulder, Colorado.
1999 The Ecological Role of Biodiversity in Agroecosystems. *Agriculture Ecosystems & Environment* 74:19-31.
2002 Agroecology: the Science of Natural Resource Management for Poor Farmers in Marginal Environments. *Agriculture Ecosystems & Environment* 93:1-24.

Altieri, Miguel A. and L. C. Merrick
1987 In Situ Conservation of Crop Genetic Resources Through Maintenance of Traditional Farming Systems. *Economic Botany* 41:86-96.

Altieri, Miguel A. and V. M. Toledo
2005 Natural Resource Management among Small-scale Farmers in Semi-arid Lands: Building on Traditional Knowledge and Agroecology. *Annals of Arid Zone* 44:365-385.
2011 The Agroecological Revolution in Latin America: Rescuing Nature, Ensuring Food Sovereignty and Empowering Peasants. *The Journal of Peasant Studies* 38(3):587-612.

Ames, Bruce
2006 Low Micronutrient Intake May Accelerate the Degenerative Diseases of Aging through Allocation of Scarce Micronutrients by Triage. *Proceedings of the National Academy of Sciences* 103(47):17589-17594.

Anderson, Anthony B., Peter Herman May, and Michael J. Balick
1991 *The Subsidy from Nature: Palm Forests, Peasantry, and Development on an Amazon Frontier.* Columbia University Press, New York.

Anderson, E. N.
1996 Gardens of Chunhuhub. *Arbeitsblatter* 14:63-76.

Anderson, M. Kat
2005 *Tending the Wild: Native American Knowledge and the Management of California's Natural Resources.* University of California Press, Berkeley, California.

Ankli, Anita, Otto Sticher, and Michael Heinrich
1999 Medical Ethnobotany of the Yucatec Maya: Healers' Consensus as a Quantitative Criterion. *Economic Botany* 53(2):144-160.

Anselmetti, F. S., D. Ariztegui, D. A. Hodell, M. B. Hillesheim, M. Brenner, A. Gilli, J. A. McKenzie, and A. D. Mueller
2006 Late Quaternary Climate-induced Lake Level Variations in Lake Petén Itzá, Guatemala, Inferred from Seismic Stratigraphic Analysis. *Palaeogeography, Palaeoclimatology, Palaeoecology* 230(1-2):52– 69.

Anselmetti, Flavio S., David A. Hodell, Daniel Ariztegui, Mark Brenner, and Michael F. Rosenmeier
2007 Quantification of Soil Erosion Rates Related to Ancient Maya Deforestation. *Geology* 35(10):915-918.

Aragón-Moreno, A. A., G. A. Islebe, and N. Torrescano
2012 A ~3800-yr, High-Resolution Record of Vegetation and Climate Change on the North Coast of the Yucatán Peninsula. *Review of Palaeobotany and Palynology* 178:35-42.

Arias Reyes, Luis Manuel
1995a La Caceria en Yaxcaba, Yucatán. In *La Milpa En Yucatán: Un Sistema De Producción Agrícola Tradicional,* edited by E. Hernández Xolocotzi, E. B. Baltazar, and S. L. Tacher, pp. 271-285, Vol. 1. Colegio De Postgraduados, Montecillo, México.
1995b La Produccion Milpera Actual en Yaxcaba, Yucatán. In *La Milpa En Yucatán: Un Sistema De Producción Agrícola Tradicional,* edited by E. Hernandez Xolocotzi, E. B. Baltazar, and S. Levy Tacher, pp. 171-199, Vol. 1. Colegio De Postgraduados, Montecillo, México.

Arnold, Jeanne E. and Anabel Ford
1980 A Statistical Examination of Settlement Patterns at Tikal, Guatemala. *American Antiquity* 45(4):713-726.

Arvigo, Rosita and Michael J. Balick
1993 *Rainforest Remedies: One Hundred Healing Herbs of Belize.* 1st ed. Lotus Press, Twin Lakes, Wisconsin.

Ashmore, Wendy (editor)
1981 *Lowland Maya Settlement Patterns.* 1st ed. University of New Mexico Press, Albuquerque, New Mexico.

Atran, Scott
1993 Itza Maya Tropical Agro-Forestry. *Current Anthropology* 34(5):633-700.
1999 Managing the Maya Commons: The Value of Local Knowledge. In *Ethnoecology: Situated Knowledge/Located Lives,* edited by V. D. Nazarea, pp. 190-214. University of Arizona Press, Tucson, Arizona.

Atran, Scott, Ximena Lois, and Edilberto Ucan Ek'
2004 *Plants of the Petén Itza Maya,* Vol. 38. Regents of the University of Michigan, Ann Arbor, Michigan.

Atran, Scott and D. Medin
1997 Knowledge and Action: Cultural Models of Nature and Resource Management in Mesoamerica. In *Environment, Ethics, and Behavior*, edited by M. Bazerman, D. Messick, A. Tenbrunsel, and K. Wade-Bezoni. New Lexington Press, San Francisco.

Atran, Scott, Douglas Medin, Norbert Ross, Elizabeth Lynch, John Coley, Edilberto Ukan Ek', and Valentina Vapnarsky
1999 Folkecology and Commons Management in the Maya Lowlands. *Proceedings of the National Academy of Sciences of the United States of America* 96(13):7598-7603.

Atran, Scott, Douglas Medin, Norbert Ross, Elizabeth Lynch, Valentina Vapnarsky, Edilberto Ucan Ek', John Coley, Christopher Timura, and Michael Baran
2000 *Folkecology, Cultural Epidemiology, and the Spirit of the Commons: A Garden Experiment in the Maya Lowlands, 1995-2000*. University of Michigan, Northwestern University, Centre National de la Recherche Scientifique, Herbolaria Maya, Northeastern University.

Balée, William
2006 The Research Program of Historical Ecology. *Annual Review of Anthropology* 35:75-98.
2010 Amazonian Dark Earths. *Tipití: Journal of the Society for the Anthropology of Lowland South America* 8(1):1-18

Balick, Michael J., Michael H. Nee, and Daniel E. Atha
2000 *Checklist of the Vascular Plants of Belize with Common Names and Uses*. Memoirs of the New York Botanical Garden. The New York Botanical Garden Press, Bronx, New York.

Barkin, David
2002 The Reconstruction of a Modern Mexican Peasantry. *Journal of Peasant Studies* 30(1):73-90.

Barrera Vásquez, Alfredo
1980 *Diccionario Maya Cordemex*. Ediciones Cordemex, Mérida, Yucatán, México.

Barrera Vásquez, Alfredo, Arturo Gómez-Pompa, and C. Vázquez-Yanes
1977 El Manejo de las Selvas por los Mayas: Sus Implicaciones Silvícolas y Agrícolas. *Biotica* 2(2):47-60.

Barrera-Bassols, Narciso and Victor M. Toledo
2005 Ethnoecology of the Yucatec Maya: Symbolism, Knowledge and Management of Natural Resources. *Journal of Latin American Geography* 4:9-41.

Basehart, Harry W.
1973 Mescalero Apache Subsistence Patterns. In *Technical Manual: Survey of the Tularosa Basin*, pp. 145-181. Human Systems Research, Tularosa, New Mexico.

Bates, Marston
1952 *Where Winter Never Comes: A Study of Man and Nature in the Tropics*. Charles Scribner's Sons, New York.

Beach, Timothy
1998 Soil Catenas, Tropical Deforestation, and Ancient and Contemporary Soil Erosion in the Petén, Guatemala. *Physical Geography* 19(5):378-405.

Beach, Timothy, N. Dunning, Sheryl Luzzadder-Beach, D. E. Cook, and J. Lohse
2006 Impacts of the Ancient Maya on Soils and Soil Erosion in the Central Maya Lowlands. *Catena* 65(2):166-178.

Beach, Timothy, Sheryl Luzzadder-Beach, Nicholas Dunning, Jon Hageman, and Jon Lohse
2002 Upland Agriculture in the Maya Lowlands: Ancient Maya Soil Conservation in Northwestern Belize. *Geographical Review* 92(3):372-397.

Beaglehole, E.
1937 *Notes on Hopi Economic Life: Yale University Publications in Anthropology, No. 15.* Yale University, New Haven.

Beckerman, Stephen
1977 The Use of Palms by the Barí Indians of the Maracaibo Basin. *Principes—Journal of the Palm Society* 21(4):143-154.
1983 Does the Swidden Ape the Jungle? *Human Ecology* 11(1):1-12.

Benbrook, Charles, Xin Zhao, Jaime Yáñez, Neal Davies, and Preston Andrews
2008 New Evidence Confirms the Superiority of Plant-Based Organic Foods. *State of Science Review: Nutritional Superiority of Organic Foods.* The Organic Center. Boulder, Colorado.

Berget, Carolina
2012 *Invasion of Bracken Fern in Southern México: Local Knowledge and Perceptions in Two Indigenous Communities in the Chinantla Region, Oaxaca, México.* Master's thesis, Environmental Studies Department, Florida International University, Miami, Florida.

Bernsten, Richard H. and Robert W. I. Herdt
1977 Towards an Understanding of Milpa Agriculture: The Belize Case. *Journal of Developing Areas* 11(3):373-392.

Betz, Virginia
1997 Early Plant Domestication in Mesoamerica. *Athena Review* 2(1):24-31.

Bierhorst, John
1985 *A Nahuatl-English Dictionary and Concordance to the 'Cantares Mexicanos' With an Analytic Transcription and Grammatical Notes.* Stanford University Press, Stanford, California.

Binford, Michael W., Mark Brenner, Thomas J. Whitmore, Antonia Higuera-Gundy, E. S. Deevey, and Barbara Leyden
1987 Ecosystems, Paleoecology and Human Disturbance in Subtropical and Tropical America. *Quaternary Science Reviews* 6(2):115-128.

Bishop, T. A. M.
1935 Assarting and the Growth of the Open Fields. *The Economic History Review* 6(1):13-29.

Blake, Michael, Brian S. Chisholm, John E. Clark, Barbara Voorhies, and Michael W. Love
1992 Prehistoric Subsistence in the Soconusco Region. *Current Anthropology* 33(1):83-94.

Boege, Eckhart
2008 El Patrimonio *Biocultural de los Pueblos Indígenas de México.* Instituto Nacional de Antropología e Historia y Comisión Nacional para el Desarrollo de los Pueblos Indígenas, México.

Bonham-Carter, G. F.
1999 Integration of Geological Datasets for Gold Exploration in Nova Scotia. *Photogrammetric Engineering and Remote Sensing* 54:1585-1592.

Booth, Barbara D., Stephen D. Murphy, and Clarence J. Swanson
2003 Weed Ecology in *Natural and Agricultural Systems.* CABI, Cambridge, Massachusetts.

Boserup, Ester
1965 *The Conditions of Agricultural Growth: The Economics of Agrarian Change Under Population Pressure.* Aldine Publishing Company, New York.
1981 *Population and Technological Change: A Study of Long-Term Trends.* University of Chicago Press, Chicago.

Bradley, Raymond S.
1999 *Paleoclimatology: Reconstructing Climates of the Quaternary.* 2nd ed. International Geophysics Series 68. Academic Press, San Diego, California.

Bray, Francesca
1986 *The Rice Economies: Technology and Development in Asian Societies*. Blackwell, New York.
1994 Agriculture for Developing Nations. *Scientific American* 271(1):30-37.
2015 Global Networks and New Histories of Rice. In *Rice: Global Networks and New Histories*, edited by F. Bray, P. Coclanis, E. Fields-Black, and D. Schafer, pp. 1-35. Cambridge University Press, New York.

Brenner, Mark
1994 Lakes Salpeten and Quexil, Petén, Guatemala, Central America. In *Global Geological Record of Lake Basins*, edited by E. Gierlowski-Kordesch and K. R. Kelts, pp. 337-380. vol. 1. Cambridge University Press, Cambridge, Massachusetts.

Brenner, Mark, Michael F. Rosenmeier, David A. Hodell, and Jason H. Curtis
2002 Paleolimnology of the Maya Lowlands: Long-term Perspectives on Interactions among Climate, Environment, and Humans. *Ancient Mesoamerica* 13(1):141-157.

Brenner, M., D. A. Hodell, J. H. Curtis, M. F. Rosenmeier, F. S. Anselmetti, and D. Ariztegui
2003 Paleolimnological approaches for Inferring Past Climate Change in the Maya Region: Recent Advances and Methodological Limitations. In *The Lowland Maya Area: Three Millennia at the Human Wildland Interface*, edited by A. Gómez-Pompa, M. F. Allen, Scott L. Fedick and J. J. Jimenez-Osornio. UC Riverside, Riverside.

Brook, Kyle and Claudia Knudson
2014 *El Pilar Archaeological Reserve of Maya Flora and Fauna: Maya Forest Land Cover from Above*. On file at the MesoAmerican Research Center, University of California, Santa Barbara.

Brookfield, Harold
2001 *Exploring Agrodiversity*. Colombia University Press, New York.

Brown, Paula and Aaron Podolefsky
1976 Population Density, Agricultural Intensity, Land Tenure, and Group Size in the New Guinea Highlands. *Ethnology* 15:211-238.

Bryant, V. M. and S. A. Hall
1993 Archaeological Palynology in the United States: A Critique. *American Antiquity* 58: 277-286.

Bullard, William R., Jr.
1960 Maya Settlement Pattern in Northeastern Petén, Guatemala. *American Antiquity* 25(3):355-372.
1964 Settlement Pattern and Social Structure in the Southern Maya Lowlands During the Classic Period. In *XXXV Congreso Internacional de Americanistas*, pp. 279-287. vol. 1, México City.

Burn, Michael J. and Francis E. Mayle
2008 Palynological Differentiation Between Genera of the Moraceae Family and Implications for Amazonian Palaeoecology. *Review of Palaeobotany and Palynology* 149:15.

Burn, Michael J., Francis E. Mayle, and Timothy J. Killeen
2010 Pollen-based Differentiation of Amazonian Rainforest Communities and Implications for Lowland Palaeoecology in Tropical South America. *Palaeogeography, Palaeoclimatology, Palaeoecology* 295:18.

Burroughs, W. J.
2005 *Climate Change in Prehistory: The End of the Reign of Chaos*. Cambridge University Press, New York.

Bush, Mark B.
1995 Neotropical Plant Reproductive Strategies and Fossil Pollen Representation. *The American Naturalist* 145(4):594-609.
2000 Deriving Response Matrices from Modern Central American Pollen Rain. *Quaternary Research* 54:132-144.

Bush, Mark B. and Robert Rivera
1998 Pollen Dispersal and Representation in a Neotropical Rain Forest. *Global Ecology and Biogeography* 7(5):14.
2001 Reproductive Ecology and Pollen Representation among Neotropical Trees. *Global Ecology and Biogeography* 10(4):359-367.

Caballero, Javier
1992 Maya Homegardens: Past, Present and Future. *Etnoecológica* 1(1):35-54.

Camacho Villa, Tania Carolina
2011 *Making Milpa, Making Life in La Mera Selva*. Ph.D. thesis, Graduate School of Social Sciences, Wageningen University, Wageningen, The Netherlands.

Campbell, David G.
2005 *A Land of Ghosts: The Braided Lives of People and the Forest in Far Western Amazonia*. Houghton Mifflin Company, Boston.
2007 Don Berto's Garden: Language, Biodiversity, and a Story of Salvation. In *Orion Magazine*. Electronic document. orionmagazine.org/article/don-bertos-garde/. March 2015.
2010 Pre-Columbian Botanical Extinction in Amazonia: Was There a Neotropical "Langdauernderkrieg?" In *Amaz'Hommes*, edited by E. Barone-Visigalli and A. Roosevelt, pp. 173-188. Ibis Rouge, Matoury, France.

Campbell, David. G., Anabel Ford, Karen Lowell, Jay Walker, Jeffrey K. Lake, Constanza Ocampo-Raeder, Andrew Townesmith, and Michael Balick
2006 The Feral Forests of the Eastern Petén. In *Time and Complexity in the Neotropical Lowlands: Studies in Historical Ecology*, edited by W. Balée and C. Erickson, pp. 21-55. Columbia University Press, New York.

Campbell, David G., John Guittar, and Karen S. Lowell
2008 Are Colonial Pastures the Ancestors of the Contemporary Maya Forest? *Journal of Ethnobiology* 28(2):278-289.

Capers, Robert S., Robin L. Chazdon, Alvaro Redondo Brenes, and Braulio Vilchez Alvarado
2005 Successional Dynamics of Woody Seedling Communities in Wet Tropical Secondary Forests. *Journal of Ecology* 93:1071-1084.

Carberry, Peter S., Wei-li Liang, Stephen Twomlow, Dean P. Holzworth, John P. Dimes, Tim McClelland, Neil I. Huth, Fu Chen, Zvi Hochman, and Brian A. Keating
2013 Scope for Improved Eco-Efficiency Varies among Diverse Cropping Systems. *Proceedings of the National Academy of Sciences* 110(21):8381-8386.

Carr, David L., Laurel Suter, and Alisson Barbieri
2005 Population Dynamics and Tropical Deforestation: State of the Debate and Conceptual Challenges. *Population and Environment* 27:89-113.

Carr, Robert F. and James E. Hazard
1961 *Maps of the Ruins of Tikal, El Petén, Guatemala*. Museum Monographs, Tikal Report 11. University of Pennsylvania Museum, Philadelphia, Pennsylvania.

Carrillo-Bastos, Alicia, Gerald A. Islebe, Nuria Torrescano-Valle, and Norma Emilia Gonzalez
2010 Holocene Vegetation and Climate History of Central Quintana Roo, Yucatán Peninsula, México. *Review of Palaeobotany and Palynology* 160:8.

Carrillo-Bastos, Alicia, Gerald A. Islebe and Nuria Torrescano-Valle
2012 Geospatial analysis of pollen records from the Yucatan peninsula, Mexico. *Vegetation History and Archaeobotany* 21:429–437.

Casas, Alejandro, Adriana Otero-Arnaiz, Edgar Perez-Negron, and Alfonso Valiente-Banuet
2007 In situ Management and Domestication of Plants in Mesoamerica. *Annals of Botany*, 100: 1101-1115.

Chase, Arlen F. and Diane Z. Chase
1987 *Investigations at the Classic Maya City of Caracol, Belize: 1985-1987*. Monograph 3. Pre-Columbian Art Research Institute, San Francisco, California.

1994 *Studies in the Archaeology of Caracol, Belize*. Pre-Columbian Art Research Institute, San Francisco, California.

1998 Scale and Intensity in Classic Period Maya Agriculture: Terracing and Settlement at the "Garden City" of Caracol, Belize. *Culture & Agriculture* 20(2/3):60-70.

2003 Minor Centers, Complexity and Scale in Lowland Maya Settlement Archaeology. *Perspectives on Ancient Maya Rural Complexity* 49:108-118.

Chase, Arlen F., Diane Z. Chase, John F. Weishampe, Jason B. Drake, Ramesh L. Shrestha, K. Clint Slatton, Jaime J. Awe, and William E. Carter

2011 Airborne LiDAR, Archaeology, and the Ancient Maya Landscape at Caracol, Belize. *Journal of Archaeological Science* 38:387-398.

Chase, Arlen F., Lisa J. Lucero, Vernon L. Scarborough, Diane Z. Chase, Rafael Cobos, Nicholas P. Dunning, Scott L. Fedick, Vilma Fialko, Joel D. Gunn, Michelle Hegmon, Gyles Iannone, David L. Lentz, Rodrigo Liendo, Keith Prufer, Jeremy A. Sabloff, Joseph A. Tainter, Fred Valdez Jr., and Sander E. van der Leeuw

2014 Tropical Landscapes and the Ancient Maya: Diversity in Time and Space. In *The Resilience and Vulnerability of Ancient Landscapes: Transforming Maya Archaeology through IHOPE*. Archeological Papers of the American Anthropological Association 24:11-29.

Chase, Arlen F. and Vernon L. Scarborough (editors)

2014a *The Resilience and Vulnerability of Ancient Landscapes: Transforming Maya Archeology through IHOPE*. Archeological Papers of the American Anthropological Association 24.

Chase, Arlen F. and Vernon L. Scarborough

2014b Resiliency, and IHOPE-Maya: Using the Past to Inform the Present. In *The Resilience and Vulnerability of Ancient Landscapes: Transforming Maya Archaeology through IHOPE*. Archeological Papers of the American Anthropological Association 24:1-10.

Chase, Diane Z. and Arlen F. Chase

2002 Classic Maya Warfare and Settlement Archaeology at Caracol, Belize. *Estudios de Cultura Maya* 22:33-51.

Chazdon, Robin L.

2008 Chance and Determinism in Tropical Forest Succession. In *Tropical Forest Community Ecology*, edited by W. P. Carson and S. A. Schnitzer. Blackwell Publishers, Oxford, UK.

2014 *Second Growth: The Promise of Tropical Forest Regeneration in an Age of Deforestation*. University of Chicago Press, Chicago, Illinois.

Chazdon, Robin L. and Felix G. Coe

1999 Ethnobotany of Woody Species in Second-Growth, Old-Growth and Selectively Logged Forest of Northeastern Costa Rica. *Conservation Biology* 13(6):1312-1322.

Chazdon, Robin L., Celia A. Harvey, Oliver Komar, Daniel M. Griffith, Bruce G. Ferguson, Miguel Martínez-Ramos, Helda Morales, Ronald Nigh, Lorena Soto-Pinto, Michiel van Breugel, and Stacy M. Philpott

2009 Beyond Reserves: A Research Agenda for Conserving Biodiversity in Human-modified Tropical Landscapes. *Biotropica* 41(2):142-153.

Cincotta, Richard P., Jennifer Wisnewski, and Robert Engleman

2000 Human Population in the Biodiversity Hotspots. *Nature* 404:3.

Clark, John E. and David Cheetham

2002 Mesoamerica's Tribal Foundations. In *The Archaeology of Tribal Societies*, edited by W. A. Parkinson, pp. 278-339. Archaeological Series International Monographs in Prehistory, Ann Arbor, Michigan.

de Clerk, F. A. J. and P. Negreros-Castillo

2000 Plant Species of Traditional Mayan Homegardens of Mexico as Analogs for Multistrata Agroforests. *Agroforestry Systems* 48(3):303-317.

Cleveland, David A.
   2013 *Balancing on a Planet: The Future of Food and Agriculture.* University of California Press, Berkeley, California.
Coe, William R.
   1965 Tikal, Guatemala and Emergent Maya Civilization: Excavations Reveal Evidence of Early Complex-living at a Prime Maya Indian Site. *Science* 147(3664):1401-1419.
Coffey, Kevin T., Axel K. Schmitt, Anabel Ford, Frank J. Spera, Constance Christensen, and Jennifer Garrison
   2014 Volcanic Ash Provenance from Zircon Dust with an Application to Maya Pottery. In *Geology,* pp. 595-598. vol. 42. The Geological Society of America, Boulder, Colorado.
CONAP
   2004 Plan Maestro Monumento Cultura El Pilar en la Reserva de la Biosfera Maya. Reserva Arqueológica El Pilar para Flora y Fauna Maya, Guatemala.
Conklin, Harold
   1957 *Hanunóo Agriculture: A Report on an Integral System of Shifting Cultivation in the Philippines.* FAO Food and Agriculture Organization of the United Nations, Rome, Italy.
Conklin, Harold C.
   1954 An Ethnoecological Approach to Shifting Agriculture. In *Transactions of the New York Academy of Sciences,* edited by R. W. Miner, pp. 133-142. vol. 17. The New York Academy of Sciences, New York.
   1971 An Ethnoecological Approach to Shifting Agriculture. In *Readings in Cultural Geography,* edited by P. L. Wagner and M. W. Mikesell, pp. 457-464. University of Chicago Press, Chicago.
Cook, O. F.
   1921 *Milpa Agriculture, A Primitive Tropical System.* The Smithsonian Institution. Washington DC.
Cooper-Driver, G.
   1990 Defense Strategies in Bracken *(Pteridium aquilinum* (L.) Kuhn). *Annals of the Missouri Botanical Garden* 77(2):281-286.
Correa Navarro, Pedro Joaquin
   1997 *La Agricultura de Solar en la Zona Henequenera Yucateca. Su Evolucion y Sus Posibilidades de Mejoramiento Productivo.* Master's thesis, Phytotechnology, Universidad Autonoma Chapingo, Texcoco, México.
Cortés, Hernán
   1985[1526] *Cartas de Relación.* Crónicas de América. Dastin, S.L., Madrid.
Corzo Márquez, Amilcar Rolando, and Norman B. Schwartz
   2008 Traditional Home Gardens of Petén, Guatemala: Resource Management, Food Security, and Conservation. *Journal of Ethnobiology* 28(2):305-317.
Covich, Alan P.
   1978 A Reassessment of Ecological Stability in the Maya Area: Evidence from Lake Studies of Early Agricultural Impacts on Biotic Communities. In *Prehispanic Maya Agriculture,* edited by P. Harrison and B. L. Turner, pp. 145-155. University of New Mexico Press, Albuquerque, New Mexico.
Cowgill, Ursula M.
   1960 Soil Fertility, Population, and the Ancient Maya. *Proceedings of the National Academy of Sciences* 46:1009-1011.
   1961 *Soil Fertility and the Ancient Maya.* Transactions of the Connecticut Academy of Arts and Sciences 42. Connecticut Academy of Arts and Sciences, New Haven, Connecticut.
   1962 An Agricultural Study of the Southern Maya Lowlands. *American Anthropologist* 64(2):273-286.

Cowgill, Ursula M. and George E. Hutchinson
1963 Ecological and Geochemical Archaeology in the Southern Maya Lowlands. *Southwestern Journal of Anthropology* 19(3):267-286.

Crosby, Alfred W.
1986 *Ecological Imperialism: The Biological Expansion of Europe, 900-1900.* Studies in Environment and History. Cambridge University Press, Cambridge, United Kingdom.

Cuanalo de la Cerda, Heriberto E., and Rogelio R. Guerra Mukul
2008 Homegarden Production and Productivity in a Mayan Community of Yucatán. *Human Ecology* 36(3):423-433.

Culbert, T. Patrick and Don S. Rice
1990 *Precolumbian Population History in the Maya Lowlands.* University of New Mexico Press, Albuquerque, New Mexico.

Curtis, Jason H., Mark Brenner, David A. Hodell, Richard A. Balser, Gerald A. Islebe, and Henry Hooghiemstra
1998 A Multi-Proxy Study of Holocene Environmental Change in the Maya Lowlands of Petén, Guatemala. *Journal of Paleolimnology* 19:139-159.

Curtis, Jason H., David A. Hodell, and Mark Brenner
1996 Climate Variability on the Yucatán Peninsula (México) During the Past 3500 Years, and Implications for Maya Cultural Evolution. *Quaternary Research* 46(1):37-47.

Daniels, Amy E., Katie Painter, and Jane Southworth
2008 Milpa Imprint on the Tropical Dry Forest Landscape in Yucatán, México: Remote Sensing and Field Measurement of Edge Vegetation. *Agriculture, Ecosystems & Environment* 123(4):293-304.

Dean, Erin
2013 Contested Ecologies: Gender, Genies, and Agricultural Knowledge in Zanzibar. *Culture, Agriculture, Food and Environment* 35(2):102-111.

Deevey, Edward S., Don S. Rice, Prudence M. Rice, H. H. Vaughan, M. Brenner, and M. S. Flannery
1979 Mayan Urbanism: Impact on a Tropical Karst Environment. *Science* 206(4416):298-306.

Demarest, Arthur A., Prudence M. Rice, and Don S. Rice (editors)
2004 *The Terminal Classic in the Maya Lowlands: Collapse, Transition, and Transformation.* University Press of Colorado, Boulder, Colorado.

Den Ouden, J.
2000 *The Role of Bracken (Pteridium aquilinum) in Forest Dynamics.* Ph.D. thesis, Department of Environmental Sciences, Wageningen University, Wageningen, The Netherlands.

Denevan, William M.
1992a The Pristine Myth: The Landscape of the Americas in 1492. *Annals of the Association of American Geographers* 82(3):369-385.
1992b Stone vs. Metal Axes: The Ambiguity of Shifting Cultivation in Prehistoric Amazonia. *Journal of the Steward Anthropological Society* 20(1/2):153-165.
2011 The "Pristine Myth" Revisited. *The Geographical Review* 101(4):576-591.
2012 Rewriting the Late Pre-European History of Amazonia. *Journal of Latin American Geography* 11(1):9-24.

Denevan, William M. and Christine Padoch
1988 *Swidden-fallow Agroforestry in the Peruvian Amazon.* Advances in Economic Botany 5. New York Botanical Garden, Bronx, New York.

Diamond, Jared
2005 *Collapse: How Societies Choose to Fail or Succeed.* The Penguin Group, New York.
2012 *The World until Yesterday: What Can We Learn From Traditional Societies?* Viking, New York.

Diemont, Stewart A. W.
2006. *Ecosystem Management and Restoration as Practiced by the Indigenous Lacandon Maya of Chiapas, Mexico.* Ph.D. Dissertation, Food, Agricultural, and Biological Engineering, Ohio State University, Columbus.

Diemont, Stewart A. W., Jessica L. Bohn, Donald D. Rayome, Sarah J. Kelsen, and Kaity Cheng
2011 Comparisons of Mayan Forest Management, Restoration, and Conservation. *Forest Ecology and Management* 261:1696-1705.

Diemont, Stewart A. W. and Jay F. Martin
2009 Lacandon Maya Ecological Management: A Sustainable Design for Environmental Restoration and Human Subsistence. *Ecological Applications* 19(1):254-266.

Diemont, Stewart A. W., Jay F. Martin, and Samuel Israel Levy Tacher
2006 Energy Evaluation of Lacandon Maya Indigenous Swidden Agroforestry in Chiapas, México. *Agroforestry Systems* 66(1):23-42.

Domínguez-Vásquez, Gabriela and Gerald A. Islebe
2008 Protracted Drought During the Late Holocene in the Lacandon Rain Forest, México. *Vegetation History and Archaeobotany* 17:327-333.

Domínguez-Vázquez, Gabriela, Gerald A. Islebe, and R. Villanueva-Gutiérrez
2004 Modern Pollen Deposition in Lacandon Forest, Chiapas, México. *Review of Palaeobotany and Palynology* 131(1-2):105-116.

Douterlungne, David, Samuel I. Levy Tacher, Duncan J. Golicher, and Francisco Román Dañobeytia
2010 Applying Indigenous Knowledge to the Restoration of Degraded Tropical Rain Forest Clearings Dominated by Bracken Fern. *Restoration Ecology* 18(3):322-329.

Dull, Robert A., Richard J. Nevle, William I. Woods, Dennis K. Bird, Shiri Avnery, and William M. Denevan
2010 The Columbian Encounter and the Little Ice Age: Abrupt Land Use Change, Fire, and Greenhouse Forcing. *Annals of the Association of American Geographers* 100(4):1-17.

Dunning, Nicholas, Timothy Beach, Sheryl Luzzadder-Beach, and John G. Jones
2009 Creating Stable Landscape: Soil Conservation and Adaptation Among the Maya. In *The Archaeology of Environmental Change*, edited by C. T. Fisher, J. B. Hill, and G. M. Feinman, pp. 85-105. University of Arizona Press, Tucson, Arizona.

Dunning, Nicholas, David Wahl, Timothy Beach, John Jones, Sheryl Luzzadder-Beach, and Carmen McCane
2014 The End of the Beginning: Drought, Environmental Change, and the Preclassic to Classical Transition in the East-Central Maya Lowlands. In *The Great Maya Droughts in Cultural Context: Case Studies in Resilience and Vulnerability*, edited by G. Iannone, pp. 107-126. University Press of Colorado, Boulder, Colorado.

Dunning, Nicholas P. and Timothy Beach
2000 Stability and Instability in Prehispanic Maya Landscapes. In *An Imperfect Balance: Landscape Transformations in the Precolumbian America*, edited by D. L. Lentz, pp. 179-202. Columbia University Press, New York.
2010 Farms and Forests: Spatial and Temporal Perspectives on Ancient Maya Landscapes. In *Landscapes and Societies: Selected Cases*, edited by I. P. Martini and W. Chesworth. Springer, New York.

Dunning, Nicholas P., Timothy Beach, P. Farrell, and Sheryl Luzzadder-Beach
1998 Prehispanic Agrosystems and Adaptive Regions in the Maya Lowlands. *Culture and Agriculture* 20(2-3):87-101.

Dunning, Nicholas P., Timothy P. Beach, and Sheryl Luzzadder-Beach
2012 Kax and Kol: Collapse and Resilience in Lowland Maya Civilization. *Proceedings of the National Academy of Science* 109(10):3652-3657.

Dunning, Nicholas P., Sheryl Luzzadder-Beach, Timothy Beach, John G. Jones, Vernon Scarborough and T. Patrick Culbert
2002 Arising from the Bajos: The Evolution of a Neotropical Landscape and the Rise of Maya Civilization. *Annals of the Association of American Geographers* 92(2):267-283.

Durán Fernández, Alejandro
1999 *Estructura y Etnobotánica de la Selva Alta Perennifolia de Nahá, Chiapas.* Master's thesis, Facultad de Ciencias, Universidad Nacional Autónoma de México, México.

Early, D.
1992 The Renaissance of Amaranth. In *Chilies to Chocolate: Food the Americas Gave the World,* edited by N. Foster and L. S. Cordell, pp. 15-33. University of Arizona Press, Tucson, Arizona.

Earp, Colleen
2011 *Characterizing Invasive Species: The Case of Bracken Fern (Pteridium Aquilinum) in the Mesoamerican Biological Corridor Sian Ka'an-Calakmul, México.* Master's thesis, Geography Department, Rutgers University, New Brunswick, New Jersey.

Eastmond, Amarella and Betty Faust
2006 Farmers, Fires, and Forests: A Green Alternative to Shifting Cultivation for Conservation of the Maya Forest? *Landscape and Urban Planning* 74:267-284.

ECOSUR
2003 Cambios de Uso del Suelo y la Vegetación en el Estado de Chiapas 1975-2000. El Colegio de la Fronera Sur. San Cristóbal de Las Casas, Chiapas, México.

Emerson, R. A.
1953 A Preliminary Survey of the Milpa System of Maize Culture as Practiced by the Maya Indians of the Northern Part of the Yucatán Peninsula. *Annals of the Missouri Botanical Garden* 40:51-62.

Emery, Kitty F.
2004 Environments of the Maya Collapse: A Zooarchaeological Perspective from the Petexbatún, Guatemala, In *Maya Zooarchaeology: New Directions in Method and Theory,* edited by K.F. Emery, pp. 81-96. Los Angeles, CA: Institute of Archaeology, UCLA Press.
2007 Assessing the Impact of Ancient Maya Animal Use. *Journal for Nature Conservation* 15(3):184-195.
2010 *Dietary, Environmental, and Societal Implications of Ancient Maya Animal Use in the Petexbatun: A Zooarchaeological Perspective on Collapse* 5. Vanderbilt University Press, Nashville, Tennesse.

Emery, Kitty F. and Linda A. Brown
2012 Maya Hunting Sustainability: Perspectives from Past and Present. In *The Ethics of Anthropology and Amerindian Research,* edited by R. J. Chacon and R. G. Mendoza, pp. 79-116. Springer-Verlag, New York.

Emery, Kitty F. and Erin Kennedy Thornton
2008 Zooarchaeological Habitat Analysis of Ancient Maya Landscape Changes. *Journal of Ethnobiology* 28(2):154-178.
2012 Using Animal Remains to Reconstruct Ancient Landscapes and Climate in the Central and Southern Maya Lowlands. In *Proceedings of the General Session of the 11th International Council for Archaeozoology Conference (Paris, 23-28 August 2010),* edited by C. Lefèvre, pp. 203-225. BAR International Series 2354. Archaeopress, Oxford, UK.
2014 Tracking Climate Change in the Ancient Maya World through Zooarchaeological Habitat Analyses. In *The Great Maya Droughts in Cultural Context: Case Studies in Resilience and Vulnerability,* edited by G. Iannone, pp. 301-331. University Press of Colorado, Boulder, Colorado.

Emery, Kitty F., Lorie E. Wright, and Henry Schwarcz
2000 Isotopic Analysis of Ancient Deer Bone: Biotic Stability in Collapse Period Maya Land-use. *Journal of Archaeological Science* 27:537-550.

Erasmus, Charles J.
1965 Monument Building: Some Field Experiments. *Southwestern Journal of Anthropology* 21(4):277-301.

ETC Group
2009 Who Will Feed Us? Questions for the Food and Climate Crises. *ETC Communique* (102).

Everton, Macduff
2012 *The Modern Maya: Incidents of Travel and Friendship in Yucatán.* 1st ed. University of Texas Press, Austin, Texas.

Exploring Solutions Past
2014 Archaeology Under the Canopy. The Maya Forest Alliance. Electronic document. http://exploringsolutionspast.org/what-we-do/archaeology-under-the-canopy/. December 2014.

Faegri, K.
1966 Some Problems of Representivity in Pollen Analysis. *Paleobotanist* 15:135-140.

Fairchild, David
1945 The Ramon Tree of Yucatán. *Florida State Horticultural Society* 58:198-200.

FAO, Food and Agriculture Organization of the United Nations
2014a *The State of Food and Agriculture.* Food and Agriculture Organization of the United Nations. Copies available from www.fao.org/3/a-i4040e.pdf. December 2014.
2014b What is Soil Carbon Sequestration? Food and Agriculture Organization of the United, Electronic document. www.fao.org/soils-portal/soil-management/soil-carbon-sequestration/en/. December 2014.

Farriss, Nancy M.
1984 *Maya Society under Colonial Rule: The Collective Enterprise of Survival.* Princeton University Press, Princeton, New Jersey.
1992 *Maya Society Under Colonial Rule: The Collective Enterprise of Survival.* 5th ed. Princeton University Press, Princeton, New Jersey.

Faust, Betty B.
1998 *Mexican Rural Development and the Plumed Serpent: Technology and Maya Cosmology in the Tropical Forest of Campeche, México.* Bergin & Garvey, Westport, Connecticut.
2001 Maya Environmental Successes and Failures in the Yucatán Peninsula. *Environmental Science and Policy* 4:153-169.

Fedick, Scott L.
1988 *Prehistoric Maya Settlement and Land Use Patterns in the Upper Belize River Area, Belize Central America.* Ph.D. Dissertation, Department of Anthropology, Arizona State University, Tempe, Arizona.
1989 The Economics of Agricultural Land Use and Settlement in the Upper Belize Valley. In *Research in Economic Anthropology,* edited by P. A. McAnany and B. L. Isaac, pp. 215-253. JAI Press, Greenwich, Connecticut.
1992 An Agricultural Perspective on Prehistoric Maya Household Location and Settlement Density. In *Primer Congreso Internacional de Mayistas* pp. 87-108. Instituto de Investigaciones Filológicas; Centro de Estudios Mayas. Universidad Nacional Autónoma de México, Mexico.
1994 Ancient Maya Agricultural Terracing in the Upper Belize Area. Computer-Aided Modeling and the Results of Initial Investigations. *Ancient Mesoamerica* 5(1):107-127.
1995 Land Evaluation and Ancient Maya Land Use in the Upper Belize River Area, Belize, Central America. *Latin American Antiquity* 6(1):16-34.
1996a Landscape Approaches to the Study of Ancient Maya Agriculture and Resource Use. In *The Managed Mosaic: Ancient Maya Agriculture and Resource Use,* edited

by S. L. Fedick, pp. 335-348. University of Utah Press, Salt Lake City, Utah.
1996b *The Managed Mosaic: Ancient Maya Agriculture and Resource Use*. University of Utah Press, Salt Lake City, Utah.
2003 In Search of the Maya Forest. In *In Search of the Rain Forest*, edited by C. Slater, pp. 133-166. Duke University Press, Durham, North Carolina.
2010 The Maya Forest: Destroyed or Cultivated by the Ancient Maya. *Proceedings for the National Academy of Sciences* 107(3):953-954.
2014 A Reassessment of Water and Soil Resources in the Flatlands of the Northern Maya Lowlands. In *The Resilience and Vulnerability of Ancient Landscapes: Transforming Maya Archaeology through IHOPE*. Archeological Papers of the American Anthropological Association 24: 72-83.

Fedick, Scott L. and Anabel Ford
1990 The Prehistoric Agricultural Landscape of the Central Maya Lowlands: An Examination of Local Variability in a Regional Context. *World Archaeology* 22:18-33.

Fedick, Scott L. and Gerald Islebe
2012 The Secret Garden: Assessing the Archaeological Visibility of Ancient Maya Plant Cultivation According to Pollination Syndrome. Paper presented at the European Conference on Ecological Restoration, Budweis, Czech Republic.

Ferguson, Bruce G., John Vandermeer, Helda Morales, and Daniel M. Griffith
2003 Post-agricultural Succession in El Petén, Guatemala. *Conservation Biology* 17(3):818-828.

Ferrand, Ezgi Akpinar, Nicholas P. Dunning, David L. Lentz, and John G. Jones
2012 Use of Aguadas as Water Management Sources in Two Southern Maya Lowland Sites. *Ancient Mesoamerica* 23:85-101.

Finegan, Bryan
2004 The Biodiversity and Conservation Potential of Shifting Cultivation Landscapes. In *Agroforestry and Biodiversity Conservation in Tropical Landscapes*, edited by G. Shroth, G. de Fonseca, C. Harvey, C. Gascon, H. L. Vasconcelos, and A.-M. N. Izac, pp. 153-197. Island Press, Washington, D.C.

FLAAR
2008 Plants Utilized by the Maya from Classic Times through Today. FLAAR Asociación Mesoamerica. Electronic document. http://www.wide-format-printers.org/FLAAR_report_covers/705182_Plants_utilized_by_the_mayan.pdf.

Flannery, Kent V.
1976 *The Early Mesoamerican Village*. Academic Press, New York.

Flaster, Trish
2007 *Ramon Seed (Brosimim Alicastrum SW.) and Ramon Seed-Derived Ingredients for Use in Traditional Foods Generally Recognized as Safe (GRAS) Self-Affirmation Report*. Food and Drug Administration.

Fletcher, Roland
2009 Low-density, Agrarian-based Urbanism: A Comparative View. *Insights* 2:2-19.

Folan, William J., Lorraine A. Fletcher, and Ellen R. Kitz
1979 Fruit, Fiber, Bark, and Resin: Social Organization of a Maya Urban Center. *Science* 204(4394):697-701.

Ford, Anabel
1981 *Conditions for the Evolution of Complex Societies: The Development of the Central Lowland Maya*. Ph.D. dissertation, Department of Anthropology, University of California, Santa Barbara, Santa Barbara, California.
1985 Maya Settlement Pattern Chronology in the Belize River Area and the Implications for the Development of the Central Maya Lowlands. *Belcast Journal of Belizean Affairs* 2:13-32.

1986 *Population Growth and Social Complexity: An Examination of Settlement and Environment in the Central Maya Lowlands.* Anthropological Research Papers No. 35. Arizona State University, Tempe, Arizona.

1990 Maya Settlement in the Belize River Area: Variations in Residence Patterns of the Central Maya Lowlands. In *Prehistoric Population History in the Maya Lowlands*, edited by T. P. Culbert and D. S. Rice, pp. 167-181. University of New Mexico Press, Albuquerque, New Mexico.

1991a Economic Variation of Ancient Maya Residential Settlement in the Upper Belize River Area. *Ancient Mesoamerica* 2:35-46.

1991b Problems with the Evaluation of Population from Settlement Data: Examination of Ancient Maya Residence Patterns in the Tikal-Yaxhá Intersite Area. *Estudios de Cultura Maya* 18:157-186.

1992 The Ancient Maya Domestic Economy: An Examination of Settlement in the Upper Belize River Area. In *Primer Congreso Internacional de Mayistas* pp. 57-86. Conference presentation at the Instituto de Investigaciones Filológicas, Centro de Estudios Mayas. Universidad Nacional Autónoma de México, Mexico.

1996 Critical Resource Control and the Rise of the Classic Period Maya. In *The Managed Mosaic: Ancient Maya Agriculture and Resource Use*, edited by S. L. Fedick, pp. 297-303. University of Utah Press, Salt Lake City, Utah.

2003a *Crecimiento de Población y Complejidad Social: Asentamiento y Medio Ambiente en las Tierras Bajas Mayas.* Translated by E. H. Gaytan Monográfica 14. Centro de Investigaciones Regionales de Mesoamérica, Miami, Florida.

2003b Continuity and Sustainability in the Maya Forest: Building a Future from the Past at El Pilar. In *Cuarto Congreso Internacional de Mayistas*, pp. 380-395. Instituto de Investigaciones Filológicas; Centro de Estudios Mayas. Universidad Nacional Autónoma de México, Mexico..

2004 Integration among Communities, Centers, and Regions: The Case from El Pilar. In *The Ancient Maya of the Belize Valley: Half a Century of Archaeological Research*, edited by J. Garber, pp. 238-256. University Press of Florida, Gainesville, Florida.

2008 Dominant Plants of the Maya Forest and Gardens of El Pilar: Implications for Paleoenvironmental Reconstructions. *Journal of Ethnobiology* 28(2):179-199.

2010 Action Archaeology and the Community at El Pilar. In *Anthropology: The Human Challenge*, edited by W. A. Haviland, H. E. L. Prins, D. Walrath and B. McBride, pp. 260-262, Wadsworth, Cengage Learning.

2011a Afterword: El Pilar and Maya Cultural Heritage: Reflections of a Cheerful Pessimist. In *Contested Cultural Heritage: Religion, Nationalism, Erasure, and Exclusion in a Global World*, edited by H. Silverman, pp. 261-265. Springer, New York

2011b Legacy of the Ancient Maya: the Maya forest garden. Popular Archaeology 1, January 2011. Electronic document. http://popular-archaeology.com/issue/january-2011/article/the-legacy-of-el-pilar-the-maya-forest garden. March 2015.

2013 Ancient Maya Landscapes: A Community of Prosperous Farmers. *Current Anthropology* 54(1):110-111.

Ford, Anabel and Keith C. Clarke
2006 Predicting Late Classic Maya Settlement Patterns. *Research Reports in Belizean Archaeology* 3:193-212.

2016 Linking the Past and Present of the Ancient Maya: Lowland Land Use, Population Distribution, and Density in the Late Classic Period. In *Oxford Handbook of Historical Ecology and Applied Archaeology*, edited by C. Isendahl and D. Stump. Oxford Press, Oxford, UK, in press.

Ford, Anabel, Keith C .Clarke, and Constance Christensen
2014 The Maya Forest GIS: Regional, Local, and Site Data. On file at the MesoAmerican Research Center, University of California, Santa Barbara.

Ford, Anabel, Keith C. Clarke, and Sebastian Morlet
2011 Calculating Late Classic Lowland Maya Population for the Upper Belize River Area. *Research Reports in Belizean Archaeology* 8:75-87.

Ford, Anabel, Keith C. Clarke, and Gary Raines
2009 Modeling Settlement Patterns of the Late Classic Maya with Bayesian Methods and GIS. *Annals of the Association of American Geographers* 99(3):496-520.

Ford, Anabel and Cynthia Ellis
2013 Teaching Secrets of Conservation and Prosperity in the Maya Forest. *Research Reports in Belizean Archaeology* 10:305-310.

Ford, Anabel and Scott L. Fedick
1992 Prehistoric Maya Settlement Patterns in the Upper Belize River Area: Initial Results of the Belize River Archaeological Settlement Survey. *Journal of Field Archaeology* 19:35-49.

Ford, Anabel and Harry Glicken
1987 The Significance of Volcanic Ash Tempering in the Ceramics of the Central Maya Lowlands. *Proceedings of the 1985 Maya Ceramics Conference* 345:479-502. Washington, D.C.

Ford, Anabel and Megan Havrda
2006 Archaeology Under the Canopy: Imagining the Maya of El Pilar. In *Tourism, Consumption and Representation: Narratives of Place and Self*, edited by K. Meethan, A. Anderson, and S. Miles, pp. 67-93. CAB International, Wallingford, Connecticut.

Ford, Anabel, Allison Jaqua, and Ronald Nigh
2012 Paleoenvironmental Record, Reconstruction, Forest Succession, and Weeds in the Maya Milpa. *Research Reports in Belizean Archaeology* 9:279-288.

Ford, Anabel and Maggie Knapp
2011 El Pilar: Archaeology Under the Canopy. Popular Archaeology 4, Septeber 2011. Electronic document. http://popular-archaeology.com/issue/september-2011/article/el-pilar-archaeology-under-the-canopy. March 2015.

Ford, Anabel and Ronald Nigh
2009 Origins of the Maya Forest Garden: A Resource Management System. *Journal of Ethnobiology* 29(2):213-236.
2010 The Milpa Cycle and the Making of the Maya Forest Garden. *Research Reports in Belizean Archaeology* 7:183-190.
2014 Climate Change in the Ancient Maya Forest: Resilience and Adaptive Management across Millennia. In *The Great Maya Droughts In Cultural Context: Case Studies in Resilience and Vulnerability*, edited by G. Iannone, pp. 87-106. University Press of Colorado, Boulder, Colorado.

Ford, Anabel and William I. Rose
1995 Volcanic Ash in Ancient Maya Ceramics of the Limestone Lowlands: Implications for Prehistoric Volcanic Activity in the Guatemala Highlands. *Journal of Volcanology and Geothermal Research* 66(1-4):149-162.

Ford, Anabel, Melanie Santiago-Smith, and John Morris
2005 Community Integration and Adaptive Management at El Pilar. *Research Reports in Belizean Archaeology* 2(459-470).

Ford, Anabel and Frank Spera
2007 Fresh Volcanic Glass Shards in the Pottery Shards of the Maya Lowlands. *Research Reports in Belizean Archaeology* 4:111-118.

Forsyth, D. W.
1993a The Ceramic Sequence at Nakbe. *Ancient Mesoamerica* 4(1):31-53.
1993b La Cerámica Arqueológica de Nakbe y El Mirador, Petén. Paper presented at the III Simposio de Arqueología Guatemalteca, Guatemala.

Foster, R. J., B. J. Harmsen, B. Valdes, C. Pomilla, and C. P. Doncaster
2009 Food Habits of Sympatric Jaguars and Pumas Across a Gradient of Human Disturbance. *Journal of Zoology* 280:309-318.

Fox, John W. and Garrett W. Cook
1996 Constructing Maya Communities: Ethnography for Archaeology. *Current Anthropology* 37(5):811-830.

Freidel, David A.
1981 The Political Economics of Residential Dispersion among the Lowland Maya. In *Lowland Maya Settlement Patterns*, edited by W. Ashmore, pp. 371-382. University of New Mexico Press, Albuquerque, New Mexico.

Freidel, David A., Linda Schele, and Joy Parker
1993 *Maya Cosmos: Three Thousand Years on the Shaman's Path*. 1st ed. W. Morrow, New York.

Fry, Robert Elmer
1969 *Ceramics and Settlement in the Periphery of Tikal, Guatemala*. Ph.D. dissertation, Department of Anthropology, University of Arizona, Tucson, Arizona.

Fukuoka, Masanobu
1978 *The One-Straw Revolution*. Bantam Books, New York.

Geertz, Clifford
1963 *Agricultural Involution: The Processes of Ecological Change in Indonesia*. University of California Press, Berkeley, California.

Gill, Richardson B., Paul A. Mayewski, Johan Nyberg, Gerald H. Haug, and Larry C. Peterson
2007 Drought and the Maya Collapse. *Ancient Mesoamerica* 18(2):283-302.

Glaser, Bruno, Ludwig Haumaier, Georg Guggenberger, and Wolfgang Zech
2001 The 'Terra Preta' Phenomenon: A Model for Sustainable Agriculture in the Humid Tropics. *Naturwissenschaften* 88:37-41.

Gliessman, Stephen R.
1978 The Establishment of Bracken Following Fire in Tropical Habitats. *American Fern Journal* 68(2):41-44.
1982 Nitrogen Distribution in Several Traditional Agro-ecosystems in the Humid Tropical Lowlands of South-eastern México. *Plant and Soil* 67:105-117.
1983 Allelopathic Interactions in Crop-Weeds Mixtures. *Journal of Chemical Ecology* 9(8):991-999.
1993 Managing Diversity in Traditional Agroecosystems of Tropical Mexico. In *Perspectives on Biodiversity: Case Studies of Genetic Resource Conservation and Development*, edited by C. S. Potter, J. I. Cohen, and D. Janczewski, pp. 65-74. American Association for the Advancement of Science (AAAS), Washington, D.C.
1998 *Agroecology: Ecological Processes in Sustainable Agriculture*. Ann Arbor Press, Chelsea, Michigan.
2001 *Agroecosystem Sustainability: Developing Practical Strategies*. Advances in Agroecology Series. CRC Press, Boca Raton, Florida.
2004 Integrating Agroecological Processes into Cropping Systems Research. *Journal of Crop Improvement* 11(1-2):61-80.

Gliessman, Stephen, E. M. García, and A. Amador
1981 The Ecological Basis for the Applications of Traditional Agriculture in the Management of Tropical Agroecosystems. *Agroecosystems* 7:173-185.

Goebel, Ted, Michael R. Waters, and Dennis H. O'Rourke
2008 The Late Pleistocene Dispersal of Modern Humans in the Americas. *Science* 319:1497-1502.

Gómez-Pompa, Arturo
1987 Tropical Deforestation and Maya Silviculture: An Ecological Paradox. *Tulane Studies in Zoology and Botany* 26(1):19-37.
2004 The Role of Biodiversity Scientists in a Troubled World. *BioScience* 54(3):217.

Gómez-Pompa, Arturo, Michael F. Allen, Scott L. Fedick, and Juan J. Jimenez-Osornio (editors)
2003 *The Lowland Maya Area: Three Millennia at the Human-Wildland Interface.* Food Products Press, New York.

Gómez-Pompa, Arturo, Jose Salvador Flores, and Victoria Sosa
1987 The "Pet Kot": A Man-Made Tropical Forest of the Maya. *Interciencia* 12(1):10-15.

Gómez-Pompa, Arturo and Andrea Kaus
1990 Traditional Management of Tropical Forests in México. In *Alternatives to Deforestation: Steps Toward Sustainable Use of the Amazon Rain Forest,* edited by A. B. Anderson, pp. 45-64. Columbia University Press, New York.
1992 Taming the Wilderness Myth: Environmental Policy and Education are Currently Based on Western Beliefs about Nature Rather than on Reality. *BioScience* 42(4):271-279.
1999 From Pre-Hispanic to Future Conservation Alternatives: Lessons from México. *Proceedings of the National Academy of Sciences* 96:5982-5986.

Gómez-Pompa, Arturo, C. Vazquez-Yanes, and S. Guevara
1972 The Tropical Rain Forest: A Nonrenewable Resource. *Science* 177:762-765.

Graham, Alan
2003 In the Beginning: Early Events in the Development of Mesoamerica and the Lowland Maya Area. In *The Lowland Maya Area: Three Millennia at the Human-Wildland Interface,* edited by S. Fedick, M. Allen and A. Gómez-Pompa, pp. 31-44. Food Products Press, New York.

Graham, Elizabeth
1992 Maya Cities and the Character of a Tropical Urbanism. In *Urban Origins in Eastern Africa,* edited by P. J. J. Sinclair and A. Juma, pp. 70. Uppsala University, Department of Archaeology, Uppsala, Sweden.
1999 Stone Cities, Green Cities. In *Complex Polities in the Ancient Tropical World,* edited by E. A. Bacus and L. J. Lucero, pp. 185-194. Archeological Papers of the American Anthropological Association No. 9. American Anthropological Association, Arlington, Texas.
2006 A Neotropical Framework for *Terra Preta*. In *Time and Complexity in Historical Ecology: Studies in the Neotropical Lowlands,* edited by W. Balée and C. Erickson, pp. 57-86. Columbia University Press, New York.

Green, Rhys E., Stephen J. Cornell, Jorn P. W. Scharlemann, and Andrew Balmford
2005 Farming and the Fate of Wild Nature. *Science* 307(5709):550-555.

Greenberg, Laurie. S. Z.
1992 Garden Hunting among the Yucatec Maya: A Coevolutionary History of Wildlife and Culture. *Ethnoecologica* 1(1):23-33.

Griffith, Daniel M.
2000 Agroforestry: A Refuge for Tropical Biodiversity after Fire. *Conservation Biology* 14(1):525-526.
2004 *Succession of Tropical Rain Forest along a Gradient of Agricultural Intensification: Patterns, Mechanisms and Implications for Conservation.* Ph.D dissertation, Philosophy (Ecology and Evolutionary Biology), The University of Michigan, Ann Arbor, Michigan.

Guimaraes Vieira, Ima Celia and John Proctor
2007 Mechanisms of Plant Regeneration during Succession after Shifting Cultivation in Eastern Amazonia. *Plant Ecology* 192:303-315.

Gunn, Joel, William J. Folan, Christian Isendahl, Maria de Rosario Domínguez Carasco, Betty Faust, and Beniamino Volta
  2014 Calakmul: Agent Risk and Sustainability in the Western Maya Lowlands. In *The Resilience and Vulnerability of Ancient Landscape: Transforming Maya Archaeology through IHOPE*. Archeological Papers of the American Anthropological Association 24:101-124.

Gunn, Joel, William J. Folan and Hubert R. Robichaux
  1995 A Landscape Analysis of the Candelaria Watershed in México: Insights into Paleoclimate Affecting Upland Horticulture in the Southern Yucatán Peninsula Semi-karst. *Geoarchaeology* 10:3-42.

Gunn, Joel D., Ray T. Matheny, and William J. Folan
  2002 Climate Change Studies in the Maya Area: A Diachronic Analysis. *Ancient Mesoamerica* 13:79-84.

Hack, J. T.
  1942 *The Changing Physical Environment of the Hopi Indians of Arizona*. Papers of the Peabody Museum 35(1). Harvard University, Cambridge, Massachusetts.

Halwell, Brian
  2007 *Still No Free Lunch: Nutrient Levels in U.S. Food Supply Eroded by Pursuit of High Yields*. The Organic Center. Boulder, Colorado.

Hammond, Norman, Gair Tourtellot, Sara Donaghey, and Amanda Clarke
  1998 No Slow Dusk: Maya Urban Development and Decline at La Milpa, Belize. *Antiquity* 72(278):831-837.

Haney Jr., Emil B.
  1968 The Nature of Shifting Cultivation in Latin America, p. 30. Land Tenure Center, University of Wisconsin, Madison, Wisconsin.

Hanks, William F.
  1990 *Referential Practice: Language and Lived Space among the Maya*. The University of Chicago Press, Chicago.

Hansen, Richard D., Steven Bozarth, John Jacob, David Wahl, and Thomas Schreiner
  2002 Climatic and Environmental Variability in the Rise of Maya Civilization: A Preliminary Perspective from Northern Petén. *Ancient Mesoamerica* 13(2):273-295.

Hardin, Garrett
  1968 The Tragedy of the Commons. *Science* 162:1243-1248.

Hartke, Edwin J. and John R. Hill
  1974 Sedimentation in Lake Lemon, Monroe County, Indiana. *Environmental Study* 3 9:23.

Harvey, Celia A., Oliver Komar, Robin L. Chazdon, Bruce G. Ferguson, Bryan Finegan, Daniel M. Griffith, Miguel Martinez-Ramos, Helda Morales, Ronald Nigh, Lorena Soto-Pinto, Michiel Van Breugel, and Mark Wishnie
  2008 Integrating Agricultural Landscapes with Biodiversity Conservation in the Mesoamerican Hotspot. *Conservation Biology* 22(1):8-15.

Haug, Gerald H., Detlef Gunther, Larry C. Peterson, Daniel M. Sigman, Konrad A. Hughen, and Beat Aeschlimann
  2003 Climate and the Collapse of Maya Civilization. *Science* 299(5613):1731-1735.

Haug, Gerald H., Konrad A. Hughen, Daniel M. Sigman, Larry C. Peterson, and Ursula Rohl
  2001 Southward Migration of the Intertropical Convergence Zone through the Holocene. *Science* 293(5533):1304-1308.

Haviland, William A.
  1969 Tikal, Guatemala and Mesoamerican Urbanism. *World Archaeology* 2(2):186-196.
  1972 Family Size, Prehistoric Population Estimates, and the Ancient Maya. *American Antiquity* 37(1):135-139.

Healy, Paul F., Christophe G. B. Helmke, Jaime J. Awe, and Kay S. Sunahara
2007 Survey, Settlement, and Population History at the Ancient Maya Site of Pacbitun, Belize. *Journal of Field Archaeology* 32(1):17-39.

Hecht, Susanna B.
2007 Kayapó Savanna Management: Fire, Soils and Forest Islands in a Threatened Biome. In *Amazon Soils: Essays in Honor of Wim Sombroek*, edited by W. Woods. Springer Verlag, Berlin.
2009 Kayapó Savanna Management: Fire, Soils, and Forest Islands in a Threatened Biome. In *Amazonian Dark Earths: Wim Sombroek's Vision*, edited by W. T. W. Woods, J. Lehmann, C. Steiner, A. WinklerPrins, and L. Rebellato, pp. 143-161. Springer, New York.

Heckenberger, Michael J., J. Christian Russell, Carlos Fausto, Joshua R. Toney, Morgan J. Schmidt, Edithe Pereira, Bruna Franchetto, and Afukaka Kuikuro
2008 Pre-Columbian Urbanism, Anthropogenic Landscapes, and the Future of the Amazon. *Science* 321(5893):1214-1217.

Hernández Xolocotzi, Efraím
1985 *Xolocotzia: Obras de Efraím Hernández Xolocotzi.* 1a ed 1. Revista de Geografía Agrícola, México.

Hernandez Xolocotzi, Efraím, Eduardo Bello Baltazar, and Samuel Israel Levy Tacher
1995 *La Milpa en Yucatán: Un Sistema de Producción Agrícola Tradicional*, Vols. 1 and 2. Colegio de Postgraduados, México.

Hervik, Peter
1999 The Mysterious Maya of National Geographic. *Journal of Latin American Anthropology* 4:166-197.

Hillesheim, Michael B., D. A. Hodell, Barbara W. Leyden, Mark Brenner, Jason H. Curtis, Flavio S. Anselmetti, Daniel Ariztegui, David G. Buck, Thomas Guilderson, Michael F. Rosenmeier, and Douglas W. Schnurrenberger
2005 Climate Change in Lowland Central America During the Late Deglacial and Early Holocene. *Journal of Quaternary Science* 20(4):363-376.

Hirshberg, Richard Irwin, Joan F. Hirshberg, and Betty J. Meggers
1957 Meggers' Law of Environmental Limitation on Culture. *American Anthropologist.* 59(5):890-892.

Hodell, David A., Flavio S. Anselmetti, Daniel Ariztegui, Mark Brenner, Jason H. Curtis, Adrian Gilli, Dustin A. Grzesik, Thomas J. Guilderson, Andreas D. Müller, Mark Bush, Alexander Correa-Metrio, Jaime Escobar, and Steffen Kutterolf
2008 An 85-ka Record of Climate Change in Lowland Central America. *Quaternary Science Reviews* 27:1152-1165.

Hodell, David A., Mark Brenner, Jason H. Curtis, and Thomas Guilderson
2001 Solar Forcing of Drought Frequency in the Maya Lowlands. *Science* 292(5520):1367-1370.

Hodell, David A., M. Brenner, J. H. Curtis, R. M. Medina Gonzalez, M. F. Rosenmeier, and T. P. Guilderson
2002 The Little Ice Age in Mesoamerica. *American Geophysical Union*, abstract #PP61B-10. Electronic document. http://adsabs.harvard.edu/abs/2002AGUFMP-P61B..10H. March 2015.

Hodell, David A., Jason H. Curtis, and Mark Brenner
1995 Possible Role of Climate in the Collapse of Classic Maya Civilization. *Nature* 375:391-394.

Hodell, David A., Alexandra V. Turchyn, Camilla J. Wiseman, Jaime Escobar, Jason H. Curtis, Mark Brenner, Adrian Gilli, Andreas D. Mueller, Flavio Anselmetti, Daniel Ariztegui, and Erik T. Brown

2012 Late Glacial Temperature and Precipitation Changes in the Lowland Neo-tropics by Tandem Measurement of $\delta^{18}O$ in Biogenic Carbonate and Gypsum Hydration Water. *Geochimica et Cosmochimica Acta* 77:352–368.

Hofling, Charles A.
2004 Language and Cultural Contacts Among Yukatekan Mayans. *Collegium Antropologicum* 28(1):241-248.

IA, Institute of Archaeology, Belize
2006 *El Pilar Management Plan: El Pilar Landscape Gateway between Two Nations.* National Institute of Archaeology, Government of Belize. Belmopan, Belize.

IFAD, International Fund for Agricultural Development
2014 The Future of World Food and Nutrition Security: Investing in Smallholder Agriculture—An International Priority. International Fund for Agricultural Development, Rome. Electronic document. http://www.ifad.org/pub/factsheet/food/food-security_e.pdf. March 2014.

Iannone, Gyles (editor)
2014 *The Great Maya Droughts In Cultural Context: Case Studies in Resilience and Vulnerability.* University Press of Colorado, Boulder, Colorado.

Iannone, Gyles, Jason Yaeger, and David Hodell
2014 Assessing the Great Maya Droughts: Some Critical Issues. In *The Great Maya Droughts in Cultural Context: Case Studies in Resilience and Vulnerability,* edited by G. Iannone, pp. 51-70. University Press of Colorado, Boulder, Colorado.

Illich, Ivan
1981 *Shadow Work.* Marion Boyars, London.

Isakson, S. Ryan
2009 No Hay Ganancia en la Milpa: The Agrarian Question, Food Sovereignty, and the On-Farm Conservation of Agrobiodiversity in the Guatemalan Highlands. *Journal of Peasant Studies* 36(4):725-759.

Isendahl, Christian
2002 *Common Knowledge: Lowland Maya Urban Farming at Xuch.* Ph.D. thesis, Department of Archaeology and Ancient History, Uppsala University, Uppsala, Sweden.

Isendahl, Christian, Nicholas P. Dunning, and Jeremy A. Sabloff
2014 Growth and Decline in Classic Maya Puuc Political Economies. In *The Resilience and Vulnerability of Ancient Landscapes: Transforming Maya Archaeology through IHOPE.* Archeological Papers of the American Anthropological Association 24:43-55.

Islebe, Gerald. A., Henry Hooghiemstra, Mark Brenner, Jason H. Curtis, and David A. Hodell
1996b A Holocene Vegetation History from Lowland Guatemala. *The Holocene* 6:265-271.

Islebe, Gerald A, H. Hooghiemstra, and R. Van't Veer
1996a Holocene Vegetation and Water Table History from Two Bogs of the Cordillerade Talamanca, Costa Rica. *Vegetation* 124:155–171.

Islebe, Gerald A. and Odilon Sánchez
2001 History of Late Holocene Vegetation at Quintana Roo, Caribbean Coast of México. *Plant Ecology* 160(2):187-192.

Jacke, Dave, and Eric Toensmeier
2005 *Edible Forest Gardens.* Chelse Green Publishing,Vermont.

Johnson, Allen W. and Timothy K. Earle
1987 *The Evolution of Human Societies: From Foraging Group to Agrarian State.* Stanford University Press, Stanford, California.

Johnston, Kevin, Fernando Moscoso Moller, and Stefan Schmitt
1992 Casas No-Visibles De Los Mayas Clásicos: Estructuras Residenciales Sin Plataformas Basales En Itzan, Petén. In *V Simposio de Investigaciones Arqueológicas en Guatemala*, edited by J. P. Laporte, H. Escobedo, and S. Brady. Museo Nacional de Arqueología y Etnología, Guatemala.

Johnston, Kevin J.
2002 Protrusion, Bioturbation, and Settlement Detection during Surface Survey: The Lowland Maya Case. *Journal of Archaeological Method and Theory* 9(1):1-67.
2003 The Intensification of Pre-Industrial Cereal Agriculture in the Tropics: Boserup, Cultivation Lengthening, and the Classic Maya. *Journal of Anthropological Archaeology* 22(2):126-161.

Jones, Grant D.
1998 *The Conquest of the Last Maya Kingdom*. University of Stanford Press, Stanford, California.

Jones, Lea D.
1986 *Lowland Maya Pottery: The Place of Petrological Analysis*. BAR International Series 288. British Archaeological Reports, Oxford, UK.

Karthik, Teegalapalli, Gopi Govindhan Veeraswami, and Prasanna Kumar Samal
2009 Forest Recovery Following Shift Cultivation: An Overview of Existing Research. *Tropical Conservation Science* 2(4):374-387.

Katz, Solomon, M. L. Hediger, and L. A. Valleroy
1974 Traditional Maize Processing Techniques in the New World: Traditional Alkali Processing Enhances the Nutritional Quality of Maize. *Science* 184:765-773.

Kellman, Martin and Rosanne Tackaberry
1997 *Tropical Environments: The Functioning and Management of Tropical Ecosystems*. Routledge, New York.

Kellman, Martin C. and C. D. Adams
1970 Milpa Weeds of the Cayo District, Belize (British Honduras). *Canadian Geographer/Le Géographe Canadien* XIV(4):323-343.

Kelly, Isabel T. and Angel Palerm
1952 *The Tajin Totonac*. U. S. Govt. Print. Office, Washington, D.C.

Kelly, Robert L. and David H. Thomas
2013 *Archaeology*. 6th ed. Wadsworth Cengage Learning, New York.

Kennett, Douglas J., Sebastian F. M. Breitenbach, Valorie V. Aquino, Yemane Asmerom, Jaime Awe, James U. L. Baldini, Patrick Bartlein, Brendan J. Culleton, Claire Ebert, Christopher Jazwa, Martha J. Macri, Norbert Marwan, Victor Polyak, Keith M. Prufer, Harriet E. Ridley, Harald Sodemann, Bruce Winterhalder, and Gerald H. Haug
2012 Development and Disintegration of Maya Political Systems in Response to Climate Change. *Science* 338:788-791.

Kennett, Douglas J., Dolores R. Piperno, John G. Jones, Hector Neff, Barbara Voorhies, Megan K. Walsh, and Brendan J. Culleton
2010 Pre-pottery Farmers on the Pacific Coast of Southern México. *Journal of Archaeological Science* 37(2010):3401-3411.

Kennett, Douglas J., Barbara Voorhies, and Sarah B. McClure
2002 Los Cerritos: An Early Fishing-Farming Community on the Pacific Coast of México. *Antiquity* 76:631-632.

Kintz, Ellen R.
1990 *Life Under the Tropical Canopy: Tradition and Change Among the Yucatec Maya*. Case Studies in Cultural Anthropology. Holt, Rinehart and Winston, Inc., Fort Worth.

Kolb, Charles C.
1985 Demographic Estimates in Archaeology: Contributions from Ethnoarchaeology on Mesoamerican Peasants. *Current Anthropology* 26(5):581-599.

LVC, La Via Campesina
2014 The International Peasant's Voice. La Via Campesina. Electronic document. http://viacampesina.org/en/index.php/organisation-mainmenu-44/what-is -la-via-campesina-mainmenu-45. December 2014.

Lal, R.
2004 Soil Carbon Sequestration Impacts on Global Climate Change and Food Security. *Science* 304:1623-1627.

Lambert, J. D. H. and J. T. Arnason
1982 Ramon and Maya Ruins: An Ecological Not an Economic Relation. *Science* 216(4543):298-299.

Lentz, David L. and Brian Hockaday
2009 Tikal Timbers and Temples: Ancient Maya Agroforestry and the End of Time. *Journal of Archaeological Science* 36:1342-1353.

Lentz, D. L., S. Woods, A. Hood and M. Murph
2012 Agroforestry and Agricultural Production of the Ancient Maya at the Chan Site. In *Chan: An Ancient Maya Farming Community*, edited by C. Robin, pp 89-112. University Press of Florida, Gainesville, Florida.

Lentz, David L., Nicholas P. Dunning, Vernon L. Scarborough, Kevin S. Magee, Kim M. Thompson, Eric Weaver, Christopher Carr, Richard E. Terry, Gerald Islebe, Kenneth B. Tankersley, Liwy Grazioso Sierra, John G. Jones, Palma Buttles, Fred Valdez, and Carmen E. Ramos Hernandez
2014 Forests, Fields, and the Edge of Sustainability at the Ancient Maya City of Tikal. *Proceedings of the National Academy of Science* 111:18513-18518.

Leung, Woot-tsuen Wu and Marina Flores
1961 INCAP-ICNND Food Composition Table for Use in Latin America. Interdepartmental Committee on Nutrition for National Defense, National Institutes of Health, Bethesda, Maryland.

Levi, Laura J.
1996 Sustainable Production and Residential Variation: A Historical Perspective on Pre-Hispanic Domestic Economies in the Maya Lowlands. In *The Managed Mosaic: Ancient Maya Agriculture and Resource Use*, edited by S. Fedick, pp. 92-106. University of Utah Press, Salt Lake City, Utah.
2002 An Institutional Perspective on Prehispanic Maya Residential Variation: Settlement and Community at San Estevan, Belize. *Journal of Anthropological Archaeology* 21:120-141.
2003 Space and the Limits to Community. In *Perspectives on Ancient Maya Rural Complexity*, edited by G. Iannone and S. Connell, pp. 89-93. Cotsen Institute of Archaeology, Los Angeles.

Levy Tacher, Samuel I.
2000 *Sucesión Causada por Roza-Tumba-Quema en las Selvas de Lacanhá Chansayab, Chiapas*. Ph.D. thesis, Botany, Colegio de Postgraduados, Montecillo, México.
2012 Applying Traditional Knowledge to Forest Restoration in Lacandon Forest, México. In *Ecological Restoration for Protected Areas: Principles, Guidelines and Best Practices*, edited by K. Keenelyside, N. Dudley, S. Cairns, C. Hall, and S. Stolton. IUCN, Gland, Switzerland.

Levy Tacher, Samuel Israel and J. Rogelio Aguirre Rivera
2005 Successional Pathways Derived from Different Vegetation Use Patterns by Lacandon Maya. *Journal of Sustainable Agriculture* 26(1):49-82.

Levy Tacher, Samuel Israel, J. Rogelio Aguirre Rivera, María Magdalena Martínez Romero, and Alejando Durán Fernández
2002 Caracterización del Uso Tradicional de la Flora Espontánea en la Comunidad Lacandona de Lacanhá, Chiapas, México. *Interciencia* 27(10):512-520.

Levy Tacher, Samuel Israel and John Duncan Golicher
2004 How Predictive is Traditional Ecological Knowledge? The Case of the Lacandon Maya Fallow Enrichment System. *Interciencia* 29(9):496-503.

Leyden, Barbara W.
1984 Guatemalan Forest Synthesis After Pleistocene Aridity. *Proceedings of the National Academy of Sciences of the United States of America-Biological Sciences* 81(15):4856-4859.
1987 Man and Climate in the Maya Lowlands. *Quaternary Research* 28(3):407-417.
2002 Pollen Evidence for Climatic Variability and Cultural Disturbance in the Maya Lowlands. *Ancient Mesoamerica* 13(1):85-101.

Leyden, Barbara W., Mark Brenner, David A. Hodell, and Jason H. Curtis
1993 Late Pleistocene Climate in the Central American Lowlands. In *Climate in Continental Isotopic Records*, edited by P. K. Swart, pp. xiii, 374. 78 ed. Geophysical Monograph. American Geophysical Union, Washington, D.C.

Liendo, Rodrigo, Elizabeth Solleiro-Rebolledo, Berenice Solis-Castillo, Sergei Sedov, and Arturo Ortiz-Perez
2014 Population Dynamics and Its Relation to Ancient Landscapes in the Northwestern Maya Lowlands: Evaluating Resilience and Vulnerability. In *The Resilience and Vulnerability of Ancient Landscapes: Transforming Maya Archaeology through IHOPE*. Archeological Papers of the American Anthropological Association 24: 84-100.

Linares, Olga F.
1976 "Garden Hunting" in the American Tropics. *Human Ecology* 4(4):331-349.

Lohse, Jon C.
2005 Preceramic Occupations of Belize. *Research Reports in Belizean Archaeology* 2:441-458.
2010 Archaic Origins of the Lowland Maya. *Latin American Antiquity* 21(3):312-352.

Lohse, Jon C., Jaime Awe, Cameron Griffith, Robert Rosenswig, and Fred Valdez
2006 Preceramic Occupations in Belize: Updating the Paleoindian and Archaic Record. *Latin American Antiquity* 17(2):209-226.

Lope-Alzina, Diana G. and Patricia L. Howard
2012 The Structure, Composition and Functions of Homegardens: Focus on the Yucatán Peninsula. *Etnoecologica* 9(1):17-41.

Lopez Morales, Francisco Javier
1993 *Arquitectura Vernácula en México*. 1a. ed. Fondo Internacional para la Promoción de la Cultura Unesco: Editorial Trillas, México.

Lucero, Lisa
2002 The Collapse of the Classic Maya: A Case for the Role of Water Control. *American Anthropologist* 104(3):814-826.

Lucero, Lisa J., Scott L. Fedick, Nicholas Dunning, David L. Lentz, and Vernon L. Scarborough
2014 Water and Landscape: Ancient Maya Settlement Decisions. In *The Resilience and Vulnerability of Ancient Landscapes: Transforming Maya Archaeology through IHOPE*. Archeological Papers of the American Anthropological Association 24:30-42.

Lundell, Cyrus Longworth
1933 The Agriculture of the Maya. *Southwest Review* XIX:65-77.
1937 *The Vegetation of Petén. With an Appendix: Studies of Mexican and Central American Plants - 1*. Carnegie Institution of Washington, Washington, D.C.

Maat, Harro
2015 Commodities and Anticommodities: Rice on Sumatra 1915-1925. In *Rice: Global Networks and New Histories*, edited by F. Bray, P. Coclanis, E. Fields-Black, and D. Schafer, pp. 335-354. Cambridge University Press, New York.

Machtmes, Krisianna
2011 Plants and Animals, Partners in Pollination, America's Research-based Learning Network. LSU AgCenter. Electronic document. www.extension.org/pages/29464/plants-and-animals-partners-in-pollination#.VHOoUovF8Rp. December 2014.

MacNeish, Richard S.
1982 *Third Annual Report of the Belize Archaic Archaeological Reconnaissance*. Robert S. Peabody Foundation for Archaeology.

Macri, Martha J. and Anabel Ford (editors)
1997 *The Language of Maya Hieroglyphs*. Pre-Columbian Art Research Institute, San Francisco.

Mann, Charles C.
2005 *1491: New Revelations of the Americas before Columbus*. Alfred A. Knopf, New York.

MARC, MesoAmerican Research Center
2014 Adaptive Management. MesoAmerican Research Center, University of California, Santa Barbara. Electronic document. www.marc.ucsb.edu/research/conservation-philosophy/adaptive-management. December 2014.

Mariaca Méndez, Ramón (editor)
2012 *El Huerto Familiar en el Sureste de México*. Estado de Tabasco & El Colegio de la Frontera Sur, Villahermosa, Tabasco, México.

Martínez Torres, María Elena, and Peter Rosset
2010 La Vıa Campesina: the Birth and Evolution of a Transnational Social Movement. *Journal of Peasant Studies* 37 (1):149-175.

Maya Forest Gardeners
2015 Plant Resources of the El Pilar Maya Forest Garden Network. Electronic document. www.mayaforestgardeners.org/db-plant.php. March 2015.

Maya Nut Institute
2014 Finding Balance Between People, Food, and Forest. Electronic document. http://mayanutinstitute.org/. December 2014.

Mayewski, Paul A., Eelco E. Rohling, J. Curt Stager, Wibjöm Karlen, Kirk A. Maasch, L. David Meeker, Eric A. Meyerson, Francoise Gasse, Sirley van Kreveld, Karin Holmgren, Julia Lee-Thorp, Gunhild Rosqvist, Frank Rack, Michael Staubwasser, Ralph R. Schneider, and Eric J. Steig
2004 Holocene Climate Variability. *Quaternary Research* 62:243-255.

McAnany, Patricia and Shoshanna Parks
2012 Casualties of Heritage Distancing: Children, Ch'orti' Indigeneity, and Copán Archaeoscape. *Current Anthropology* 53(1):80-107.

McAnany, Patricia A.
1993 The Economics of Social Power and Wealth Among Eighth-Century Maya Households. In *Lowland Maya Civilization in the Eighth Century A.D.*, edited by J. A. Sabloff and J. S. Henderson, pp. 65-89. A symposium at Dumbarton Oaks, 7th and 8th October 1989. Dumbarton Oaks. Dumbarton Oaks Research Library and Collection, Washington, D.C.
1995 *Living with the Ancestors: Kinship and Kingship in Ancient Maya Society*. 1st ed. University of Texas Press, Austin, Texas.

McCann, J. M., W. I. Woods and D. W. Meyer
2001 Organic Matter and Anthrosols in Amazonia: Interpreting the Amerindian Legacy. In *Sustainable Management of Soil Organic Matter*, edited by R. M. Rees, B. C. Ball, D. G. Campbell, and A. Watson, pp. 180-189. CAB International, Wallingford, UK.

McClung de Tapia, Emily
1992 The Origins of Agriculture in Mesoamerica and Central America. In *The Origins of Agriculture: An International Perspective*, edited by C. W. Cowan and P. J. Watson, pp. 143-171. Smithsonian Institution Press, Washington, D.C.

McElwee, Pamela
2009 Reforesting "Bare Hills" in Vietnam: Social and Environmental Consequences of the 5 Million Hectare Reforestation Program. *Ambio* 38(6):325-333.

McNeil, Cameron L.
2012 Deforestation, Agroforestry, and Sustainable Land Management Practices among the Classic Period Maya. *Quaternary International* 249:19-30.

McNeil, Cameron L., David A. Burney, and Lida Pigott Burney
2010 Evidence Disputing Deforestation as the Cause for the Collapse of the Ancient Maya Polity of Copan, Honduras. *PNAS* 107:1017-1022.

Medellin, Rodrigo A.
1991 The Selva Lacandona: An Overview. *Tropical Conservation and Development Program Newsletter* 24:1-15.
1994a Mammal Diversity and Conservation in the Selva Lacandona, Chiapas, México. *Conservation Biology* 8(3):780-799.
1994b Seed Dispersal of Cecropia Obtusifolia by Two Species of Opossums in the Selva Lacandona, Chiapas, Mexico. *Biotropica* 26(4):400-407.

Medellin, Rodrigo A. and Miguel Equihua
1998 Mammal Species Richness and Habitat Use in Rainforest and Abandoned Agricultural Fields in Chiapas, México. *Journal of Applied Ecology* 35(1):13-23.

Medellin, Rodrigo A. and Osiris Gaona
1999 Seed Dispersal by Bats and Birds in Forest and Disturbed Habitats of Chiapas, México. *Biotropica* 31(3):478-485.

Medina-Elizalde, Martin and Eelco J. Rohling
2012 Collapse of Classic Maya Civilization Related to Modest Reduction in Precipitation. *Science* 335:956-959.

Meggers, Betty Jane
1954 Environmental Limitation on the Development of Culture. *American Anthropologist* 56:801-824.

MesoAmerican Research Center
2015 The Anceint Maya House and Forest Garden at Tzunu'un. Electronic document. www.marc.ucsb.edu/research/maya-forest-is-a-garden/ancient-maya-house-forest garden-Tzunuun. March 2015.

Merlet, Sébastien
2009 *Étude de l'utilisation des SIG dans le Cadre d'un Projet Archéologique Milti-échelles.* Master's thesis, Graduate School of Surveyors and Surveyors National Conservatory of Arts and Crafts Le Mans, France.
2010 Détermination des Besoins d'une Population Maya Durant la Période du Classique Tardif au Moyen d'un Modéle Prédictif. *Revue XYZ* 123(2):17-24.

Metcalfe, Jessica Z., Christine D. White, Fred J. Longstaffe, Gabriel Wrobe, Della Collins Cook, and K. Anne Pyburn
2009 Isotopic Evidence for Diet at Chau Hiix, Belize: Testing Regional Models of Hierarchy and Heterarchy. *Society for American Archaeology* 20(1):15-36.

Metcalfe, S.E., M.D. Jones, S.J. Davies, A. Noren, and A. MacKenzie
2010 Climate Variability over the Last Two Millennia in the North American Monsoon Region, Recorded in Laminated Lake Sediments from Laguna de Juanacatlán, México. *The Holocene* 20(8):1195-1206.

de Miguel, Jesus Garcia
2000 *Etnobotanica Maya: Origen y evolucion de los Huertos Familiares de la Peninsula de Yucatán, México.* Ph.D. thesis, Escuela Técnica Superior de Ingenieros Agronómos y de Montes, Universidad de Cordoba, Cordoba, Spain.

Mittermeier, Russell A., Norman Myers, and Cristina Goettsh Mittermeier
2000 *Hotspots: Earth's Biologically Richest and Most Endangered Terrestrial Ecoregions.* CEMEX, México.

Montgomery, David R.
2007a Is Agriculture Eroding Civilization's Foundation? *GSA Today* 17(10):4-9.
2007b Soil Erosion and Agricultural Sustainability. *PNAS* 104(33):13268–13272.

Monthus, Florent
2004 *Weights of Evidence and Maya Settlement.* Master's thesis, Engineering, Ecole Superieure des Geometres et Topographes Le Mans, France.

Morley, Robert J.
2000 *Origin and Evolution of Tropical Rain Forests.* John Wiley & Sons, New York.

Mueller, A. D., F. S. Anselmetti, D Ariztegui, M. Benner, M.B. Hillesheim, D. A. Hodell, and J. A. McKenzie
2006 Climate Drying and Forest Decline (~4.0-3.0 calkyrBP) Preceding Sedentary Maya Occupation in the Lowlands of the Petén, Guatemala. *Geophysical Research Abstracts* 8:1784.

Mueller, Andreas D., Flavio S. Anselmetti, Daniel Ariztegui, Mark Brenner, David A. Hodell, Jason H. Curtis, Jaime Escobar, Adrian Gilli, Dustin A. Grzesik, Thomas P. Guilderson, Steffen Kutterolf, and Michael Plötze
2010 Late Quaternary Palaeoenvironment of Northern Guatemala: Evidence from Deep Drill Cores and Seismic Stratigraphy of Lake Petén Itza. *Sedimentology* 57:1220-1245.

Mueller, Andreas D., Gerald A. Islebe, Michael B. Hillesheim, Dustin A. Grzesik, Flavio S. Anselmetti, Daniel Ariztegui, Mark Brenner, Jason H. Curtis, David A. Hodell, and Kathryn A. Venz
2009 Climate Drying and Associated Forest Decline in the Lowlands of Northern Guatemala During the Late Holocene. *Quaternary Research* 71:133-141.

Nadal, Alejandro and Timothy A. Wise
2004 *The Environmental Costs of Agricultural Trade Liberalization: México-U.S. Maize Trade Under NAFTA.* The Working Group on Development and Environment in the Americas, Discussion Paper No. 4. Electronic document. http://ase.tufts.edu/gdae/pubs/rp/dp04nadalwisejuly04.pdf. March 2015.

NRC, National Research Council
1984 *Amaranth: Modern Prospects for an Ancient Crop.* National Academy Press. Washington, D.C. Electronic document. http://pdf.usaid.gov/pdf_docs/PNAAQ614.pdf. March 2015.

Nations, James D.
1979 *Population Ecology of the Lacandon Maya.* Ph.D. Dissertation, Department of Anthropology, Southern Methodist University, Dallas, Texas.
2006 *The Maya Tropical Forest: People, Parks, and Ancient Cities.* University of Texas Press, Austin, Texas.

Nations, James D. and Ronald Nigh
1980 The Evolutionary Potential of Lacandon Maya Sustained-Yield Tropical Forest Agriculture. *Journal of Anthropological Research* 36(1):1-30.

Nations, James D., Christopher J. Rader, and Ingrid Q. Neubauer (editors)
1999 *Thirteen Ways of Looking at a Tropical Forest: Guatemala's Maya Biosphere Reserve.* Conservation International, Washington, D.C.

Neff, Hector, Deborah M. Pearsall, John G. Jones, Bárbara Arroyo, Shawn K. Collins, and Dorothy E. Freidel
2006b Early Maya Adaptive Patterns: Mid-Late Holocene Paleoenvironmental Evidence from Pacific Guatemala. *Latin American Antiquity* 17(3):287-315.

Neff, Hector, Deborah Pearsall, John G. Jones, Barbara Arroyo de Pieters, and Dorothy E. Freidel
2006a Climate Change and Population History in the Pacific Lowlands of Southern Mesoamerica. *Quaternary Research* 65:390-400.

Negreros-Castillo, P. and R. B. Hall
2000 Sprouting Capability of 17 Tropical Tree Species after Overstory Removal in Quintana Roo, México. *Forest Ecology and Management* 126:399-403.

Nesheim, Ingrid, Rune Halvorsen, and Inger Nordal
2010 Plant Composition in the Maya Biosphere Reserve: Natural and Anthropogenic Influences. *Plant Ecology* 208(1):93-122.

Netting, Robert McC.
1965 Household Organization and Intensive Agriculture: The Kofyar Case. *Africa: Journal of the International African Institute* 35(4):422-429.
1968 Hill Farmers of Nigeria: Cultural Ecology of the Kofyar of the Jos 1974 Agrarian Ecology. *Annual Review of Anthropology* 3:21-56.
1977 Maya Subsistence: Mythologies, Analogies, Possibilities. In *The Origins of Maya Civilization*, edited by R. E. W. Adams, pp. 299-333. University of New Mexico Press, Albuquerque, New Mexico.
1993 *Smallholders, Householders: Farm Families and the Ecology of Intensive, Sustainable Agriculture*. Stanford University Press, Stanford, California.

Netting, Robert McC., M. P. Stone, and Glenn Davis Stone
1989 Kofyar Cash Cropping: Choice and Change in Indigenous Agricultural Development. *Human Ecology* 17:299-319.

Nigh, Ronald
1999 The Contested Mosaic: Biodiversity Conversation and Human Livelihood in the Lacandon Rainforest (Chiapas, México). Paper presented at the Open Meeting of the Human Dimensions of Global Environmental Change Research Community, Shonan Village, Kanagawa, Japan.
2008 Trees, Fire and Farmers: Making Woods and Soil in the Maya Forest. *Journal of Ethnobiology* 28(2):231-243.

Nigh, Ronald and Stewart Diemont
2013 The Maya milpa: fire and the legacy of living soil. *Frontiers in Ecology and the Environment* 11 (s1):e45-e54. Electronic document. http://www.esajournals.org/doi/pdf/10.1890/120344

Nikolic, Nina, Rainer Schultze-Kraft, Miroslav Nikolic, Reinhard Bocker, and Ingo Holz
2008 Land Degradation on Barren Hills: A Case Study in Northeast Vietnam. *Environmental Management* 2008(42):19-36.

Ollerton, Jeff, Rachek Winfree, and Sam Tarrant
2011 How Many Flowering Plants are Pollinated by Animals? *Oikos* 120:321-326.

Orrego Corzo, Miguel and Rudy Larios Villalta
1983 *Tikal, Petén: Reporte de las Investigaciones Arqueologicas en el Grupo 5E-11*. Instituto de Antropologia e Historia de Guatemala, Parque Nacional Tikal, Guatemala.

Ortega, Salvador Montiel and Luis Manuel Arias Reyes
2008 La Cacería Tradicional en el Mayab Contemporáneo: Una Mirada Desde la Ecología Humana. *Avance y Perspectiva* Abril-Junio:21-27.

Packham, J. R., D. J. L. Harding, G. M. Hilton, and R. A. Stuttard
1992 *Functional Ecology of Woodlands and Forests*. Chapman & Hall, London [England].

Padoch, Christine
1982 Land Use in New and Old Areas of Iban Settlement. *Borneo Research Bulletin* 14(1):3-14.

Palerm, Angel
    1967 Agricultural Systems and Food Patterns. In *Handbook of Middle American Indians*, edited by R. Wauchope and M. Nash, pp. 26-52,Vol 6. Social Anthropology, Austin, Texas, University of Texas Press, Austin Texas.
    1976 Agriculture and Food Patterns. In *Handbook of Middle American Indians* edited by R. Wauchope and N. Manning, pp. 26-52, Vol. 6. University of Texas Press, Austin, Texas.

Palka, Joel
    2005 *Unconquered Lacandon Maya: Ethnohistory and Archaeology of Indigenous Culture Change*. University Press of Florida, Gainesville, Florida.

Parsons, David, Luis Ramırez-Aviles, Jerome H. Cherney, Quirine M. Ketterings, Robert W. Blake, and Charles F. Nicholson
    2009 Managing Maize Production in Shifting Cultivation Milpa Systems in Yucatán, Through Weed Control and Manure Application. *Agriculture, Ecosystems and Environment* 133(1-2):123-134.

Patiño Valera, Fernando, Roberto Centeno Erguerra, and Juana Marín Chávez
    2003 Conservation and use of mahogany in forest ecosystems in Mexico. Electronic document. www.fao.org/docrep/005/y4586e/y4586e07.htm#TopOfPage. March 2015.

Peters, Charles M.
    1983 Observations on Maya Subsistence and the Ecology of a Tropical Tree. *American Antiquity* 48(3):610-615.
    2000 Precolumbian Silviculture and Indigenous Management of Neotropical Forests. In *Imperfect Balance: Landscape Transformations in the Precolumbian Americas*, edited by D. L. Lentz, pp. 203-223. Columbia University Press, New York.

Peterson, J. B., E. G. Neves, and Michael J. Heckenberger
    2001 Gift from the Past: Terra Preta and Prehistoric Amerindian Occupation in Amazonia. In *Unknown Amazon*, edited by C. McEwan, pp. 86-105. British Museum, London.

Peterson, Larry C., Gerald H. Haug, Konrad A. Hughen and Ursula Rohl
    2000 Rapid Changes in the Hydrologic Cycle of the Tropical Atlantic During the Last Glacial. *Science* 290:1947-1951.

Peterson, Larry C. and Gerald H. Haug
    2005 Climate and the Collapse of Maya Civilization: A Series of Multi-Year Droughts Helped to Doom an Ancient Culture. *American Scientist* 93(4):322-329.

Pilcher, Jeffrey M.
    1998 *¡Qué vivan los tamales! Food and the Making of Mexican Identity*. Diálogos. University of New Mexico Press, Albuquerque, New Mexico.

Piperno, Dolores
    2011 Prehistoric Human Occupation and Impacts on Neotropical Forest Landscapes during the Late Pleistocene and Early/Middle Holocene. In *Tropical Rainforest Reponses to Climatic Change*, edited by M. B. Bush, J. R. Flenley, and W. D. Gosling. Cambridge University Press, Cambridge, United Kingdom.

Piperno, Dolores R.
    2006 Quaternary Environmental History and Agricultural Impact on Vegetation in Central America. *Annals of the Missouri Botanical Garden* 93(2):274-296.

Piperno, Dolores R. and Deborah M. Pearsall
    1998 *The Origins of Agriculture in the Lowland Neotropics*. Academic Press, San Diego, California.

Piperno, Dolores R. and Karen E. Stothert
    2003 Phytolith Evidence for Early Holocene Cucurbita Domestication in Southwest Ecuador. *Science* 299:1054-1057.

Ploeg, Jan Douwe van der
2013 Peasant-driven Agricultural Growth and Food Sovereignty. Paper presented at the Food Sovereignty: A Critical Dialogue International Conference. Electronic document. www.yale.edu/agrarianstudies/foodsovereignty/pprs/8_van_der_Ploeg_2013. pdf. March 2015.

Pohl, Mary D., Dolores R. Piperno, Kevin O. Pope, and John G. Jones
2007 Microfossil Evidence for Pre-Columbian Maize Dispersals in the Neotropics from San Andrés, Tabasco, México. *Proceedings of the National Academy of Sciences* 104:6870-6875.

Pohl, Mary D., Kevin O. Pope, John G. Jones, John S. Jacob, Dolores R. Piperno, Susan D. deFrance, David L. Lentz, John A. Gifford, Marie E. Danforth, and J. Kathryn Josserand
1996 Early Agriculture in the Maya Lowlands. *Latin American Antiquity* 7(4):355-372.

Polanyi, Karl
2001[1944] *The Great Transformation: The Political and Economic Origins of Our Time.* Beacon Press, Boston.

Pope, Kevin O., Mary E. Pohl, John G. Jones, David L. Lentz, Christopher von Nagy, Francisco J. Vega, and Irvy R. Quitmyer
2001 Origin and Environmental Setting of Ancient Agriculture in the Lowlands of Mesoamerica. *Science* 292.1370-1373.

Primack, Richard, David Bray, Hugo Galleti, and Ismael Ponciano (editors)
1998 *Timber, Tourists, and Temples: Conservation and Development in the Maya Forest of Belize, Guatemala, and México.* Island Press, Washington, D.C.

Pugh, Timothy W., José Rómolo Sánchez, and Yoko Shiratori
2012 Contact and Missionization at Tayasal, Petén, Guatemala. *Journal of Field Archaeology* 37(1):3-19.

Puleston, Dennis E.
1968 *Brosimum Alicastrum as a Subsistence Alternative for the Classic Maya of the Central Southern Lowlands.* Master's thesis, Department of Anthropology, University of Pennsylvania, Philadelphia.
1973 Ancient Maya Settlement Patterns and Environment at Tikal, Guatemala: Implications for Subsistence Models. Ph.D. Dissertation. Department of Anthropology, University of Pennsylvania, Philadelphia.
1974 Intersite Area in the Vicinity of Tikal and Uaxactun. In *Mesoamerican Archaeology*, edited by N. Hammond, pp. 303-312. Duckworth, London.
1982 Appendix 2: The Role of Ramon in Maya Subsistence. In *Maya Subsistence: Studies in Memory of Dennis E. Puleston,* edited by Kent Flannery, pp 353-366. Academic Press, New York.
1983 *Tikal Report No. 13: The Settlement Survey of Tikal.* University Museum Monograph 48 No. 13. The University Museum, University of Pennsylvania, Philadelphia.

Puleston, Dennis E. and O. Puleston
1971 An Ecological Approach to the Origins of Maya Civilization. *Archaeology* 24(4):330-337.
1972 A Processual Model for the Rise of Classic Maya Civilization in the Southern Lowlands. *Proceedings of the 40th International Congress of Americanists* 2:119-124. Roma-Genoa, Italy.

Pyburn, K. Anne
1998 Smallholder in the Maya Lowlands: Homage to a Garden Variety Ethnographer. *Human Ecology* 26(2):267-286.

Quintana-Ascencio, Pedro Francisco, Mario Gonzales-Espinosa, Neptali Ramiraz-Marcial, Gabriela Domínguez-Vázquez, and Miguel Martinez-Ico
1996 Soil Seed Banks and Regeneration of Tropical Rain Forest from Milpa Fields at the Selva Lacandona, Chiapas, México. *Biotropica* 28(2):192-209.

Rackham, Oliver
  2006 *Woodlands*. Collins New Naturalist. HarperCollins UK, London.
Raines, G. L., G. F. Bonham-Carter, and L. D. Kemp
  2000 Weights of Evidence - An Arcview Extension for Predictive Probabilistic Modeling Document. University of Campinas, São Paulo. Brazil. Electronic document. www.ige.unicamp.br/sdm/default_e.htm. December 2014.
Rätsch, Christian
  1992 Their Word for World is Forest: Cultral Ecology and Religion among the Lacandone Maya Indians of Southern México. *Jahrbuch für Ethnomedizin und Bewusstseinsforschung* 1:17-32.
Redfield, Robert and Alfonso Villa Rojas
  1962 *Chan Kom, A Maya Village*. University of Chicago Press, Chicago.
Redman, C. L.
  1999 *Human Impact on Ancient Environments*. University of Arizona Press, Tucson, Arizona.
Reina, Ruben E.
  1967 Milpas and Milperos: Implications for Prehistoric Times. *American Anthropologist, New Series* 69(1):1-20.
Repussard, Antoine, Henry P. Schwarcz, Kitty F. Emery, and Erin K. Thornton
  2014 Oxygen Isotopes from Maya Archaeological Deer Remains: Experiments in Tracing Droughts Using Bones. In *The Great Maya Droughts in Cultural Context: Case Studies in Resilience and Vulnerability*, edited by G. Iannone, pp. 231-253. University Press of Colorado, Boulder, Colorado.
Rice, Don S.
  1976 *The Historical Ecology of Lakes Yaxhá and Sacnab, El Petén, Guatemala*. Ph.D. dissertation, Anthropology, Pennsylvania State University, University Park, State College, Pennsylvania.
  1996 Paleolimnological Analysis in the Central Petén, Guatemala. In *The Managed Mosaic: Ancient Maya Agriculture and Resource Use*, edited by S. L. Fedick, pp. 193-206. University of Utah Press, Salt Lake City, Utah.
Rice, Don S. and Dennis E. Puleston
  1981 Ancient Maya Settlement Patterns in the Petén, Guatemala. In *Lowland Maya Settlement Patterns*, edited by W. Ashmore, pp. 121-156, University of New Mexico Press, Albuquerque, New Mexico.
Rice, Don S. and Prudence M. Rice
  1990 Population Size and Population Change in the Central Petén Lakes Region, Guatemala. In *Precolumbian Population History in the Maya Lowlands*, edited by T. P. Culbert and D. S. Rice, pp. 123-148. University of New Mexico Press, Albuquerque, New Mexico.
Rico-Gray, Victor, Jose G. Garcia-Franco, Alexandra Chemas, Armando Puch, and Paulino Sima
  1990 Species Composition, Similarity, and Structure of Mayan Homegardens in Tixpeual and Tixcacaltuyub, Yucatán, México. *Economic Botany* 44(4):470-487.
Roberts, Paul
  2008 *The End of Food*. Houghton Mifflin Harcourt, New York.
Robin, Cynthia
  2001 Peopling the Past: New Perspectives on the Ancient Maya. *PNAS* 98(1):18-21.
  2002 Outside of Houses: The Practices of Everyday Life at Chan Nòohol, Belize. *Journal of Social Archaeology* 2:245-268.
  2004 Social Diversity and Everyday Life within Classic Maya Settlements. In *Mesoamerican Archaeology: Theory and Practice*, edited by J. A. Hendon and R. A. Joyce, pp. 148-168. Blackwell Publishing, Malden, Massachusetts.

2012 *Chan: An Ancient Maya Farming Community.* University Press of Florida, Gainesville, Florida.

2013 *Everyday Life Matters: Maya Farmers at Chan.* University Press of Florida, Gainesville, Florida.

Rojas Rabiela, Teresa

1990 La Agricultura en la Epoca Prehispanica. In *La Agricultura en Tierras Mexicanas Desde sus Orígenes hasta Nuestros Días,* edited by T. R. Rabiela. Editorial Grijalbo-CONACULTA, México.

Roman Dañobeytia, Francisco, Samuel Israel Levy Tacher, J. Rogelio Aguirre Rivera, David Douterlungne, and Antonio Sanchez Gonzalez

2009 *Arboles de la Selva Lacandona Utiles para la Restauración Ecológica.* El Colegio de la Frontera Sur, San Cristóbal de Las Casas, Chiapas, México.

Roman Dañobeytia, Francisco, Samuel Israel Levy Tacher, James Aronson, Ricardo Ribeiro Rodrígues, and Jorge Castellanos Albores

2011 Testing the Performance of Fourteen Native Tropical Tree Species in Two Abandoned Pastures of the Lacandon Rainforest Region of Chiapas, México. *Restoration Ecology* 20(3):378–386.

Romero-Balderas, Karina G., Eduardo J. Naranjo, Helda H. Morales, and Ronald B. Nigh

2006 Danos Ocasionados por Vertebrados Silvestres al Cultivo de Maiz en la Selva Lacandona, Chiapas, México. *Interciencia* 31(4):276-283.

Rosen, Arlene Miller

2007 *Civilizing Climate: Social Responses to Climate Change in the Ancient Near East.* AltaMira Press, Lanham, Maryland.

Rosenmeier, Michael F., David A. Hodell, Mark Brenner, Jason H. Curtis, and Thomas P. Guilderson

2002 A 4,000-Year Lacustrine Record of Environmental Change in the Southern Maya Lowlands, Petén, Guatemala. *Quaternary Research* 57(2):183-190.

Rosenswig, Robert M.

2006a Northern Belize and the Soconusco: A Comparison of the Late Archaic to Formative Transition. *Research Reports in Belizean Archaeology* 3:59-71.

2006b Sedentism and Food Production in Early Complex Societies of Soconusco, México. *World Archaeology* 38(2):330-355.

Rosenswig, Robert M. and M. A. Masson

2001 Seven New Preceramic Sites Documented in Northern Belize. *Mexicon* XXIII:138-140.

Rosenswig, Robert M., Deborah M. Pearsall, Marilyn A. Masson, Brendan J. Culleton, and Douglas J. Kennett

2014 Archaic Period Settlement and Subsistence in the Maya Lowlands: New Starch Grain and Lithic Data from Freshwater Creek, Belize. *Journal of Archaeological Science* 41:308-321.

Ross, Nanci J.

2008 *The Impact of Ancient Maya Forest Gardens on Modern Tree Species Composition in NW Belize.* Ph.D. dissertation, Ecology, University of Connecticut.

2011 Modern Tree Species Composition Reflects Ancient Maya "Forest Gardens" in Northwest Belize. *Ecological Applications* 21(1):75-84.

Ross, Nanci J. and Thiago F. Rangel

2011 Ancient Maya Agroforestry Echoing Through Spatial Relationships in the Extant Forest of NW Belize. *Biotropica* 43(2):141-148.

Roys, Ralph L.

1952 Conquest Sites and Subsequent Destruction of Maya Architecture in the Interior of Northern Yucatán. *Contributions to American Anthropology and History* 11:129-182.

1976 *The Ethno-Botany of the Maya.* ISHS Reprints on the Latin America and the Caribbean. Institute for the Study of Human Issues, Philadelphia.

Rue, D. J.
1989   Archaic Middle American Agriculture and Settlement: Recent Pollen Data from Honduras. *Journal of Field Archaeology* 16:177-184.

Rushton, Elizabeth A. C., Sarah E. Metcalfe, and Bronwen S. Whitney
2012 A Late-Holocene Vegetation History from the Maya Lowlands, Lamanai, Northern Belize. *The Holocene* 23(4):485-493.

Sanchez, P. A.
2012 Soils. In *Tropical Rain Forest Ecosystems: Biogeographical and Ecological Studies*, edited by H. Lieth and M. J. A. Werger, pp. 73-88. Elsevier Science Publishers, New York.

Sanders, W. T
1981 Classic Maya Settlement Patterns and Ethnographic Analogy. In *Lowland Maya Settlement Patterns*, edited by W. Ashmore, pp. 351-369. University of New Mexico, Albuquerque, New Mexico.

Scarborough, Vernon L.
2003 *The Flow of Power: Ancient Water Systems and Landscapes*. A School of American Research Resident Scholar Book. School of American Research, Santa Fe, New Mexico.

Scarborough, Vernon L. and William R. Burnside
2010 Complexity and Sustainability: Perspectives on the Ancient Maya and Modern Balinese. *American Antiquity* 75(2):327-363.

Scarborough, Vernon L. and Fred Valdez
2014 The Alternative Economy: Resilience in the Face of Complexity from the Eastern Lowlands. In *The Resilience and Vulnerability of Ancient Landscapes: Transforming Maya Archaeology through IHOPE*. Archeological Papers of the American Anthropological Association 24:124-141.

Scarborough, Vernon L. and Lucero, L.
2011 The Non-Hierarchical Development of Complexity in the Semitropics: Water and Cooperation. *Water History* 2:185-205.

Schele, Linda and David A. Freidel
1990 *A Forest of Kings: The Untold Story of the Ancient Maya*. 1st ed. William Morrow, New York.

Schele, Linda and Peter Mathews
1998 Palenque: Hanab-Pakal's Tomb. In *The Code of Kings*, pp. 119-123. Scribner, New York.

Schlesinger, Victoria
2001 *Animals and Plants of the Ancient Maya: A Guide*. University of Texas Press, Austin, Texas.

de Schlippe, Pierre
1956 *Shifting Cultivation in Africa*. Routledge & Kegan Paul Limited, London.

Schmook, Brigit, Colin Vance, Peter Klepeis, Eric Keys, and Mirna E. Canul
2004 Características de los Ejidos al Sur de los Estados de Campeche y Quintana Roo, pp. 22. Proyecto de la Region Sur de Peninsula de Yucatán, Chetumal, Quintana Roo, México.

Schneider, L. C.
2004 *Understanding Bracken Fern (Pteridium aquilinum (L.) Kuhn) Invasion in the Southern Yucatan Peninsular Region through Integrated Land-Change Science*. Ph.D. thesis, Geography, Clark University, Worcester, Massachusetts.

Scholes, Mary C. and Robert J. Scholes
2013 Dust Unto Dust. *Science* 342:565-567.

Schulze, Mark D. and David F. Whitacre
1999 *A Classification and Ordination of the Tree Community of Tikal National Park, Petén, Guatemala*. Bulletin of the Florida Museum of Natural History, Vol 41. University of Florida, Gainsville, Florida.

Schwartz, Norman B.
1990 *Forest Society: A Social History of Petén, Guatemala*. University of Pennsylvania Press, Philadelphia.
1999 Tables of Plants in the Milpa. In *Field Notes 1960-1977*. On File at the Meso-American Research Center, University of California, Santa Barbara.

Schwartz, Norman B. and Amilcar Rolando Corzo Márquez
2015 Swidden Counts: A Petén, Guatemala Milpa System: Production, Carrying Capacity and Sustainability in the Southern Maya Lowlands. *Journal of Anthropological Research* 71(1):69-93.

Scott, James C.
1998 *Seeing Like a State: How Certain Schemes to Improve the Human Condition Have Failed*. Yale University Press, New Haven, Connecticut.
2009 *The Art of Not Being Governed*. Yale Agrarian Studies Series. Yale University Press, New Haven, Connecticut.

Service, Elman Rogers
1962 *Primitive Social Organization: An Evolutionary Perspective*. Random House Studies in Anthropology. Random House, New York.
1975 *Origins of the State and Civilization: The Process of Cultural Evolution*. Norton, New York.

Sheets, Payson D.
1992 *The Ceren Site: A Prehistoric Village Buried by Volcanic Ash in Central America*. Case Studies in Archaeology Series. Harcourt Brace Jovanovich College Publishers; Shepard, Mark
2013 *Restoration Agriculture: Real-World Permaculture for Farmers*. Acres U.S.A, Austin, Texas.

Siebert, Stephen, Jill Belsky, Sangay Wangchuk, and James Riddering
2014 The End of Swidden in Bhutan: Implications for Forest Cover and Biodiversity. In *A Growing Forest of Voices*, edited by M. Cairns. Earthscan, London.

Siebert, Stephen F. and Jill M. Belsky
2014 Historic Livelihoods and Land Uses as Ecological Disturbances and their Role in Enhancing Biodiversity: An Example from Bhutan. *Biological Conservation* 177(2014):82-89.

Sirjean, Elise
2003 *Creation and Validation of a Predictive Model of Ancient Maya Settlements with a Statistical Method*. Master's thesis, Ecole Superieure des Geometres et Topographes, Conservatoire National des Arts et Metiers, Le Mans, France.

Smalley, John and Michael Blake
2003 Sweet Beginnings: Stalk Sugar and the Domestication of Maize. *Current Anthropology* 44(5):675-703.

Smith, Bruce D.
1998 Origins of Agriculture Enhanced: Between Foraging and Farming. *Science* 279(5357):1651-1652.

Smith, Jr., C. Earle and Marguerita L. Cameron
1977 Ethnobotany in the Puuc, Yucatán. *Economic Botany* 31(2):93-110.

Smithsonian Institution
2014 Plants and Animals, Partners in Pollination. *Smithsonian Education*. vol. 2014. Smithsonian Center for Learning and Digital Access. Electronic document. www.smithsonianeducation.org/educators/lesson_plans/partners_in_pollination/. December 2014.

Smyth, Michael P.
1991 *Modern Maya Storage Behavior: Ethnoarchaeological Case Examples from the Puuc Region of Yucatán*. University of Pittsburgh Latin America Archaeology Publications, Pittsburg, Pennsylvania.

Snook, Laura
1998 Sustaining Harvests of Mahogany (*Swietenia macrophylla* King) from México's Yucatán Forests: Past, Present, and Future. In *Timber, Tourists, and Temples*, edited by L. R. Primech, D. Bray, and H. Galleti. Island Press, San Francisco.
2005 Sustaining Mahogany: Research and Silviculture in México's Community Forests. *Bios Forets des Tropiques* 285(3):55-65.

Snook, Laura K., Patricia Negreros-Castillo and Jennifer O'Connor
2005 Supervivencia y Crecimiento de Plántulas de Caoba en Aperturas Creadas en la Selva Maya de Belize y México. *Recursos Naturales y Ambiente* 44:91-99.

Snook, Laura K. and Riamondo Capitanio
2012 Restoring Valuable Diversity through Patch Clearcuts in Tropical Forests: Slash and Burn is Best. *Bioversity International*. Electronic document. http://elti.fesprojects .net/ISTF%20Conference%202012/laura_snook_istfconference2012.pdf. December 2014.

Snook, Laura K. and Patricia Negreros-Castillo
2004 Rengenerating Mahogany (*Swietenia macrophylla* King) on Clearings in México's Maya Forest: The Effects of Clearing Method and Cleaning on Seedling Survival and Growth. *Forest Ecology and Management* 189(2004):143-160.

Snow, Dean R.
2006 Picturing the Pre-Columbian Americas. *Science* 312(5778):1313.

Soleri, Daniela and David A. Cleveland
1993 Hopi Crop Diversity and Change. *Journal of Ethnobiology* 13(2):203-231.

Sowervine, Jennifer C.
2004 Territorialisation and the Politics of Highland Landscapes in Vietnam: Negotiating Property Relations in Policy, Meaning and Practice. *Conservation & Society* 2(1):97-136.

Stahl, Peter W. and Deborah M. Pearsall
2012 Late Pre-Columbian Agroforestry in the Tropical Lowlands of Western Ecuador. *Quaternary Institute* 249:43-52.

Staller, John E.
2010 *Maize Cobs and Cultures: History of Zea mays L.* Springer Berlin, Heidelberg, Germany.

Steele, James, Jonathan Adams and Tim Sluckin
1998 Modelling Paleoindian Dispersals. *World Archaeology* 30(2):285-305.

Steggerda, Morris
1941 *Maya Indians of Yucatán.* Carnegie Institution of Washington Publication 531. Carnegie Institution of Washington, Washington, D.C.

Steinberg, Michael K.
1998 Political Ecology and Cultural Change: Impacts on Swidden-Fallow Agroforestry Practices among the Mopan Maya in Southern Belize. *Professional Geographer* 50(4):407-417.
2005 Mahogany (*Swietenia macrophylla*) in the Maya Lowlands: Implications for Past Land Use and Environmental Change? *Journal of Latin American Geography* 4(1):127-134.

Stone, Glenn Davis, M. Priscilla Stone, and Robert McC. Netting
1990 Seasonality, Labor Scheduling, and Agricultural Intensification in the Nigerian Savanna. *American Anthropologist* 92(1):7-23.

Strauss-Debenedetti, S. and F. A. Bazzaz
1991 Plasticity and Acclimation to Light in Tropical Moraceae of Different Sucessional Positions. *Oecologia* 87:377-387.

Stuart, James W.
1990 Maize Use by Rural Mesoamerican Households. *Human Organization* 49(2):135-139.

Stump, Daryl
2013 On Applied Archaeology, Indigenous Knowledge, and the Usable Past. *Current Anthropology* 54(3):268-298.

Suazo, I.
1998 *Aspectos Ecologicos de la Especie Invasora Pteridium Aquilinum (L.) Kuhn en una Selva Homeda de la Region de Chajul, Chiapas, México*. Master's thesis, Facultad de Biologia, Universidad Michoacana de San Nicolas de Hidalgo, Morelia, Michoacán, México.

Sunahara, Kay Sachiko
2003 *Ancient Maya Ceramic Economy in the Belize River Valley Region: Petrographic Analyses*. Ph.D. dissertation, Anthropology, McMaster University, Hamilton, Ontario, Canada.

Sweeney, Stuart, Douglas G. Steirgerwald, Frank Davenport and Hallie Eakin
2013 Mexican Maize Production: Evolving Organizational and Spatial Structures Since 1980. *Applied Geography* 39(2013):78-92.

Tambiah, Stanley J.
1976 The Galactic Polity: The Structure of Traditional Kingdoms in Southeast Asia. *Annals New York Academy of Sciences* 293:69-97.

Tankersley, Kenneth B., Vernon L. Scarborough, Nicholas Dunning, Warren Huff, Barry Maynard, and Tammie L. Gerke
2011 Evidence for Volcanic Ash Fall in the Maya Lowlands from a Reservoir at Tikal, Guatemala. *Journal of Archaeological Science* 38:2925-2938.

Teeccino
2014 *Ramon Seeds*, edited by C. MacDougall. Electronic document. http://teeccino .com/about/246/Ram%C3%B3n-Seeds.html. December 2014.

Terán, Silvia and Christian H. Rasmussen
1994 La Milpa en Mesoamérica. In *La Milpa de los Mayas*, pp. 124. Talleres Gráficos del Sudeste, Mérida, Yucatán, México.
1995 Genetic Diversity and Agricultural Strategy in 16th Century and Present-Day Yucatecan Milpa Agriculture. *Biodiversity and Conservation* 4(4):363-381.
2008 *Jinetes del Cielo Maya: Dioses y Diosas de la Lluvia en Xocen*. Ediciones de la Universidad Autonoma de Yucatán, Merida, Yucatán, México.
2009 *La Milpa de los Mayas: La Agricultura de los Mayas Prehispánicas y Actuales en el Noreste de Yucatán*. Universidad Nacional Autonoma de Mexico, Mérida, Yucatán, México.

Terán, Silvia, Christian H. Rasmussen, and Olivio May Cauich
1998 *Las Plantas de la Milpa entre los Mayas: Etnobotánica de las Plantas Cultivadas por Campesinos Mayas en las Milpas del Noreste de Yucatán, México*. Fundación Tun Ben Kin, A.C., Yucatán, México.

Terrell, John Edward and John P. Hart
2008 Domesticated Landscapes. In *Handbook of Landscape Archaeology*, edited by B. David and J. Thomas, pp. 328-332. Left Coast Press, Inc. Walnut Creek, California.

Terrell, John Edward, John P. Hart, Sibel Barut, Nicoletta Cellinese, Antonio Curet, Tim Denham, Chapurukha M. Kusimba, Kyle Latinis, Rahul Oka, Joel Palka, Mary E. D. Pohl, Kevin O. Pope, Patrick Ryan Williams, Helen Haines, and John E. Staller
2003 Domesticated Landscapes: The Subsistence Ecology of Plant and Animal Domestication. *Journal of Archaeological Method and Theory* 10(4):323-368.

TNC, The Nature Conservancy
2014 Maya Forest. Electronic document. www.nature.org/ourinitiatives/regions/northamerica/mexico/placesweprotect/ maya-forest.xml. March 2015.

Toledo, Victor M.
1990 El Proceso de Ganaderización y la Destrucción Biológica y Ecológica de México. *Medio Ambiente y Desarrollo en México* 1:191-222.
2010 Indigenous Peoples. In *Encyclopedia of Biodiversity*, edited by S. Levin, pp. 2-3. Academic Press, San Diego, California.

Toledo, Víctor M., Narciso Barrera-Bassols, Eduardo García-Frapolli, and Pablo Alarcón-Chaires
2008 Uso Múltiple y Biodiversidad entre Los Mayas Yucatecos (México). *Interciencia* 33:345-352.

Toledo, Victor M., Benjamin Ortiz Espejel, Leni Cortés, Patricia Moguel, and María de Jesús Ordoñez
2003 The Multiple Use of Tropical Forests by Indigenous Peoples in Mexico: A Case of Adaptive Management. *Conservation Ecology* 7(3):9.

Torre-Cuadros, Maria de Los Angeles La and Gerald A. Islebe
2003 Traditional Ecological Knowledge and Use of Vegetation in Southeastern México: A Case Study from Solferino, Quintana Roo. *Biodiversity and Conservation* 12:2455-2476.

Tourtellot, Gair
1983 Assessment of Classic Maya Household Composition. In *Prehistoric Settlement Pattern Studies: Retrospect and Prospect*, edited by E. Z. Vogt and R. M. Leventhal, pp. 35-54. University of New Mexico Press, Albuquerque, New Mexico.

Tourtellot, Gair, Jeremy A. Sabloff, and Michael P. Smyth
1990 Room Counts and Population Estimation for Terminal Classic Sayil in the Puuc Region, Yucatán, México. In *Precolumbian Population History in the Maya Lowlands*, edited by T. P. Culbert and D. S. Rice, pp. 245-261. University of New Mexico Press, Albuquerque, New Mexico.

Townsend, Patricia K.
2009 *Environmental Anthropology From Pigs to Policies*. Waveland Press, Long Grove, Illinois.

Trigger, Bruce G.
2003 *Understanding Early Civilizations: A Comparative Study*. Cambridge University Press, Cambridge, United Kingdom.

Turner, B. L.
1978 Ancient Agricultural Land Use in the Central Maya Lowlands. In *Pre-Hispanic Maya Agriculture*, edited by P. D. Harrison and B. L. Turner, pp. 163-183. University of New Mexico Press, Albuquerque, New Mexico.
1990 Population Reconstruction of the Central Maya Lowlands: 1000 B.C. to A.D. 1500. In *Precolumbian Population History in the Maya Lowlands*, edited by T. P. Culbert and D. S. Rice, pp. 301-324. 1st ed. University of New Mexico Press, Albuquerque, New Mexico.

Turner, B. L., Jacqueline Geoghegan, and David R. Foster (editors)
2004 *Integrated Land-Change Science and Tropical Deforestation in the Southern Yucatán*. Oxford University Press, New York.

Turner, B. L., R. E. Kasperson, P. A. Matson, J. M. McCarthy, R. W. Corell, Lindsey Christensene, Noelle Eckley, Jeanne X. Kasperson, Amy Luers, Marybeth L. Martello, Colin Polskya, Alexander Pulsiphera, and Andrew Schiller
2003 A Framework for Vulnerability Analysis in Sustainability Science. *Proceedings of the National Academy of Sciences* 100:8074-8079.

Turner, B. L., and Jeremy A. Sabloff
2012 Classic Period Collapse of the Central Maya Lowlands: Insights about Human–Environment Relationships for Sustainability. *Proceedings of the National Academy of Science* 109(35):13908-13914.

Turner, B. L., S. Cortina Villar, D. Foster, J. Geoghegan, E. Keys, P. Klepeis, D. Lawrence, P. Macario Mendoza, S. M. Manson, Y. Ogneva-Himmelberger, D. Pérez Salicrup A. B. Plotkin, R. Roy Chowdhury, B. Savitsky, L. Schneider, B. Schmook, and C. Vance
2001 Deforestation in the Southern Yucatán Peninsula Region: An Integrative Approach. *Forest Ecology and Management* 154(3):343-370.

Turner, Ian M.
2001 *The Ecology of Trees in the Tropical Rain Forest.* Cambridge Tropical Biology Series. Cambridge University Press, Cambridge, Umited Kingdom.

Turrent, Antonio, Timothy A. Wise, and Elise Garvey
2012 *Achieving México's Maize Potential.* Global Development and Environment Institute, Somerville, Maryland. Electronic document. www.ase.tufts.edu/gdae/poli cy_research/MexMaize.html. March 2015.

Udo, R. K.
1965 Disintegration of Nucleated Settlement in Eastern Nigeria. *Geographical Review* 60:53-67.

UN, United Nations
2004 World Population to 2300. Department of Economic and Social Affairs. United Nations, New York. Electronic document. http://www.un.org/esa/population/ publications/longrange2/WorldPop2300final.pdf.

Valdez-Hernández, Mirna, Odilón Sánchez, Gerald A. Islebe, Laura K. Snook, and Patricia Negreros-Castillo
2014 Recovery and Early Succession after Experimental Disturbance in a Seasonally Dry Tropical Forest in México. *Forest Ecology and Management* 334(2014):331-343.

Van Vliet, Nathalie, Ole Mertz, Torben Birch-Thomsen, and Birgit Schmook
2013 Is There a Continuing Rationale for Swidden Cultivation in the 21st Century? *Human Ecology* 41:1-5.

Vandermeer, John and Ivette Perfecto
2013 Complex Traditions: Intersecting Theoretical Frameworks in Agroecological Research. *Agroecology and Sustainable Food Systems* 37:76–89.

Vanderwarker, Amber M.
2006 *Farming, Hunting, and Fishing in the Olmec World.* University of Texas Press, Austin, Texas.

Vargas-Contreras, Jorge A., Rodrigo A. Medellin, Griselda Escalona-Segura, and Ludivina Interian-Sosa
2009 Vegetation Complexity and Bat-Plant Dispersal in Calakmul, México. *Journal of Natural History* 43:219-243.

Vaughan, Hague H., Edward S. Deevey Jr., and S. E. Garrett-Jones
1985 Pollen Stratigraphy of Two Cores from the Petén Lake District, With an Appendix on Two Deep-Water Cores. In *Prehistoric Lowland Maya Environment and Subsistence Economy,* edited by M. Pohl, pp. 73-89. Papers of the Peabody Museum of Archaeology and Ethnology, Vol. 77. Harvard University Press, Cambridge, Massachusetts.

Vieyra-Odilon, Leticia and Heike Vibrans
2001 Weeds as Crops: The Value of Maize Field Weeds in the Valley of Toluca, México. *Economic Botany* 55(3):426-443.

Villa Rojas, Alfonso
1945 *The Maya of East Central Quintana Roo* 559. Carnegie Institution, Washington, D.C.

Voeks, Robert A.
  2004 Disturbance Pharmacopoeias: Medicine and Myth from the Humid Tropics. *Annals of the Association of American Geographers* 94(4):868-888.
Voorhies, Barbara
  1982 An Ecological Model of the Early Maya of the Central Lowlands. In *Maya Subsistence: Studies in Memory of Dennis Edward Puleston*, edited by K. V. Flannery, pp. 65-95. Studies in archaeology. Academic Press, New York.
  1998 The Transformation from Foraging to Farming in Lowland Mesoamerica. In *The Managed Mosaic: Ancient Maya Agriculture and Resource Use*, edited by S. L. Fedick, pp. 17-29. University of Utah Press, Salt Lake City, Utah.
  2004 *Coastal Collectors in the Holocene: The Chantuto People of Southwest México*. University Press of Florida, Gainesville, Florida.
Wahl, David, Roger Byrne, Thomas Schreiner, and Richard Hansen
  2006 Holocene Vegetation Change in the Northern Petén and its Implications for Maya Prehistory. *Quaternary Research* 65:380-289.
  2007 Palaeolimnological Evidence of Late-Holocene Settlement and Abandonment in the Mirador Basin, Petén, Guatemala. *The Holocene* 17(6):813-820.
Wahl, David, Francisco Estrada-Belli, and Lysanna Andersona
  2013 Prehispanic Human-Environment Interactions in the Holmul Region of the Southern Maya Lowlands. *Palaeogeography, Palaeoclimatology, Palaeoecology* 397(80):17-31.
Warman, Arturo
  2003 *Corn and Capitalism: How a Botanical Bastard Grew to Global Dominance*. Latin America in Translation. The University of North Carolina Press, Chapel Hill, North Carolina.
Wauchope, Robert
  1938 *Modern Maya Houses: A Study of their Archaeological Significance*. 1st ed. Carnegie Institution of Washington, Washington, D.C.
Webster, David
  2002 *The Fall of the Ancient Maya: Solving the Mystery of the Maya Collapse*. Thames & Hudson, London.
Webster's
  1927 Arable. In *New Webster's International Dictionary of the English Language*, edited by F. A. W. T. Harris. G & C Merriam, Springfield, Massachusetts.
  2010 *Webster's New World College Dictionary*. Wiley Publishing, Cleveland, Ohio.
Weis, Tony
  2010 The Accelerating Biophysical Contradictions of Industrial Capitalist Agriculture. *Journal of Agrarian Change* 10(3):315-341.
Wernecke, Daniel Clark
  1994 *Aspects of Urban Design in an Ancient Maya Center: El Pilar, Belize*. Master's thesis, The College of Social Science, Florida Atlantic University, Boca Raton, Florida.
  2005 *A Stone Canvas: Interpreting Maya Building Materials and Construction Technology*. Ph.D. thesis, Graduate School of the University of Texas at Austin, , Austin, Texas.
West, Robert C.
  1964 Surface Configuration and Associated Geology of Middle America. *Handbook of Middle American Indians* 1:33-83.
White, Christine D. and Henry P. Schwarcz
  1989 Ancient Maya Diet: As Inferred from Isotopic and Elemental Analysis of Human Bone. *Journal of Archaeological Science* 16(5):451-474.
White, D. A. and C. S. Hood
  2004 Vegetation Patterns and Environmental Gradients in Tropical Dry Forests of the Northern Yucatán Peninsula. *Journal of Vegetation Science* 15:151-160.

Whitmore, Thomas M. and Billie Lee Turner
1992 Landscapes of Cultivation in Mesoamerica on the Eve of the Conquest. *Annals of the Association of American Geographers* 82(3):402-425.
2005 *Cultivated Landscapes of Middle America on the Eve of Conquest.* Oxford University Press, Oxford, UK.

Wikipedia
2015 Arable Land. Electronic document. http://en.wikipedia.org/wiki/Arable_land. December 2015.

Wilk, Richard
2013 Anthropology Until Only Yesterday. *American Anthropologist* 115(3):514-533.

Wilken, Gene C.
1971 Food-Producing Systems Available to the Ancient Maya. *American Antiquity* 36(4):432-448.
1987 *Good Farmers: Traditional Agricultural Resource Management in México and Central America.* University of California Press, Berkeley, California.

Wilkinson, T. J.
2014 Comparative Landscape Analysis: Contrasting the Middle East and Maya Regions. In *The Resilience and Vulnerability of Ancient Landscapes: Transforming Maya Archaeology through IHOPE.* Archeological Papers of the American Anthropological Association 24:183-200.

Willey, Gordon R.
1956 The Structure of Ancient Maya Society: Evidence from the Southern Lowlands. *American Anthropologist* 58:777-782.

Willey, Gordon R., William R. Bullard, Jr., John B. Glass, and James C. Gifford
1965 *Prehistoric Maya Settlements in the Belize Valley.* Peabody Museum, Cambridge, Massachusetts.

Wilson, E. O.
2002 *The Future of Life.* Alfred A. Knopf, New York.

Wise, Timothy A.
2007 *Policy Space for Méxican Maize: Protecting Agro-biodiversity by Promoting Rural Livelihoods.* Global Development and Environment Institute at Tufts University. Somerville, MA. Electronic document. www.ase.tufts.edu/gdae/policy_research/mexicanmaize.html. March 2015.
2010 Agricultural Dumping Under NAFTA: Estimating the Costs of US Agricultural Policies to Mexican Producers. Global Development and Environment Institute at Tufts University. Somerville, Massachusetts. Electronic document. www.ase.tufts.edu/gdae/policy_research/agnafta.html. March 2105.

Woods, William I. and Joseph M. McCann
1999 The Anthropogenic Origin and Persistence of Amazonian Dark Earths. *The Yearbook of Latin Americanist Geographers* 25:7-14.

Woodward, Michelle R.
2000 Considering Household Food Security and Diet at the Classic Period Village of Ceren, El Salvador (A.D. 600). *Mayab* 13:11.

Woodworth, Paddy
2013 *Our Once and Future Planet: Restoring the World in the Climate Change Century.* The University of Chicago Press, Chicago.

Wyatt, Andrew
2012 Agricultural Practices at the Chan Site: Farming and Political Economy in an Ancient Maya Community. In *Chan: An Ancient Maya Farming Community*, edited by C. Robin, pp. 71-88. University of Florida Press, Gainesville, Florida.

Zetina Gutiérrez, María de Guadalupe
  2007 Ecología Humana de las Rancherías de Pich, Campeche: Un Análisis Dia-
  crónic. MS, Ecologia Humana, Centro de Investigación Y Estudios Avanzados del
  Instituto Politècnico Nacional, Merida, México.

Zetina Gutiérrez, María de Guadalupe and Betty B. Faust
  2011 De la Agroecología a la Arqueología Demográfica: ¿Cuántas Casas por Famil-
  ia? *Estudios de Cultura Maya* XXXVIII:97-120.

INDEX

Page numbers in *italics* refer to tables or illustrations.
Italicized *n* refers to a note number.

ABOUT THE AUTHORS

Anabel Ford is director of the MesoAmerican Research Center at the University of California, Santa Barbara, and President of the nonprofit organization Exploring Solutions Past: The Maya Forest Alliance. She has done extensive research on patterns of Maya settlement and landscape ecology, and is recognized for the archaeological discovery of the ancient Maya city center of El Pilar, on the border of Belize and Guatemala.

Ronald Nigh is a professor at Centro Investigaciones y Estudios Superiores en Antropología Social (CIESAS) in Chiapas, Mexico. He is the author of numerous studies and articles on agricultural, ecological, and environmental issues of concern to indigenous peoples in Mesoamerica. He is also director of Dana, a non-government organization that coordinates an experimental garden in San Cristobal de Las Casas for training and support of young Maya farmers involved in agroecological transition.